Values and Development in Southern Africa

This book is a product of CODESRIA's Comparative Research Network

Values and Development in Southern Africa

Edited by

Hans Müller
Pinkie Mekgwe
Marvellous Mhloyi

CODESRIA

Council for the Development of Social Science Research in Africa
DAKAR

© CODESRIA 2013
Council for the Development of Social Science Research in Africa
Avenue Cheikh Anta Diop, Angle Canal IV
BP 3304 Dakar, 18524, Senegal
Website: www.codesria.org

ISBN: 978-2-86978-554-0

Typesetting: Daouda Thiam
Cover Design: Ibrahima Fofana

Distributed in Africa by CODESRIA
Distributed elsewhere by African Books Collective, Oxford, UK
Website: www.africanbookscollective.com

The Council for the Development of Social Science Research in Africa (CODESRIA) is an independent organisation whose principal objectives are to facilitate research, promote research-based publishing and create multiple forums geared towards the exchange of views and information among African researchers. All these are aimed at reducing the fragmentation of research in the continent through the creation of thematic research networks that cut across linguistic and regional boundaries.

CODESRIA publishes *Africa Development*, the longest standing Africa based social science journal; *Afrika Zamani*, a journal of history; the *African Sociological Review*; the *African Journal of International Affairs*; *Africa Review of Books* and the *Journal of Higher Education in Africa*. The Council also co-publishes the *Africa Media Review*; *Identity, Culture and Politics: An Afro-Asian Dialogue*; *The African Anthropologist* and the *Afro-Arab Selections for Social Sciences*. The results of its research and other activities are also disseminated through its Working Paper Series, Green Book Series, Monograph Series, Book Series, Policy Briefs and the CODESRIA Bulletin. Select CODESRIA publications are also accessible online at www.codesria.org.

CODESRIA would like to express its gratitude to the Swedish International Development Cooperation Agency (SIDA/SAREC), the International Development Research Centre (IDRC), the Ford Foundation, the MacArthur Foundation, the Carnegie Corporation, the Norwegian Agency for Development Cooperation (NORAD), the Danish Agency for International Development (DANIDA), the French Ministry of Cooperation, the United Nations Development Programme (UNDP), the Netherlands Ministry of Foreign Affairs, the Rockefeller Foundation, FINIDA, the Canadian International Development Agency (CIDA), the Open Society Foundations (OSFs), TrustAfrica, UN/UNICEF, the African Capacity Building Foundation (ACBF) and the Government of Senegal for supporting its research, training and publication programmes.

Contents

Contributors

Hennie Kotzé: Political Science, Centre for International and Comparative Politics, Dean of Faculty of Arts and Social Sciences, Stellenbosch University, South Africa.

Stefanie Schulein: Political Science, Researcher, Centre for International and Comparative Politics, Stellenbosch University, South Africa.

Musonda Lemba: Demography, Department of Social Development Studies, University of Zambia, Zambia.

Pinkie Mekgwe: English Literature, University of Botswana, formerly Programme Officer, CODESRIA, Dakar, Senegal.

Marvellous Mhloyi: Demography and Sociology, Chair of Department of Sociology, Centre for Population Studies, University of Zimbabwe, Zimbabwe.

Hans Müller: Social Theory and Decision-making, Centre for Knowledge Dynamics and Decision-making, University of Stellenbosch.

Tania van Heerden: Economics, Centre for Knowledge Dynamics and Decision-making, University of Stellenbosch.

Noah Taruberekera: Demography, Centre for Population Studies, University of Zimbabwe and Research Manager, Population Services International, Zimbabwe.

Preface

Any attempt to do comparative research with substantial empirical components, whether these are qualitative or quantitative or both, as it should be is fraught with obstacles. To do so without significant funding of the empirical work is to try the impossible. We wanted to do all of this across a minimum of six countries in Southern Africa. The focus on development and values gives our work intellectual direction and significance, as this is not something that has been done before. The support that we got from the South African National Research Foundation and the University of Stellenbosch, and facilitated by individuals like Robert Kriger and Johan Groenewald, allowed us to get together as a network and thrash out the project details from 2001 onwards. It was a significant idea and worth attempting.

With the bestowing of a CODESRIA Comparative Research Network award in 2005, we began to believe that we would actually be able to make a dream come true. The support from CODESRIA and individuals like Ebrima Sall, Abdon Sofonou and, in the phase, Awa Diop, made a book possible. However, we are still some away from the real aim of the network in that we had to make do with empirical data generated by others and in terms of different research agendas.

The eventual comments of the anonymous but most gracious and insightful reviewers have helped us reflect very critically on what we were able to achieve, given the circumstances. They have added significantly to the outcome. They have also reinforced our opinion that this is a project that has significance. It is unfinished in some ways, but we believe that a path has been laid out and concepts presented that could help build a road.

The content of the respective chapters is the responsibility of the authors and the editors; and although we have taken due care to reference published and documented contributions to our thought processes, we were not able to do that for the contribution of the members of the network who did not contribute a chapter or section. They simply formed our thoughts and words in far-reaching ways. We are most grateful to these members and accept the blame of every misunderstood or wrong interpretation of their comments in workshops in Pretoria, Dakar and Stellenbosch. Thank you, Marcelino, Amos, Gaspar and Fred. It was an honour and a pleasure to work with you and our friendship is a cherished one.

Hans Müller
Stellenbosch

Section I

Introducing the Issues

1

Introduction

Hans Müller, Pinkie Mekgwe and Marvellous Mhloyi

Our Cause

Africa's most important challenge is the uneven development within and between countries and the pressing issues relating to poverty in Southern Africa and the continent as a whole. We acknowledge that development has been on Africa's agenda for a long time and progress has been variable. We contend that development has been limited partly due to the level at which discussion of the challenges and interventions made to tackle them have been conducted. Our contribution focuses on the social and cultural dimensions of development dynamics and, in particular, the role of values in shaping development. Values are at the core of the hopes and aspirations of individuals, communities and societies; while they also inform worldviews and therefore co-determine the path that individuals, communities and societies follow to realise their aspirations. We do not aim to analyse and then prescribe. Our aim is to understand as best as we can the values that motivate and inform African communities and societies; and then facilitate a dialogue about sustainable development in that context among academics and intellectuals, policy-makers and decision-makers and the communities. We take a minimalist view of what development is, in an attempt to reconstitute the development debate at a different level. The aim is neither a technical imposition from outside, nor a normative position that excludes dissenters of that position. The aim is to facilitate a dialogue.

Our methodology is informed by the realisation that the conceptual definition of social and cultural values is difficult; that empirical and comparative perspectives from both qualitative and quantitative data would be necessary; and, last but not least, that the available data is insufficient and sometimes misleading. On the quantitative level, some comparative data that is available was developed in terms that are more appropriate in industrialized and Western contexts, while other data-sets do not deal directly with the issues that we consider central to our quest. Furthermore, we are well aware of the limitations of working with aggregate data on large populations when attempting to deal with a complex social issue or series of issues. On the qualitative level, the obvious problem was finding data that would enable consistent interpretation across the region as most qualitative insights are particular and not conceived from a comparative point of view. Therefore, attempts at developing capacity to collect data in terms of the conceptualisation of issues that we address are ongoing and this publication can only be seen as a start on a more comprehensive process and task.

The Southern African Values Comparative Research Network was set up in 2005 with support from CODESRIA, the South African National Research Foundation and Stellenbosch University. The network brought together researchers from different disciplines from six Southern African countries to investigate social and cultural values, and the social dynamics associated with values in the region. We decided to focus on the link between values and development as a first attempt at developing perspectives on the very popular, but diffuse and ideologically fraught concern with the role of values in society. Funding constraints limited the research activities to conceptual argumentation and secondary analysis of existing data.

The Imperative of Development

Development is the African agenda – if one can navigate the ideological constructions of the term by outside institutions and capitalism generally and just focus on creating a better life for Africans. African people are mostly poor and often have very little real choices in a wide variety of aspects of human existence. Extreme poverty exists in large parts of Africa. There is massive inequality within some comparatively wealthy countries, and significant inequality in most African countries. All poor people are plagued by loss of freedom and dignity and are often not able to effectively participate in their countries' political, economic, legal and social processes. Poverty, therefore, causes the victims to suffer social exclusion or political repression or any combination of these factors. Societies that experience poverty are under continuous threat of ecological disaster and disease. In a global perspective, the relatively poor position of Africa is glaring.

In purely income terms, the picture is fairly clear: African countries dominate the lower reaches of global income scales.

> In 1998, over 80% of the people in the world's lowest quintile outside China and India lived in Africa. The entire populations of Benin, Chad, Congo, Malawi and Togo ... and Tanzania are in the lowest quintile. 80% of the population of Burkina Faso, Burundi, Central African Republic, Ethiopia, Gambia, Guinea Bissau, Kenya, Madagascar, Mali, Mozambique,

Niger, Nigeria, Rwanda, Sierra Leone, Uganda and Zambia, and 60% of people of Ghana, Mauritania, and Senegal, also belong to the world's lowest quintile. Only Botswana, Gabon, Guinea and South Africa have less than 20% of their citizens in the world's lowest quintile (Sala-i-Martin, 2002:38).[1]

In growth terms, the picture in Africa seems to be more promising as 14 out of 43 countries in Sub-Saharan Africa have recorded average growth rates of 5 per cent per year between 2000 and 2008 (World Bank data). However, when we look at human development in a broader sense than income, we realise that not much has changed in spite of high growth in many African countries in the past decade. Of the 31 countries listed as exhibiting Low Human Development in the 2005 Human Development Index, only six are not strictly Sub-Saharan African countries, and only one is not strictly an African country (UNDP, 2005). All these factors and more make development a moral and practical imperative for any African person, in spite of the very real and structurally important causes that lie outside Africa.[2]

At the same time, it is quite imperative that some erroneous perceptions about Africa be dispelled and ideological and biased analyses be confronted. An example of this is the very simple fact which Mkandawire points out with regard to Deaton and Miller's view that African economies are very much open to 'external conjuncture and the role of foreign expertise', and that African economies do well when the rest of the world grows and do badly when the rest of the world is in decline (Mkandawire 2001b:303). The point is that development is neither the antithesis of the African state nor does it have to be undemocratic, as Botswana and Mauritius both prove the possibility of African developmental states (Mkandawire 2001b:309-310). However, many African states are at the bottom of a long list of states where large sections of society, and many communities suffer the humiliation of grinding poverty and exclusion on a sustained basis. Africans cannot and do not want anything else than a change in that reality.

It is, therefore, assumed for now that development at least means positive and sustained change in the freedom of choice and living conditions of the poor and marginalised. Of course, the whole point of a real definition of development also needs to say how development is to occur; but for now, we settle for a parsimonious definition. If the poor and marginalised do not benefit in a sustained manner, development has not occurred in an African society. Of course, such a benchmark would be much more controversial in relatively more developed parts of the world than Africa. Given the circumstances sketched above, such a parsimonious definition cannot be controversial in Africa.

Development in Africa will not necessarily follow the path of the industrial modernisation that took Europe and the Western world from the traditional societies to the current affluence. It is clear that attempts to impose development in Africa from outside, in terms of a theory of modernisation or capitalist or socialist versions of the theory of modernisation, have failed, even though no application would satisfy the theoretical purist. The current context seems to be dominated by debates on neo-liberalism and globalisation. Neo-liberalism and globalisation are often seen as two faces of the same coin – a coin that excludes Africa deliberately or, at least, effectively (Nyamnjoh 2004:42; Mhone and Bond 2002).

The debate about development and modernisation theory and even globalisation may be a sidetrack even if it is interesting. Positive and sustained change in the freedom of choice and living conditions of the poor has been mostly absent in African societies in the past 40 years. Furthermore, on average, positive and sustained change in freedom of choice and living conditions has not even been effected in most African societies. Development in Africa has to mean that societies as a whole develop and that the most marginalised and poor also benefit significantly. This has not been happening in Africa during the past two or three decades unlike in other parts of the world where positive change has happened. In fact, African nations are doing worse and can offer fewer opportunities for their people than before.

The question is why societies in other parts of the world have been able to increase the standard of living and at least some important dimensions of freedom of choice for marginalised people? Why has development happened in other places in the world and not in Africa? Why are there such immense differences within Africa?

The Imperative of Cultural and Social Insight in Development

In a context where Africa is a unitary cultural concept to many, if not most non-Africans, African poverty seems to have a logical and self-evident link with African culture. Another dimension of Africa that should be logical and self-evident to most non-Africans is the colonial and continued post-colonial imprint of exploitation and devastation in the way businesses are run, governments instituted and function, global rules of trade operate and education and health are kept under pressure.

However, what seems to be self-evident and logical, and what is really the case, is often far apart. First of all, the racist conflation of African poverty and lack of development with African culture is quite powerful as a trope in the global media and popular perception outside of Africa. Not only is Africa diverse, it is also not to be captured in singular and linear explanations. For that reason, we need to delve into the seemingly self-evident explanations of the development paths of African communities and societies and Africa a whole. Seeing that the cultural and the social are both the most difficult and the most susceptible to superficial and often racist explanations for poverty, it seems apt that scholars tackle the issues head on. It is imperative that the cultural and social explanations for poverty and underdevelopment in Africa be investigated. It is imperative that the social and cultural dynamics of development in Africa be understood. An interpretation of African development that does not take the cultural and social dynamics of development processes into account would only seem better than one that blames African culture for poverty as it would ignore the people of Africa in its definition of development.

In a public institution and especially the multi-lateral agency context, one has to recognise that there has been a growing interest in social capital explanations for development and the lack of development (Utting 2006:2). This is clear in the approach of various international institutions to the analysis of poverty as well as a broader consciousness of social and cultural issues in theoretical arguments about development. In general terms, it serves the African development agenda well to be suspicious of this interest in social capital. The failure of development as a project of a teleological conception of modernisation (Kothari and Minogue 2002:2-12), and specifically as a failure of the policy-makers and donors to have the effects that they assumed would follow from their interventions, has lead to some agitation in the ranks of the development agencies (Stiglitz 2002). One of the major issues has been the way in which terms like participation and social values and indigenous knowledge have been instrumentalised and used in the continued neo-liberal development agenda (Cornwall and Brock 2006).

The World Bank has changed its approach to culture in spite of the neo-liberal assumptions that accompany the use of the social capital terminology (Fine 2001; Francis 2002), aside from the fact that often it is still only an afterthought and a residual category for the World Bank and other like institutions (Elson 2002:1; Cornwall and Brock 2006). The United Nations has also increased its focus on cultural and social dimensions of development (Mkandawire 2001a). Furthermore, the post-basic-needs era has seen considerable and significant interest in the notions of trust, networks and freedom (Marini 2004; Fukuyama 1995; Putnam 1995; Sen 1999) and thus, by implication or directly in the notions of culture and values.

It seems less surprising then that the recent Commission for Africa (CFA) stated their interest in the social and cultural dimensions of development explicitly:

> The overall lesson is that outside prescriptions only succeed where they work with the grain of African ways of doing things. They fail where they ignore, or do not understand, the cultural suppositions of the people they seek to address. The international community must make greater efforts to understand the values, norms and allegiances of the cultures of Africa and in their policy-making display a greater flexibility, open-mindedness and humility (2005c:33).

We think that these efforts will be well served by cultural and social analysis that emanates from within Africa, and that provides content to statements like that of the CFA. The 'African way of doing things' cannot be left as an open-ended phrase as all the stereotypes and uninformed interpretations will simply occupy the empty space left by such statements. One also has to be careful that the interest in culture and values does not follow the route that has often been taken in business organisations where attempts are made to manipulate and control this new aspect of the brief of executives. Instrumentalisation of objects of management is in the genetics of management as a discipline and politicians and development agencies are also often similarly tempted (for a serious critique of the CFA see: Bush 2007:25-48).

What about Culture?

The question is 'what' specific role culture and social values play and could play. This is not articulated directly in the Millennium Development Goal strategies (emanating from UN resolution 55/2, 2000b)[3] or in other important international policy documents. These issues are to be articulated more clearly in order to show how the claim that values play a definitive role in development is not the same as blaming the victims, that this claim is not a simplistic conclusion that 'the fates of countries are effectively *sealed* by the nature of their respective cultures' (Sen 2004a:38, his italics). It is also important if we are to be able to define practical ways of drawing on culture for development. Culture is a resource because it is a framework of meaning and social structure. In general terms, culture and values can motivate development by intelligent and organic policies, agencies and leadership. At the same time, there may indeed also be important inhibiting or contradictory cultural forces to be reckoned with when designing and implementing development policy.

However, opinions about the exact meaning of values and culture in Africa vary. First of all the obvious point must again be made: there is no single set of African values or one African culture but many clusters and contradictions within clusters of values and many cultures within and outside of Africa that can be called African but are not the same. African values are often sanctified (thereby also reduced to a singular set) as primal examples of communal support and solidarity – especially by politicians (Müller 2000) and some Pan-Africanist philosophers and writers (Oyeshile 2004; Teffo 1999). When making such statements, the focus is often on African culture as it is portrayed as having been in the past and with a somewhat selective view demanded by the logic of opposing the West. Therefore, the logic is then often to complain that these values have been compromised or lost due to non-African influences like materialism or capitalism (Nkrumah 1964:74; Gyekye 1997; Lassiter 1999a). The assumption seems to be that change brought about by forces that have their origin outside of Africa is necessarily, or at least, mostly to the detriment of African culture and African people.

The opposite of that line of thought is the very direct argument that values associated with development are often distasteful to traditional societies. Alcalde (1991:114-16), Grondona, (2000) and Montaner (2000) cite the notions and constructs of human triumph over nature, the orientation towards the future, individualism and self-interest, frugality, and work as moral activity or instrument to get ahead, as rare in many non-Western countries. Etounga-Manguelle is even more controversial and argues, among other things, that Africans are slaves of their environment as this is seen as an 'immutable order'. This supposedly leads to an attitude and behaviour where nothing is done to prepare for the future; where 'the entire social body accepts, as a natural fact, the servitude imposed by the strong man of the moment'; where the community suppresses the individual; where material accumulation is not a priority; and where, lo and behold, Africans are by and large irrational and 'to some extent cannibalistic' (2000:68-75). This is in line with the general argument that traditional societies cannot sustain and deal with market-oriented development and are therefore limited in terms of economic growth potential (Landes 2000; Harrison 2000; Huntington 2000; Landes 1998). These arguments assume or directly argue a static definition of African (and non-Western) culture and a universalist model of development.

In this context, it seems wise to concur with Sen that the key question is not 'whether' values matter, but 'how' they matter (Sen 2004a:37-38) and to push the point further, and ask 'how what' values matter. It is universally true that value orientations can be supportive, but also an impediment to achieving developmental goals of governments and other agencies. In that sense, African values are indeed of key importance for the future development of Africa. However, being specific and investigating the complexities of values and culture matter more than acceptance of the general point that values matter. Such statements become empty or susceptible to prejudices and ideological embroidery of various kinds if not followed up with research. This applies to specific statements like those of Etounga-Manguelle and others. It is easy to make statements about seemingly self-evident features of African societies. It is, however, a very different matter to understand the complex dynamics that lead to some of the most disturbing features of African societies, and to understand the ambiguity that is hidden in the bland depiction of these features by sensationalist media and superficial analyses.

To follow Sen's argument further, there are a number of ways in which values and culture 'do not matter' and cannot and should not be conceived. Cultural prejudice and political asymmetry tied together can be a lethal concoction; cultural determinism supported with scanty evidence has lead to later embarrassment (remember the 'Asian condition' and the way in which culture has been reified and manipulated over a long time in Rwanda and recently in Kenya and South Africa?), but may very well lead to current investment blunders. Culture does not work in isolation from other social influences and is not 'uniquely pivotal in determining our lives and identities' (Sen 2004a:43-52). It is the dynamic between cultures and between cultural and political-economy and geography and disease, etc., that has to be studied and understood before we know 'how' culture and values matter.

The book is about the cultural and social dimensions of the development challenges of Africa, and specifically Southern Africa. However, it makes no sense to discuss this dimension of the matter without due recognition of the structurally induced reasons for underdevelopment and poverty in Africa.

Global Systemic Dimensions

Global systemic causes of both economic and political nature are the most obvious and probably also the most significant for Africa's comparative lack of development. Colonialism and imperial exploitation, international political-economic systems of trade, credit, technological and intellectual exchange, recent financial and competitive business globalisation, entrenched structures of dependence resulting in weak African states and weak institutions are key aspects (Osagha 1999:182-195). To this list, one has to add the slave trade, colonial and post-colonial production for export and internal predatory malpractice – especially by states that function as the dominion of an elite and that is fed and kept erect by the vagaries of international political and economic needs. Institutionalised exploitation and degradation are still rampant in some countries and threaten others, while states are weak in many countries (Clapham 1996:3, 163-167).

However, some impressions that seem obvious may not be correct. According to some analysts there is no proof that African governance is comparatively worse than other regions (UN 2005:146). Other types of reasons are cited as being critical in Africa. The same important UN report lists the following:

- very high transport costs and small markets;
- low-productivity agriculture;
- a very high disease burden;
- a history of adverse geopolitics;
- very slow diffusion of technology from abroad (UN 2005:148).

The same report argues that a poverty trap exists on national or regional level.

> The starting conditions in Africa in the 1960s were far behind those of other parts of the developing world. Contrary to casual discourse (the common comparison of Ghana and Korea in the 1960s, for example),

African countries at the time of independence had very few individuals with higher education, very few paved roads, almost no electrification of rural areas where the bulk of the population lived, and food yields far below those of other parts of the developing world. Africa had a much harder path to follow, and was much more vulnerable to getting stuck in a poverty trap' where countries are too poor to invest in their own development (UN 2005:152).

It seems that the list of critical reasons that are unique to Africa as well as the starting conditions, point to specific and unique systemic features that characterise Africa.[4]

While significant aid and support goes towards alleviating or solving some of these problems and conditions, the outlook on changing these global systemic dimensions of African poverty in general and the poverty trap of many African countries in particular is not clear. There seems to be some convergence between initiatives like NEPAD, the UN Millennium Development Goals and other multilateral initiatives, but the level of convergence cannot be specified in a quick overview. What one can, however, point out without fear of contradiction is that the development emphasis should be on systemic issues. The same applies to governmental initiatives on unilateral and multilateral levels. It may be that the reason why systemic issues are not addressed systemically is because it would threaten vested interests in the global systems (see Amin 1997:12-45 for a 1990s critique, Bush 2007, and many more for a more recent critique) and the implications of a systemic change would at least uncover the type of independence that was created in African nations in decolonisation. However, if we knew how to intervene on the political level, it is even more difficult to know how to intervene in the social and cultural area of development without again manipulating cultural and social institutions and relationships.

At the same time, it does not help pointing out that African culture is critical to the success of development initiatives and not finding out how this is important. It is here that the significance of our research lies.

The Significance of our Research

The research presented here is important for at least three reasons. Firstly, it adds substance to general statements regarding the role of culture in African development and, secondly, it reflects on the limitations of existing approaches and data. Lastly, it makes a unique reconstitution of the development debate in Southern Africa possible.

We attempt to say something about the content of how values matter in development in a manner that is empirically informed and theoretically engaged. In that sense, it is a real attempt at giving some definition to the simple platitude that the African way of doing things should be recognised in that it is a step in the development of a Southern African perspective on the role of values in development, and the role of specific values in communities and societies in Southern Africa in particular.

Secondly, it is an attempt at interpreting the existing data-sets on social and cultural values within a comparative framework and with the aim of understanding the cultural and social dimension of development in Southern Africa. The World Values Survey and its origin, the European Values Study, must rate as important international surveys that provide data and challenge conceptualisation of the role of values in society and the interaction between values and other dimensions of social interaction and structure. These types of data-sets are to be analysed in terms that will be familiar to the researcher in this field to see how much can be learnt from these data-sets about African development issues. In the process, it also becomes clear what some of the important limitations of these existing empirical data-sets are.

Finally, the study is significant in that it provides a theoretical argument and the beginning of an empirical perspective on the role of values in development in Africa that may facilitate a dialogue about African development. Such a dialogue is more useful than either the imposition of a technical process or the announcement of a normative framework. 'Where sustainable development is conceived as a unifying ethic, its implementation is pursued in terms of defining the content of that ethic and winning adherents to its practice – an effort at achieving ethical consensus. Where it is conceived as a set of formally comparable dimensions, its analysis and measurement becomes a technical exercise reserved for experts. We argue for a third view, a pluralistic conception of sustainability not as a fixed end but as a dialogue of values, a view that accentuates the need to identify and strengthen social institutions to manage value conflict at different scales' (Ratner 2004:51). Such a dialogue could enable development to become a dynamic African concept instead of a foreign imposition.

The dialogue can happen at many levels. First of all there is the immediate academic and intellectual interest that a book about a controversial theme generates (if the book is good enough). Then, there is the policy environment where it seems that there is increased consciousness that values and culture do play a distinct and important role in development and should play a much larger role in development policy and development projects. We would like to deconstruct some of the easy ideas about values and culture that are sometimes found in this arena and provide ways in which policy discussions can deal with this cluster of issues in a more serious and sophisticated manner. If the book is to lead to more quantitative studies where the concepts presented can be discussed in focus group or action research settings, there would be some benefit from having a number of controversial but important issues to place on the table.

The Structure of the Book

Chapter One is this introduction that is meant to present the main issues without too much debate on the merits of this or that way of formulating the case and giving some perspective on where the project fits in a bigger scheme of things. Chapter Two of the book deals with matters that have been dealt with in a very simple and unqualified manner in the introduction. It makes the case for the Southern African region as unit of analysis with reference to the interwoven nature of geo-political and economic dynamics of the region as well as its historical and cultural linkages. It then defines what we mean by social and cultural values and by the notions of development and poverty. Of course, we need to take a position on these matters as there is a plethora of definitions and approaches in these fields. We then set out the objectives of the study in a slightly more structured and argued manner than in the introduction and specify areas of concentration. We also deal with methodological issues that relate to our task in some detail as the comparative method is a reasoned mode of operation in our case – even if we understand and explain the limitations thereof.

Chapters One and Two also form the first section of the book as we thought it sensible to divide the book into three main sections. The first section sets the scene, the second reflects theoretically and the third attempts to explore the theoretical concepts empirically. The theoretical section comprises two chapters: the first locating the issue of culture in development literature generally and the second proposing content to the cultural dimensions that are at stake in development.

Chapter Three, therefore, sets out the main lines of the history of development theory and of empirical research relating to development in Africa and Southern Africa as specifically as possible. The point is not to regurgitate all the theories and empirical research that has ever been put forward, but to review these with the aim of establishing what has been done that speaks to our own interest in the cultural and social dimensions of development. We argue that the state of the art in development theory and in empirical research is lacking in that it does not provide a nuanced and contemporary perspective on the impact and potential of values in development.

Chapter Four puts forward the content of what we believe should be investigated about values following Sen's point that it is not so much whether values and culture matter, but how and what it is that is at work when it is said that values matter in development. We argue that cosmology in general and specific aspects of cosmology matter; that notions and values associated with power matter; that values relating to personal relationships matter; and that, lastly, certain personal characteristics that are valued and desirable matter. These arguments are laid out in terms of literature that we consider noteworthy, but the value aspects and ordering of these aspects is the product of our discussions as a network. It is preliminary in that it consists of the aspects that we would consider important to do research on in the field. We are well aware of the tendentious nature of these choices and follow it up with what we found possible in terms of secondary data analysis. Of course, further and much more comprehensive research is needed to establish a more than exploratory framework for such a theoretical position.

Chapters Five, Six and Seven, therefore, are chapters that lay out the arguments for and the results of exploratory analyses of existing data-sets and other material. These three chapters form Section Three of the book.

Chapter Five trawls through the Afrobarometer data on opinions and views of the countries in the region that we have data for and in terms of the content that we find important and that can remotely be investigated within the aspects covered in the Afrobarometer. Interesting results are found regarding some of the aspects that we profile theoretically, but the limitations of mass opinion surveys as a means to values analysis also become clearer.

Chapter Six reviews data on the demography of two countries in terms that are important to value change. We review the three components of population growth, fertility, mortality and migration, variables with an intricate interrelationship with development. The variables not only create social conditions, but are also the expression of deeply held values. We find development or lack of such, as important determinants of these variables; yet development is also deeply affected by these components. An understanding of these relationships provides a launch pad for relevant policies.

Chapter Seven deals with the world of work, which is the most obvious proving ground for theories and perceptions of African specificity regarding values that supposedly determine development. We, firstly, look at work values that are supposed to run on a continuum from instrumental to expressive interest in work. The model holds up well for Europe and points to instrumental work values associating with social conditions in which getting and holding a job is more important than expressing yourself at work. Expressive values are found at the higher end of the social ladder where work security and working conditions are no longer issues to contend with. The expectation that Africans would tend to have an instrumental orientation to work was disappointed however, confusing the expectation of a cultural effect in work orientation. Africans are more like Europeans than would be expected with the given theoretical approach, considering the economic conditions under which they work. We follow this up with another, even more classical expectation that the Protestant Christians (or in our time those who defer satisfaction for religious reasons) would be more hardworking and thrifty than those who are Catholic (or those who live from the fruit of their labour, are fatalistic and do not see an economic relationship between what they do in life and thereafter). This expectation is confounded on a fundamental level as the standard constructs needed for such an analysis do not succeed. The expectation is also confused by the results which show that the only more or less interesting avenue along which to pursue the religious line of questioning about work ethos would be the impact of Pentecostalism and evangelicalism in Africa. The expectation that religion would have the same kind of effect on work ethos than that of Europe is not fulfilled and the similarity with the Latin American experience in this regard is pointed out.

The last chapter draws some conclusions regarding the limitations and benefits of our research as we see it, and scopes some dimensions of future research that we consider to be useful and feasible.

Notes

1. The same Sala-i-Martin has presented statistical evidence that inequality has declined in the world as a whole and that this is due, in some way, to globalisation in the 1980s and 1990s. The 'evidence' for this claim is disputed (Firebaugh and Goesling 2004; Wade 2004) but the positive change Sala-i-Martin directs our attention to does not lie in Africa but in Asian economic growth and therefore does not really concern us.

2. While development is a practical imperative for Africans, the causes for Africa's underdevelopment and poverty are complex and cannot simply be ascribed to one or the other agent or cluster of agents. These causes are structural, but not in the objectivist sense of the word as if these structures are institutions or systems that can be identified and, if changed, will lead to a solution. The causes of poverty and development are social and as with all other social phenomena, these causes lie in the structure of patterns of action, reflexive responses to these patterns and resultant rules that can be deduced from the interaction between what went before and how it is instituted again and again. Of course, not all agents in the social system operate with the same power or under the same constraints. To say this in less theoretical language: neither capitalism not the World Bank, nor a particular predatory African state can be held solely responsible for the existence of poverty and the underdevelopment of African societies. The entire social edifice of global relationships, including the governments, development and aid agencies, development intermediaries, business and local communities, etc. have over time created or allowed or not resisted effectively the development of a dire situation. While not all participants have the same position in the system and effective power is relative, the solutions will lie in transformative action on all levels.

3. The Millennium Development Goals were adopted within the UN system in 2000 and comprise 8 goals broken down in 21 targets and 60 indicators. The goals themselves are: 1: Eradicate extreme poverty and hunger; 2: Achieve universal primary education; 3: Promote gender equality and empower women; 4: Reduce child mortality; 5: Improve maternal health; 6: Combat HIV/AIDS, malaria and other diseases; 7: Ensure environmental sustainability; 8: Develop a Global Partnership for Development

4. It is disturbing that this very same United Nations report does not discuss culture or social values in any significant manner throughout the text – culture only appears as a word in the text as part of agriculture. However, this is in keeping with Jeffrey Sachs's (the major author of the text) argument that culture does not really matter much in development (Sachs 2000)!

2

Background, Problem and Methodology

Hans Müller, Hennie Kotzé and Stefanie Schulein*

Definitions

This chapter explains the basic issues, choices and assumptions that launch the rest of the study. It includes defining some of the key terms to be used in the study, i.e. "values" and "development", but starts with an explanation of the choice to focus on Southern Africa and specifically the six countries that are covered by the network. We continue with the statement of the objectives of the study in a more formal manner than above, and explain the areas of concentration based on that. Lastly, the methodological choice to compare is explained and some of the pitfalls and problems of that choice are discussed with reference to our own work that follows the framing that the first chapter provides.

Southern Africa

The study focuses on Southern Africa and six countries in particular. The six countries were picked in terms of practical considerations and can be seen as a convenient sample. However, the six countries are also a good distribution of countries in the region. The countries we were able to include in the network are Tanzania, Mozambique, South Africa, Botswana, Zimbabwe and Zambia.

One might consider the case for the inclusion other Southern African countries separately from the existence of a network of collegial cooperation established and co-funded by CODESRIA that lead to the convenience sample that delimits the rest of the research reported here. The countries with relatively small populations left out in a strictly Southern African Development Community member states population are Namibia, Swaziland and Lesotho. The countries with larger populations left out are Malawi, Angola and the Democratic Republic of Congo (DRC). The Francophone island states left out are the Seychelles, Madagascar and

Mauritius. Arguments can be advanced for the inclusion of any selection of these countries with the exception (at the time of the conception of the project) of Angola and DRC. Both these countries were still in the last throes of civil war and serious destabilisation in 2001 and survey data of the type handled in the empirical analyses were not available then.

In general terms, through migrationsof linguistically-related groups from further north centuries ago, the communities and societies of the Southern African region have been in interaction through economic exchange, religious influence, migration, political power struggles and alliances, etc. The colonial history is also one of interaction with four blocks constituted by the four main colonial authorities, namely Britain, Portugal, Germany and the Belgian king and later the Belgian state. Here, the forms of interaction again included religion, migration, economic exchange and politics, but the content was decidedly different with the effects of slavery, missionary activity, colonial rule, migrant labour systems, disenfranchisement, imposition of political borders, trading political relationships from afar, etc.

Apartheid became the next major feature of the political economy of the region after the decolonisation of Angola and Mozambique. The alliance of the Frontline States, the instigation, support and direct involvement of the South African regime in civil war in Mozambique and Angola and independence struggles in Zimbabwe and Namibia, and the existence of apartheid with significant economic but dwindling (later) political support cannot be unravelled here; but this does show how intertwined the Southern African region was prior to democratisation in South Africa, and hints at how interdependent the region will continue to be.[1]

With the reconstitution of the region after the democratisation of South Africa in the 1990s, a new order has been emerging. From the seventies onwards in the apartheid era, the Frontline States were working together politically and sometimes economically in an attempt to break the stranglehold of South Africa on the region. In 1980, they formed the Southern African Development Co-ordination Conference and it is this body that was transformed into the Southern African Development Community in 1992 with 14 member countries (SADC, 1992). SADC has a large number of regional projects and agreements and plans. These are not just important instances of regional interaction. We can take the activities that are associated with SADC[2] as symbols of other types of constant interaction through all sorts of institutional arrangements, business ventures, government and non-governmental initiatives, etc. Southern Africa is a region not only in name, but also in terms of activity and institutional agreements. Many essential aspects are similar across countries in the region, and certainly across the countries that form part of the Comparative Network. Therefore, a research design formed in the Most Similar Systems Design mode is applicable.

Some of these essential aspects include the fact that there are significant linguistic overlaps and exchange as well as cross-border community relationships between the populations of these countries; they have seen similar cultural and religious transformations; have been exploited economically through slavery in some cases and through exploitative colonial regimes and foreign business interests in all cases; have gone through liberation struggles led by nationalist and mostly socialist-oriented liberation movements; now struggle to make progress from a low base in a globalised economic environment of extreme competition and trade barriers that are mostly unfavourable to African countries. The important differences that could be considered as independent variables are the varying levels of industrialisation and economic sophistication and therefore the type of integration into the world economy. The social and political cultures that go with a population that is mostly urbanised, the development of a sizeable middle-class and liberal constitutional and legal dispensation could also be considered. This sets South Africa apart from the rest. Furthermore, we might expect some impact from the type of post-colonial economic regime in that some countries went for a much more rigorous or specific form of socialism. The cases of Mozambique and Tanzania are important in this regard. Civil War is the last prominent dimension that may have a noticeable effect. Mozambique, the Congo and Angola have had their share of this type of tragedy, but only Mozambique forms part of our study in some chapters.

Values

Our Approach to Values

To analyse the values of ordinary people is to discover the ideas of the good, notions about meaning, significance and coherence, points of motivation and symbols of identity. These come from concrete forms of interaction such as community, family, friendships, religious and other civil organisations as well as the interaction between these localised and personal relations and the larger more abstract and distant systems and structures. The institutions and the political, economic, social, legal and scientific systems of society only make sense and are only made sense of in terms of the 'stocks of knowledge' (Ingram 1987:116) that societies and individuals hold.

In spite of possibly thousands of attempts at defining values, a definition of social values would mostly refer to the idea that values are 'conceptions of the desirable that guide behaviour over the long term' (Coetzee 1989; Halman 1991; Joubert 1992; McLaughlin 1965; van Deth and Scarbrough; 1995b). We argue that there are three important assumptions associated with this definition. These assumptions eventually determine the significance of the term as well as the research methodology.

- Values are of heuristic nature in that they enable us to interpret and categorise our own and other people's general approach to life. Values appear in attitudes, opinions, preferences, etc. patterns can be discerned. When we observe social interaction and behaviour. If we focus our attention on attitudes, opinions, beliefs and moral judgements, we argue that a distinct pattern in a wide array of these observable aspects can be interpreted as evidence of constraints. These constraints are evidence of a value orientation. It is still an interpreted constraint, and thus an interpreted value orientation. But that is what value analysis is for. It makes it possible to understand the general orientations that guide or underlie behaviour over the long term.

- Values are non-empirical (McLaughlin 1965) conceptions of the desirable in the sense that they cannot be observed directly. It is, thereby, assumed that values are latent variables underlying opinions, attitudes, beliefs and moral judgements. These can be regarded as manifestations of values focusing on a particular object or class of objects while values are more general and enduring. However, as people act on their opinions, attitudes, judgements and beliefs, they learn from the experience and that affects their values. In that sense, there is a reciprocal relation between values and manifestations of values.

- Values engage moral considerations because of the implied moral dimension of conceptions of 'desirability' in distinction to simple 'desire'. Conceptions of desirability are social and historical. We engage in moral discourses in relation to particular issues that we face and have to take decisions on in everyday life as well as in momentous circumstances. These issues relate to contexts of interaction and social structures and thus we are engaging with others when we form and change values. In addition, the others that we meet in this engagement are not all part of one seamless series of exchanges, but part of a complex array of relations, and structures. That means that values have to be studied with due regard for the particular historical and social context within which they are found.

If we, therefore, take the cultural approach outlined below with the approach to values stated here, we define social values as cultural and cultured conceptions of the desirable that guide behaviour over the longer term. These conceptions are formed and embedded by the structures of society and manifestations and instruments of power.

Because values discourses have such powerful but hidden normative associations obscured the seemingly self-evident nature of the ethical precepts carried in the values discourse, we find it necessary to point to a fourth logic of the definition of values that we adhere to.

> Values are always expressed in a context of the exertion and contestation of power. As values are normative expressions they operate within the sphere of ideology. Because the expression of values is an expression of what ought to be, values discourses intend change to a desired, normative situation or the establishment of the normativity of a current situation. This implies that values analysis should always also be analysis of power and especially hidden structures of power. Values, when instituted in a discourse, are too easily just the expression of the ideology of the dominant class (Touraine 1974:144; Touraine 1977:37)

There is no self-evident set or number of values that play a role in development; just as there is no self-evident role of values in poverty. This has to be observed and interpreted in historical and social context. There is evidence that values are, indeed, path-dependent, implying that values may differ between people and groups of people because they have followed different trajectories in the (recent) past. But it is important to define what has to be taken into consideration and for that purpose a provisional and working definition of poverty and development has to be formulated.

Economists now realise that human beings are not just self-interested rational decision-makers, but cultured beings that have different ideas about rationality and that are not only motivated by self-interest. Human values are the 'outcomes of environments in which individuals develop and live, within boundaries set by genetic predispositions' (Ben-Ner and Putterman 1998:58). These 'genetic predispositions' relate to basic human needs and how humanity has learnt to satisfy these needs through cooperation and mutual solidarity. The environment within which this deep structure is played out is affected by socialisation of the individual in terms of the conditions within which he or she grows up and forms a world-view. These conditions are affected by the institutions of the time, major events that have a deep impact and technologies that bring about major shifts in the way we live and make a living (Ben-Ner and Putterman 1998:17-51).

Sociologists and political scientists have been arguing for some time that different cultures are the product of different strategies of dealing with economic, technological and political change, but add that these cultures also shape the environment (Inglehart 1990:3). In fact, the rise of sociology and political science as subjects in modern science has at its root the attempt to understand the change brought about by industrialisation and the establishment of modern societies in the nation-state system (Giddens 1971).

Empirical research is always trying to pin down particular formative factors in the development of particular values. This is notoriously difficult but not unimportant. Inglehart finds that '[f]ormal education, one's current social milieu and perhaps life-cycle effects all seem to shape one's value priorities. But the impact of a given generation unit's formative experiences seems to be the most significant variable...' (Inglehart 1977:96). Inglehart argues that generations are influenced by two dynamics. These are explained by the 'scarcity hypothesis' and by the 'socialization hypothesis'. The first depends on the Maslovian need hierarchy – even if only in a very broad sense of distinguishing between material needs and needs that relate to 'esteem, self-expression and aesthetic satisfaction' (Inglehart 1997:33). The second hypothesis implies that values formed at a young age tend to have more purchase and the environment seems to have relatively little effect on values after individuals have reached adulthood (1997:33-34). A third hypothesis holds promise that goes beyond the commonly accepted ideas of socialisation and scarcity. Inglehart speaks of the 'authoritarian reflex'. By this term, he refers to the effect of rapid change and subsequent insecurity that seems to lead to fundamentalist reactions or a need for strong secular leaders (1997:38).

Values are part of a wider cultural framework and this is discussed in order to establish some basic principles.

Our Approach to Culture

Culture and values are modern concepts even if what we immediately think of in these terms is as old as humanity itself. No concept central to the self-description of society can be understood in isolation from what the concept is meant to effect in society. An essentialist but naïve concept of culture and values may maintain that culture and values are just other words for being human. However, the notions of culture and values emanate from a consciousness that we may also have control and influence over society and over human differences and that these are not just facts of social life but human constructs. The intention and hope of actively changing the way of life of a society is the root of the idea of culture. This is fundamentally modern. Obviously, the question is then how this change of culture is effected and to what aims cultural change is effected.

Baumann provides an enlightening historical perspective on the matter. In the initial stages of modernity, views on culture could be equated with 'gardening'. There was only the cultured and the uncultured (Bauman 1987:95) and the uncultured had to be kept out or 'weeded out'. In early modern society and with the advent of the nation-state system and the institution of mass education, industrial production, universal legal systems, etc., a new view of culture emerged whereby culture was to be 'legislated'. In many countries, religion, language and other aspects of culture were standardised. For that more than propaganda was needed, and institutions were built up to govern the citizens of a country. In late modernity or globalised modernity, it is no longer possible to do this kind of social engineering – even if many societies still try, and many political parties still have cultural and social engineering as the core of their ideology. The role of intellectuals and ethical research is that of 'interpreting' (Bauman 1987).

From our perspective there are important choices implied here. Looking at African culture from this gardener perspective means that the correct cultural answer to African development exists and can be instituted. Looking at African culture from a legislator perspective means that the standard cultural answer for every society can be developed by representative political processes and then enforced. Such views cannot be accepted if the diversity and continuous change that typify modern societies is taken seriously. Baumann suggests a more modest approach. Cultural research should interpret. Interpretation assumes pluralism and precludes the existence of a privileged or final normative answer to cultural issues. Culture is to be communicated and debated and not gardened to root out the weeds or legislated to homogenise all (Bauman 1987:143).

This perspective is a warning to both the investigator and researcher and the policy-maker and decision-maker. If this is not done, the Disreali observation of social and cultural manipulation in his time will be true of the relationship between our research and policy-makers and the African societies that are engaged: 'ours are nations of the seduced and the repressed; of those free to follow their needs and those forced to comply to the norms' (Bauman 1987:169).

Another aspect that has to be noted when thinking about cultural investigation and the relationship between any such investigation, and its context is the necessary relationship between culture and power. 'Culture is linked inextricably with power because some people are able to structure the world more than others; and they do so for others… Culture is structure' (Varcoe and Kilminster 1996: 217).

The connection between power and structure has been a standard issue in social theory since the notion of the two faces of power became current due to Bachrach and Baratz's critique of Dahl's argument according to which power was the ability to effect decisions (Lukes 1974; Bachrach and Baratz 1962). They pointed out that the effect of 'non-decision-making' was also the exercise of power in that it sets the agenda in a given context. They (Bachrach and Baratz 1962, following Schattschneider 1960) call this agenda-setting feature of existing social patterns the 'mobilization of bias'. Structure refers to the patterns that are set in society and in organisations and do not change overnight. Institutions and organisations are in themselves prime examples of social patterning in that they do not change overnight.

Cultural investigation should, therefore, also include institutional investigation and as institutions are critical to the political and economic patterns in any society, culture forms 'informal constraints that are part of the makeup of institutions' (North 2005:12). Institutions are manifestations of the structuration of culture and the dominant culture. Castells also argues that 'cultures manifest themselves fundamentally through their embeddedness in institutions and organisations… The culture that matters for the constitution and development of a given economic system is the one that materializes in organisational logics' (Castells 1996a:151-152). Therefore, it is imperative that a cultural analysis and attempts at moulding development initiatives with a cultural consciousness include an institutional analysis and approach.

The so-called 'third face' of power, i.e. ideology, as defined by Lukes (1974) has to be reflected on as well. Behaviourist cultural analyses do not have the inclination to think about ideology, because the object of the analysis is purely the 'empirically verifiable' behaviour rather than the interaction between meaning and behaviour and the structures within which the meaning and behaviour is placed and makes sense. However, culture is a playground of ideology and the institutions and other structures of society often both support and require ideology. Apartheid structures and ideology cannot be bettered as an example of this.

If we take the approach developed here, the key guidelines in our analysis of African culture and values have to be that:

- the intention of the analysis is to be reflected on at least, and at best focused on interpretation and mediation rather than judgement, reform or political alignment;

- institutional and other structural dimensions of the particular cultural aspect that is studied should be included in the research; and

- the ideological potential of the research and the ideological embeddedness of the cultural aspect that is being studied should be investigated and questioned.

Most observers and commentators and policy-makers now seem to say African solutions are the only ones that will work. All of these people and institutions would agree that solutions that recognise the values and culture of African people and that deal with them are needed. We suspect that this is not only recognition of the dignity of African people and their say in the development process. It is also admission that there has to be a fusion of the development process and African values and culture for the institutions and projects and policies and aid to work. We suspect that this is sometimes meant as 'gardening' and the 'weeding out' of aspects of culture that inhibit development. We also suspect that this is sometimes meant as the 'legislation' of a homogenous and politically enforced standard cultural framework – which would suit a neo-liberal agenda, as we will see later on. We would suggest that it should rather be meant as interpretation and communication that enables ordinary people to escape the threat of being forced to comply with the norms that govern outside influences and those who are seduced by freedom to follow their needs.

An interpretative view of culture understands that values and culture cannot be changed overnight and do not change from the outside. Even though some might think that values lie waiting for the next individual and government to take them and change them to suit the ends or goals of the individual or government, this is not the case. It is a much more complex and in principle unpredictable process of change that is at stake. In a globalised and connected world the process of cultural change has become even more complex as it is more reflexive (Giddens 1994; Beck 1986) than ever. This means a more sophisticated understanding of communication and mutual understanding has to be developed for the area of values and cultural exchange.

Poverty and Development

We define development as a significant and sustained change for the better in material conditions as well as social and psychological experience of a community or society – knowing full well that the term is not unambiguous (Mkandawire 2010). Any definition of development in Africa has to deal with the existing widespread and severe poverty that characterises large parts of the continent. It also has to deal with systemic matters such as the impact of globalisation and the consequent marginalisation of Africa in the world economy. Development definitions must be useful in institutional contexts in that it has to deal with political governance, economic and corporate governance, infrastructure development, capital flows, market access, human resources, etc. Development definitions also need a historical dimension in both human and environmental time. Development that could deal with these issues would require a restructuring of both the position of Africa in the world and of domestic development strategies. Lastly, and maybe even most importantly, one has to deal with the discourse on development itself, i.e. the ideological nature of the term and the space left for ideological agendas in policy-making in the very ambiguity of the term.

This is not what development theory has been about all the time, though. The practice and the theory have to meet. Not only has actual economic growth meant global and national increases in inequality (Seligson 2003) and has such economic growth not been evident in many African countries on a consistent level, but Africa has been following (if sometimes belatedly) the strictures of the World Bank and the International Monetary Fund (IMF) and other multilateral development agencies that are supposedly based on the best of what development theory had to offer (Rutten and Leliveld 2008:12-13). It is now clear that most African countries will not even reach the Millennium Development Goals (UN 2010) and the failure of development as a notion has to be considered (Kothari and Minogue 2002:2-7). Some argue that the notion of development is a foreign imposition and if we take the dominant formalised theories that cluster around modernisation as a metatheory (Kothari and Minogue 2002:7-10) this has to be acceded. However, the initial impression is different if one reads development theory texts.

Diversity of approaches to development and the fight against poverty have almost become a principle (Booth 1993a). In this regard, gender (Nussbaum and Glover 1995; Townsend 1993; Tripp 1998), class formation (Sklar 1998), rural and indigenous knowledge (Chambers 1983; Long and Villareal 1993; Prosterman et al. 1990), ecology (Adams 1993; Sutcliffe 2000), the state (Castells 1996a; Mouzelis 1994), ICTs (Ben Soltane and Adam 1999), non-governmental organisations (NGOs) (Brown and Korten 1989; Cernea 1988; Korten 1990; Schuurman 1993), New Social Movements (Sklair 2000) and culture (Putnam 1993; Serageldin and Taboroff 1994) have been studied and have been the focus of particular development programmes and policies. In different ways, all of these are relevant and legitimate dimensions that need to be tackled.

It may be that development is not the right term for this change. The notion of development has a range of general and more systematic associations that are to be declared and declined. Development often meant foreign and imposed. It has also meant capitalism, and this is still a dominant association for many commentators in the current period. These two associations have to be declined. Development cannot be imposed and development is not capitalist ideology cloaked as something else.

Development has long been associated with foreign designs for African people that assume that Africans are to follow the path taken by others, and subsequently theorised as the normative framework for development under all circumstances. However, development has been associated with this kind of evolutionism and determinism for too long. The fact that Europe has seen a particular modernisation process does not mean that Africa should follow the same steps. This is the case not only because African development takes place under different conditions, but also because a modernisation model would necessarily be an imposed model.

Modernisation theory, as we know it, makes little sense in Africa. There is no necessary connection between the, sometimes hidden, assumptions of evolutionism and determinism in modernisation theory on the one hand and development theory for Africa on the other. African development cannot mean change from traditional African society to modern society, simply because these essentialist concepts do not apply – even if they were used to define development theory and designs in Africa for quite some time. Not only are 'traditional' and 'modern' flags for a significant variety of conditions, but traditional and modern have been in conversation for a long time in Africa. This 'long conversation' (Comaroff and Comaroff 1991, 1997) has emptied out any pristine or pure form that may be conceived. No traditional society (whatever that may have meant) exists in Africa after at least 200 years of intense and deep confrontation and entanglement with first colonial Europe and, subsequently, with modern capitalism and socialism.

At the same time, modern cannot be exclusively associated with Western – unless one claims that socialism and communism are exclusively Western concepts. The notion of revolution and proletarian or peasant-based change as propounded by socialists and communists of all hues is as modern a notion as one can get.

The other question one has to discuss is the issue of whether the notion of development does not suppose capitalism and capitalist forms of development. Capitalism looms so large in the current world order that this issue cannot be finished off with historical perspectives that point to some similarity in assumptions about historical change between capitalism and socialism. Those that argue that development is more often than not a mask of capitalist change, point out that development in Africa has often meant that Africans and African goods and resources are accessed and exploited by the West. This is a critical matter not only because of critique of the *dependencia* school of thought (Frank) and world systems theory (Wallerstein). Many African commentators and intellectuals have tried to use this argument to develop the foundations of an independent view of African change – rather than 'development' as propounded by the World Bank and other international or Western agencies (Onimode 1992).

Such arguments seem to forget that historically, development has also, for a considerable period of time and in many countries, meant socialism and therefore another type of modernisation of 'backwardness' and 'traditional' society (Mafeje 1978:8, 48, 75) correctly points the disjunction between socialist ideologues and community life while still using a framework of necessary and historical progress from 'primitive' to socialist in his own work. In fact, as argued above, both socialism and capitalism are deeply dependent on ideological constructs of modernisation and of the 'backwardness' of traditional societies. If one looks at the use of the term development over a slightly longer period of time than the past decade, it becomes clear that socialism also intended to 'develop' societies and communities and that the real issue is not whether the notion of development supposes capitalism but what development means in a context where capitalism is the dominant mode of production.

We might then follow the arguments of post-development theorists (Rahnema and Bawtree 1997) and dismiss the term fully, but Matthews (2004) makes the important point that this would not be the preferred position of Africans themselves. She then follows the line set out in our initial definition of development, but adds that development in Africa cannot work on the basis of the values of development in the West as the values and the project have to be aligned.

Theorists of the RWWII development project lament the way in which African communities have failed to achieve 'development', but are blind to the possibility that some of these communities may have rejected the kind of development such theorists propose and may be actively trying to meet their needs and fulfil their aspirations in a different way (Mathews 2004:381).

If we discount the idea that development has to mean modernisation and if we discount the idea that development has to mean capitalism, one still has to deal with the question of what development is. We agree with Kebede that an historical approach is needed, as this creates space for divergence and choice and does away with the universalism and evolutionism of ideological constructs of modernisation and concomitant theories of development (Kebede 2004).

It, then, become possible to understand what Diagne means when he concurs with Sall that the notion of development means 'the exploration of the future' (Diagne 2004:57) and most importantly, that this way of thinking about development is not at all foreign to African culture. He severely criticises Mbiti's characterisation of African time as 'motion towards the past' and agrees with Gyekye that Mbiti overanalyses African languages in order to find what he already decided to argue, namely an essentialist view of African cognitive processes and culture (Diagne 2004:59-64). This kind of accusation has been levelled at Mbiti before (Lo Liyong 1988; p'Bitek 1970, 1973).

Gyekye himself argues for a 'self-created modernity' as a counter to the assumption that Western modernity has to replace some essentially African tradition, and as a counter to the assumption that Africa cannot be modern and cannot change (Gyekye 1997:286).

From the above, it is clear that we want to define development in terms that do not continue the mental colonisation that characterises most of the history of the discourse on development in Africa up to now. At the same time, we want to focus on the concrete and the historical and not be enamoured with a theoretical discourse that disregards the complexity of difficult questions that come from all sorts of different quarters.

For example, the question of who is to benefit from development remains. If development is not simply an imposed process of modernisation in terms of criteria and a path of change defined outside of Africa, and if development in not simply a process of de-liberalisation, structural adjustment and formal democratisation in order to suit the capitalist mode of production and enable exploitation in a more 'palatable' form than the present, it may still not mean that the poor will benefit. Even though we are not presuming the 'trickle-down effect' of capitalist development thought, and we are not presuming the necessity of 'breaking eggs to make an omelette' (Leninist modernisation) or 'liberalisation' (capitalist modernisation), it may be that the poorest people in societies that go through significant change still end up being victims of the process of change. Development cannot mean that this happens.

It is useful to reflect on Barrington Moore's analysis of the role of peasants in industrial modernisation. Although African development cannot be limited to the aim of industrial development, and although we have already declined an ideological reading of modernisation as an adequate or desirable model for development in Africa, Moore's historical and comparative perspective is very useful to focus attention on the question of beneficiaries from development. He argues convincingly that the peasant has always, lost even if peasants did sometimes play a very important role in creating change. On an economic level, the extension of market relationships implies the replacement of subsistence farming and on a political level, modernisation means centralised political control – both detrimental to peasant interests in important regards (1966:467-468). Even though the notion of peasant is not all that useful in the post-colonial African context where large groups of very poor are urbanised and otherwise displaced, careful consideration has to be given to the results of development for the poor.

Barrington Moore's conclusions may be the result of the questions that he asks. The consequence of change for peasants that Moore identifies may be because industrial modernisation has always been about the interests of some elite and not about development as a whole. Our interest is not industrial modernisation in the first place but development in a sustained and holistic sense. Therefore, the discussion will be limited to stating the likelihood that change may benefit particular groups to the exclusion of the poor and setting a criterion for successful development as change that is to the benefit of those at the bottom of society.

Development is for people, and this means that development has to be defined in terms of the aspirations and expectations of the people concerned (Coetzee 1989). In tandem with that approach, poverty has to be defined by ordinary people and their approach to poverty should guide attempts to alleviate or eradicate poverty (Narayan 2000).

In continuity with that, we see the data available from household surveys used in the Living Standards Measurement Surveys and the Participatory Poverty Assessments (PPA) of the World Bank and associated institutions. The PPA data focuses on the 'multiple meanings, dimensions, and experiences of poverty' (Narayan 2000:15). The data available on the meaning of poverty for the poor themselves, the role of formal and informal institutions in the lives of the poor, gender relations in that context and the relation between poverty and social fragmentation, forms important background information for the study of the values of ordinary people (of whom a sizeable proportion in Southern Africa are poor or very poor). The six main findings of the PPA studies expose the multidimensionality of poverty in the experience of the poor themselves. Poverty is associated with a lack of material well-being, but it also includes a lack of basic infrastructure, illness, lacking literacy and material assets. Furthermore, poverty signifies psychological aspects such as dependence, humiliation and social marginalisation as well. Development would mean positive change in these conditions and experiences. However, the poor cannot be made to speak in a form that is predetermined by the global institutions (Pithouse 2007); and in the case of the PPAs, the function of the data is clearly encapsulated, but the function of the World Bank and how the bank sees itself and its role in ideological terms.

For that reason, we need to discuss poverty a bit more than to list the findings of a constrained data gathering process such as the PPAs. We find that the Economy, Ecology and Exclusion group of the Africa Studies Centre of Leiden has the right approach to the matter. There has to be, detailed study of the complexity of the nature of poverty and how it links to development opportunities that will seek to understand the varied and complex ways in which resources are accessed and institutions allocate resources (Rutten and Leliveld 2008:15). We find their use of the notion of exclusion relevant, as they want to point to the way in which access is denied. This is most relevant to a view of poverty as it allows us to place the poverty concept in terms that are aligned with an attempt to account for the effects of globalisation on poor people and in the creation of poverty (2008:17).

It can be contrasted with the other two common ways of thinking about poverty. May provides a good summary of these. The first is the most obvious notion that poverty is 'the inability to attain an absolute minimum standard of living, reflected by a quantifiable and absolute indicator applied to a constant threshold...' (May 2008:27). The second is less obvious, but quite pervasive. It argues that poverty is the 'lack of resources with which to attain a socially acceptable quality of life' (2008:28). The difference lies in the norm that is used. In the one case, it is a derived international number. In the second, it is a relative social level. The third way of looking at poverty is to think of it 'as being constrained choices, unfulfilled capabilities, and exclusion' (2008:28).

This approach fits the Human Development measures of the United Nations. These were developed with significant influence of Amartya Sen's approach to development as freedom and the so-called capabilities approach. The history of this development will be considered in more detail in the next chapter, but suffice to say at the moment that our notion of development and poverty takes into account the full range of human capabilities and is not limited to an economistic or quantification model of development. We are interested in the experience of ordinary people, and as a test of the success of development, we are specifically looking at the experience of marginal groups. Along with Diagne, we are interested in how these people think about their own ability to create their own destiny. Are they able to 'explore the future' and conceptualise a future? Do they feel well and are they happy? Are they free from poverty, also in the sense that they do not suffer from a poverty of ideas about their own future and what they can do about it? Do they feel empowered enough to use resources that they have at their disposal or is hopelessness a cloud that covers their horizon? One could go on in this vein and attempt to make the list of questions universal (Nussbaum's Aristotelian list [1993] or Clarke's version of it [2002b, 2002a]). However, [t]he problem is not with listing important capabilities, but with insisting on one predetermined canonical list of capabilities, chosen by theorists without any general social discussion or public reasoning. To have such a fixed list, emanating entirely from pure theory, is to deny the possibility of fruitful public participation on what should be included and why public discussion and reasoning can lead to a better understanding of the role, reach and significance of particular capabilities (Sen 2004b:77, 81).

For that reason, we see the establishment of a multi-level dialogue about values, poverty and development as critical to the successful redefinition of development in Africa. It may well be that there is a list of universal capabilities that will mean development for all people, including poor people in Southern Africa. However, we will only know that if we have taken the trouble to engage with poor people and if we have heard and analysed the variety of verbalisations that tell us about capabilities that are relevant.

Research Objectives and Questions

Our objectives are to link cultural values in the fullest sense of the word (including institutions and all social interaction) and development conceptually and empirically, to explore specific values that are supposedly playing a significant role in perpetuating poverty and to identify values that could contribute positively to development as we have defined it above.

Determining what role values play in development and determining what role what particular values play has to be done in context. Values are not just particular to the culture of a particular community or 'nation', but also to groups and stratifications within communities and large social entities. Age, gender, ethnicity, rural-urban location, occupation and employment status, income, education, religion, ethnic background, marital status, etc are all variables that require investigation in order to establish how values play a role in development. In terms of the region which we focus on and the countries that we have data for and which we study in some or other way, it is also important to focus on the aspects in which these countries differ. These aspects have been pointed out above, but they include the level of industrialisation, urbanisation, global economic integration, middle-class formation and war trauma experience. These aspects will be highlighted where appropriate and mostly on a country level analysis.

A number of questions can be formulated and applied in terms of the differentials listed. These include:

- Do values provide a partial explanation for the pervasive poverty of African people?
- Are there certain discernable values that provide a partial explanation for the notion that Africans have allowed themselves to be exploited by outside forces and inside elites over the past decades?

- Are there certain discernable values that enable a partial understanding of the fact that many African communities have survived in the most extreme conditions in the recent past?
- Are there certain values that could play a pivotal role in the future development of Africa and its people?
- What is the interplay between demography, values and development?
- Is it possible to explain the dynamics between discernable values and value-clusters and other factors like political-economy, demographic change, geography, etc.?
- What value differences and cultural dynamics are there between countries and communities in Southern Africa that could explain development differentials?

By investigating the questions above, we could focus on a tangible list of dimensions of development possibly affected by the values of ordinary people. The aim of this book is to argue the ambitious claim as to the aspects that are to be considered when investigating the relationship between culture and development in our time. This claim is based on our interpretation of the current debates about social capital, religion, civil society, moral virtues, relationships and trust and the reasons why and how culture matters in development. But it is also based in our particular African experiences of issues that continue to come up in discourses about values in Africa. The aim is not only to argue that particular aspects are to be investigated, but also to start the investigation and to attempt to draw conclusions about the correctness and relevance of the theoretical claims made from existing material and data.

Areas of Concentration

The values notion encapsulates a wide variety of themes. With the definition provided above and the focus added by the research questions regarding the role of social and cultural values in development in Southern Africa, the matter has been reduced somewhat. However, when one considers the variety of value-related matters that might conceivably have an impact on development, the field opens up again. The need for choices is, therefore, implied again. The process of deciding on which values we find most important and the availability of data are two separate matters of course.

During a preliminary workshop and subsequent meetings and discussions, the results of our deliberations were that four clusters of values were defined. We saw these clusters as encapsulating what we thought would be important ones to investigate. These clusters refer to a fairly long list of specific values and value-oriented notions. The four value clusters are power, cosmology, human relationships and human qualities. Some aspects are, of course, crosscutting.

Power: including questions about the nature of different definitions and social role of status, success, wealth and leadership; the social role of obedience, tradition and custom; the significance of these themes for the body, for gender relations and gender definitions.

Cosmology: including the various definitions of social and general harmony and conflict; positions regarding strangers, foreigners, the unknown; the concepts of fate and causality, and their relationship to witchcraft and to multiple explanations for the same events; the notion of time; the value of human life in the greater scheme of things; the significance of these aspects for creativity and innovations, tradition and custom, risk and view of the future.

Human relationships: including patterns and conventions of communication; gender definitions and relationships; the body; notions of honour and shame; values regarding freedom, trust and tolerance, strangers, foreigners, the unknown.

Human qualities: including notions of obedience, integrity, responsibility, discipline; types of aspirations; perceived different work ethics; the role and value of imagination, creativity and innovation; and the value of human life.

In some instances, we include an aspect because existing analyses and theories focus attention on it, whether or not we deem this aspect to be particularly useful in answering the research questions that we pose. For example, Weber's Protestant Ethic is a famous argument that has seen many analyses flow from it. The African case is a rather complex setting for the operationalisation of this argument as the religion picture is not as clear as elsewhere and work is not as industrialised as elsewhere. However, the concept was operationalised and tested as far as possible. In other cases, we made educated guesses as to the relevance of particular notions and relationships and were able to establish some relevance in empirical analysis. In most cases, however, we still remained on the conceptual and theoretical level, as we were not able to test the relevance of most of the notions listed above fully or adequately.

The conceptual and theoretical arguments for the particular notions are made in the next two chapters. The empirical analysis is done in the subsequent four chapters. The analysis depends mostly on secondary analysis of existing data and therefore on the category fit and sampling arguments of the primary data collection frameworks. It is not always satisfactory, but exactly in the problems we identify, a significant number of learning points emerge.

Comparative research is not about quantitative analysis and should use both quantitative and qualitative analyses. We attempt to provide material that has that balance, but the full spectrum of such an attempt will remain outside the scope of a single publication.

Methodology

The Case for the Comparative Method

Introduction

The increased interest in cross-cultural research in recent times can be seen to be directly related to factors such as globalisation, in which individuals across the globe have become connected in new and unexpected ways. However, the history of Orientalism (Said 1979, 2004) as a subject should be a warning about ethnocentric and ideological conclusions to such research. In trying to understand the similarities and differences between cultures, cross-cultural studies bring with them a unique set of methodological challenges. These need to be comprehensively addressed if valid and reliable results are to be obtained. In essence, all cross-cultural researchers have to deal with a set of similar problems, such as the (in)equality of meanings of phenomena they wish to study across cultural groups, the appropriateness of measurement instruments across cultures, and the accuracy of data collected to answer research questions and hypotheses. More especially, these differences are greatly amplified when varying cultural contexts are taken into account,.

The most basic assumption of cross-cultural research is that comparison is possible because patterns (kinds of phenomena that occur repeatedly) can be identified. To understand why a particular community or culture is the way it is, we must compare that case with others. Nevertheless, there are those who argue that cultures are so diverse and unique that they can only be described in their own terms. From this point of view, comparison is a waste of time, if not wholly illegitimate (Ember and Ember 2001:5). It is, however, important to note that cross-culturalists do not deny the uniqueness of each culture as such. Instead, they argue that uniqueness and diversity are always present, simultaneously. Taking these dynamics into consideration, this chapter will aim to address the challenges inherent in cross-cultural research with specific reference to methodological issues.

Establishing Equivalence

Undergirding the superstructure of theory and causality within the social sciences is measurement. As noted by Torgerson (1958:89), achieving the theoretical and causal goals of a particular field 'would seem to be virtually impossible unless its variables can be measured adequately'. Two closely related concepts play an essential role in cross-cultural comparisons, namely: equivalence and bias. From a theoretical point of view the two concepts are the opposite of each other; scores are equivalent when they are unbiased (Van de Vijver and Leung 2000:7).

Neumann (2000:410-11) refers to four types of equivalence that the cross-cultural researcher should strive towards: Lexicon, Contextual, Conceptual and Measurement equivalence. Firstly, lexicon equivalence refers to the correct translation of words and phrases and also highlights the need for the researcher to make sure that words have the same meaning across cultures.

Contextual equivalence, however, refers to the correct application of terms or concepts in different social or historical contexts. For example, in different cultures with different dominant religions, a religious leader may have different roles, training and authority. A researcher who asks about "priests" within a specific culture, without taking into account the context, could make serious errors in interpretation.

Conceptual equivalence relates to the use of the same concept across divergent cultures. Here, the question arises, whether it is in fact possible to create concepts that are true, accurate, and valid representations of social life in two or more cultural settings? For instance, as noted by Neumann (2000:410), there is no Western conceptual equivalent for the Japanese 'ie', which denotes a continuing line of familial descent going back generations and continuing into the future. The researcher, therefore, needs to be aware of these conceptual limitations and make the relevant adjustments to the research design.

The final type of equivalence described by Neuman (2000:411) is measurement equivalence, referring to the measurement of the same concept in different settings. Even if a researcher develops a concept appropriate to different cultural contexts, the question remains has to whether one may not need different types of measurement to test the same concept in these different contexts. For instance, the researcher might measure a concept using an attitude survey in one culture but field research in another. Similarly, it may be necessary to use different indicators to measure the same concept in different cultures.

Differential response styles such as acquiescence and extremity ratings can also cause significant levels of measurement bias in the researcher's findings. Hui and Triandis (1989:296-309), for example, found that Hispanics tended to choose extremes on a five-point rating scale more often than did white Americans. Another common source of method bias is differential familiarity with the stimuli used. When, for example, cognitive tests are administered to cultural groups with widely different educational backgrounds, differences in stimulus familiarity may be almost impossible to overcome (Van de Vijver and Leung 1997:45-49). The application of Western methods of information gathering to non-Western contexts therefore presents particular difficulties, as many people in the developing world may not fully understand the concepts of evaluation, measurement or anonymity.

Translation-related Problems

As Hofstede (2001:21) notes, language is both the vehicle of most of cross-cultural research and part of its object. Our thinking is framed by the categories and words available in our language. One of the major challenges of any kind of research in which the language of the people under study is different from that of the write-up is, therefore, gaining conceptual equivalence or comparability of meaning. Phillips (1960:291) sees this as being 'in absolute terms, an unsolvable problem' as 'almost any utterance in any language carries with it a set of assumptions, feelings, and values that the speaker may or may not be aware of, but that the field worker, as an outsider, usually is not'.

For many researchers (Sechrest et al 1972; Brislin et al 1973; Warwick and Osherson 1973) the process of gaining comparability of meanings is greatly facilitated by the researcher (or the translator) having not only a proficient understanding of a language, but also an intimate knowledge of the culture. As noted by Birbili (2000:86), only then can the researcher pick up the full implications that a term carries for the people under study and make sure that the cultural connotations of a word are made explicit to the readers of the research report. The use of translators and interpreters 'is not merely a technical matter that has little bearing on the outcome. It is of epistemological consequence, as it influences what is "found"' (Temple, as quoted in Birbili, 2000:86).

Solutions to the Problem of Inequivalence

As noted by Landman (2000:43), the explanatory power of concepts can be greatly enhanced if they are applied to contexts in which the comparativist is most familiar. Those who engage in area studies should, therefore, have extensive knowledge of the history, economics, politics, and culture of a regional sub-set of countries in an effort to make more meaningful explanations of political and cultural phenomena. This local knowledge can identify gaps between theoretical concepts and their application, resulting in a more meaningful comparison.

A second solution involves the raising of the level of abstraction of concepts in order to allow a study to be more inclusive. For example, Inglehart (1997) applied two value continua to forty-three countries, which ranged on the one hand from citizens' concerns with 'survival' vs. 'well-being' and, on the other, from 'traditional' vs. 'legal-rational' forms of authority. In doing so, he specified his concepts so as to incorporate a wide range of countries (Landman 2000:43). However, this heightened level of abstraction also has its own limitations in terms of adequately tapping into the complexity of a given society.

The third solution follows from the first. If a truly informed comparison of countries is sought, then those seeking to compare 'should venture out of the security of the familiar [and] collaborate with other scholars who possess specialist knowledge of the countries under scrutiny' (Sanders quoted in Landman 2000:44).

It becomes clear that one of the most challenging aspects facing comparativists is the equivalence of both their theoretical concepts and the indicators for these concepts across multiple contexts. As Mayer (1989:57) argues, 'the contextual relativity of the meaning or the measures of indicators constitutes the most serious impediment to the cross-contextual validity of empirically testable explanatory theory'. The key towards overcoming this obstacle necessarily lies in careful specification of concepts, thoughtful construction of indicators that operationalise them, careful application of them to multiple contexts, and recognition of their limitations.

Selection of Countries: Most Similar and most Different Systems Design

Variously called the "comparative method", "comparable cases strategy" or "focused comparison", comparing few countries achieves control through the careful selection of countries that are analysed (Landman 2000:27). Comparison of the similarities and differences is meant to uncover what is common to each country that accounts for the observed outcome.

The method of comparing few countries is divided primarily into two types of system design: "most similar systems design" (MSSD) and "most different systems design" (MDSD). MSSD seeks to identify the key features that are different among essentially similar countries, with these differing features therefore accounting for the differing political outcomes. For example, countries may share the same basic characteristics (a, b, c), and some share the same key explanatory factor (x), but those without the key explanatory factor also lack the outcome which is to be explained (y). Thus, the presence or absence of the key explanatory factor is seen to account for this outcome. By contrast, in the MDSD design, countries selected have inherently different features, but share the same key explanatory factor (x) as well as the presence of the outcome to be explained (y) (Landman 2000:27).

MSSD is particularly well suited for those engaged in area studies. The theoretical and intellectual justification for area studies is that there is something inherently similar about countries that make up a particular geographical region of the world. Whether it is common history, language, religion, politics or culture, researchers working in area studies are essentially employing most similar systems design, and the focus on countries from these regions effectively controls for those features that are common to them while looking for those features that are not (Landman 2000:28).

However, it should be kept in mind that it is often a vast oversimplification to view individual countries which are to be analysed as homogenous units which possess a single "culture". It is, in fact, common to see studies from vast and hugely diverse countries such as India or China being used to suggest that the findings are representative of the culture of the entire nation (Patel 2001:36). Such simplistic assumptions seem to have greatly limited the value of cross-cultural studies. Thus, while employing MSSD or MDSD, one needs to remain wary of the pitfalls associated with aggregating country data, and take full cognisance of the internal variations present in these countries.

Ethnocentrism and Representation of the "Other"

Prejudices and cultural biases in judgments of other cultures work like "cognitive schemata" that have a bearing on the type of processing that takes place. Information congruent with the schemata tends to be more actively sought after and better remembered. These schemata essentially 'act as templates and reduce the rich and pluriform reality to more manageable formats' (Van de Vijver and Leung 2000:35). Value bias is, therefore, intimately related to the perspective from which one sees the world. Classification, analysis and substantive interpretation are all subject to the particular perspective of the researcher, with that which is observed in part 'being a consequence of the theoretical position that the analyst adopts in the first place' (Sanders, quoted in Landman 2000:51). One could even go as far as to argue that the very decision that cross-cultural research is worthwhile reflects a certain ethnocentric Western universalist value position (Hofstede 2001:18). Knowledge is, therefore, by no means value-free.

Ethnocentrism can be defined as the 'exaggerated tendency to think the characteristics of one's own group or race superior to those of other groups or races' (Drever 1952:86). Such tendencies often start at the level of data collection, in which surveys only deal with issues that have proven relevant in a particular (usually western) test population and for which a particular language has words. The very concepts and categories of thought which sociologists and political scientists employ in their analysis 'are very often themselves part of the very political ideology which they try to understand' (Cohen, quoted in Hofstede 2001:19). As noted above, it is, therefore, essential that instruments being put to cross-cultural use should be developed with cross-cultural input.

Subjective judgements become particularly evident when studying values. Inspection of a number of instruments designed to measure human values makes it clear that the universe of all human values is not defined, and that each author has made his or her own subjective selection from this unknown universe, with little consensus among researchers. This means that the content validity of measurements of values (their representativeness for the universe of values) is necessarily low (Hofstede 2001:7).

The representation of the "other" is also an important methodological issue which needs to be considered by comparative researchers. Researchers produce meanings and values, and create social identities through the ways in which they represent people's lived experiences. This homogenising representational discourse, however, often merely reproduces unequal social relations, especially when representation involves unequal power relationships between researchers and their participants (Donnelly 2002:59). As Cotterill (quoted in Kamler and Threadgold 2003:137) notes: 'When the researcher leaves the field and begins to work on the final account, the responsibility for how the data are analysed, interpreted [and represented] is entirely his own. From now on, the [participants] are vulnerable.

Their active role in the research process is over and whatever way it is produced is beyond their control.'

Ultimately then, defining and presenting the participants' lived reality resides in the power that uncritical and non-reflexive researchers hold. According to Cheek and Porter (1997:110), what we choose to represent or not represent, and how we represent certain views and social phenomena, reflects our own beliefs, values and assumptions about reality. In essence, what we represent, we affect as well.

Ecological and Individualistic Fallacy

While individual data comprise information about individual people, ecological data comprise information that has been aggregated for territorial units, such as voting districts, municipalities, countries, amongst others. Fallacies occur when inferences are drawn about one level of analysis using evidence from another, thereby often overestimating existing relationships between variables. The ecological fallacy relates to results obtained through the analysis of aggregate-level data being used to make inferences about individual-level behaviour, while the individualistic fallacy occurs when individual-level data are used to make inferences about aggregate-level phenomena (Landman 2000:49-50).

Data availability is one of the major sources of ecological and individualistic fallacies, since scholars may be forced to substitute data from one level to examine a research question specified at another level. For example, Landman (2000:50) argues that Inglehart (1997) commits an individualistic fallacy in his study of values in forty-three societies in *Modernization and Postmodernization*. Using a standard battery of questions ranging from the "importance of God" to "protection of the environment", Inglehart constructs "clusters" of values that cohere into distinct geographical patterns. These patterns, Inglehart argues, are meaningfully distributed around the globe according to general cultural groups. In this study, Inglehart is aggregating individual-level responses to questions to establish simplified classifications of countries based on culture. Yet as Landman (2000:51) notes, grouping percentages of individuals who responded similarly to a battery of survey questions and ascribing cultural "types" to them can be argued to be an illustration of the individualistic fallacy, which confuses systemic properties with individual characteristics.

Research that specifies questions at the individual level ought to use individual data, and vice versa for research questions that specify systemic relationships. As Neuman (2000:138) notes, sociology is a discipline that rests on the fundamental belief that a distinct level of social reality exists beyond the individual. Explanations of this level require data and theory that go beyond the individual alone. Indeed, 'cultures are not king-size individuals: They are wholes and their internal logic cannot be understood in terms used for the personality dynamics of individuals' (Hofstede 2001:17).

By contrast, the ecological fallacy is committed when ecological correlations are interpreted as if they apply to individuals. Doing so is attractive because ecological correlations are often stronger than individual correlations. For example, Robinson (1950) dealt with the relationship between skin colour and illiteracy in the United States and found that between percentages of blacks in the population and percentages of illiterates across 48 states the ecological correlation was r=.77. An ecological fallacy would lead one to infer that blacks are more likely to be illiterate than other racial groups. This conclusion is proved false, however, as across 97 million individuals the individual correlation between race and literacy was r=.2 (Hofstede 2001:16).

The Importance of Triangulation

Many researchers perceive their research methods as an 'a-theoretical tool' and therefore, fail to recognise that methods impose certain perspectives on reality (Denzin 1978:98). Seeing as each method reveals different aspects of empirical reality, triangulation is necessary in order to increase the depth of understanding an investigation can yield. According to Denzin (1978:101), triangulation includes the use of multiple data-collection procedures, multiple theoretical perspectives, and/or multiple analysis techniques.

Qualitative and quantitative techniques should, therefore, be combined if a comprehensive view of the world is to be achieved. Simply put, quantitative methods seek to show differences in number between certain objects of analysis while qualitative methods seek to show differences in kind.

Qualitative strategies such as in-depth interviews, focus groups and participant observation strive to uncover a deeper level of information in order to capture meaning, process and context. Superficial, fragmented, simplistic tests and responses are therefore avoided, operating under the presumption that phenomena cannot simply be reduced to numbers analysed according to mechanical statistical tests (Berg 1995:86). By contrast, quantitative strategies serve the positive-science ideal by providing rigorous, reliable, verifiable aggregates of data and the statistical testing of empirical hypotheses (Berg 1995:10).

Triangulation can also be seen to include the incorporation of different disciplines in the research process. Indeed, cross-cultural studies presuppose a systems approach. Any element of the total system called culture should, therefore, be eligible for analysis, regardless of the discipline that usually deals with such elements. The unwanted effects of overspecialisation such as compartmentalisation, restriction of inputs and restriction of methods can thereby be avoided (Hofstede 2001:19-20).

As Hofstede (2001:2) notes, social scientists approach social reality as the blind men from an old Indian fable approached the elephant; the one who gets hold of the leg, thinks it is a tree, the one who gets hold of the tail thinks it is a rope, but none of them understands the true nature of the whole animal. Thus, we will never be more than blind men in front of a social elephant, but by joining forces with other blind men and approaching the animal from as many different angles as possible, we may find out more about it than we could ever do alone. There is no such thing as objectivity in the study of social reality; we will always be subjective, but we may at least try to be 'intersubjective', pooling and integrating a number of subjective points of view of different observers (Hofstede 2001:2).

One qualitative method which can be seen to be particularly valuable in gaining a better conceptual understanding of people's value systems is the use of focus groups. Here, researchers strive to learn through discussion with small groups about conscious and unconscious psychological and socio-cultural characteristics and processes within societies (Berg 1995:68).

Interactions between and among group members stimulate discussions in which one group member reacts to comments made by another. This group dynamism has been described as a "synergistic group effect" (Stewart and Shamdasi, 1990:16). A far larger number of ideas, issues, topics, and even solutions to a problem can be generated through group discussion than through individual conversation. The informal atmosphere of the focus group interview structure is intended to encourage subjects to speak freely and completely about their behaviours, attitudes and opinions. It is the group energy which distinguishes focus group interviews from more conventional styles of one-on-one, face-to-face interviewing approaches (Berg 1995:85).

Aggregate Data Analysis in Developing Countries

Aggregate data collection and survey research in developing countries poses its own specific challenges beyond those encountered in most developed countries. The problems frequently include, for instance: multiple languages and dialects; lack of skilled staff; poor road systems and lack of suitable transport, lack of adequate computing facilities, poor maps; nomadic populations, lack of knowledge about ages and other items by many members of the population, and difficulties with the concept of "household" as used in censuses and surveys in most developed countries (Brink 2004:65).

As Brink (2004:181) notes, government or government subsidized institutions often manipulate data in order to present a rosier picture than what should be reflected in reality. In the study of developing countries, where survey analysis is often politically and subjectively suspect, aggregate data analysis published by an independent organization can, therefore, play a useful role in generating objective information. Nevertheless, many of the figures used and presented as country statistics in such indices are only estimates – proving that figures for certain countries remain hard to come by (Brink 2004:182). In addition, as mentioned above, gross averages and aggregates also frequently mask substantial internal variations and deviations. This is particularly the case in developing countries where the views and material conditions of the political elite often do not correspond at all to those being governed.

Conclusion

As the above analysis has indicated, the very nature of cross-cultural research presents challenges not otherwise encountered in data collection processes. Researchers must be aware of, and account for a myriad of possible pitfalls, such as styles of verbal and non-verbal interaction, equivalence of meanings and the unbiased representation of the research subject. So too, it is crucial that various research methods are used in order to provide a comprehensive, contextualised understanding of cultural differences within specific environments.

Using multiple data collection strategies as well as multiple data sources may resolve some of the problems associated with cross-cultural data collection, and improve the quality of the information collected. So too, involving researchers from the country under investigation in the research process is crucial if cultural and language differences are to be adequately dealt with in the research design. Multi-cultural and multi-disciplinary research teams also have a vital role to play in selecting appropriate research methods within specific cultural contexts.

The above overview has provided some initial insights into the challenges faced by the cross-cultural researcher. Although the rewards for those engaging in this type of research are immense, valid and reliable measurement of unambiguous and interpretable cultural differences is only possible through scrupulous theorizing, design, data collection and analysis, with the validity of the results being as good as the weakest link in this chain.

The selection of South Africa, Zimbabwe, Zambia, Tanzania and Mozambique for the network that led to the analyses in this work was due to practicalities as well as substantive reasons. These considerations were indicated at the start of the chapter. However, when one takes into consideration the discourse that has now been presented about comparative research methodology, one might consider some other alternative frames for the research as well.

The choice of doing a comparison between countries, whatever the selection of countries may be, directly implies a view on the relevant unit of analysis. The Southern African region not only comprises nation-states. One might also attempt other comparisons. Cities, developmental hubs defined by the SADC, provinces, communities, and a number of other more complex constellations could be compared.

In what follows, we depend mostly on a national comparison between data gathered in terms of national sampling. We attempt to provide thicker descriptions of the complexity that national comparisons hide away throughout the publication and in particular chapters. However, most of the data that is available depends on the position that nation-states are a valid unit of analysis. This is a contentious position in a world that is networked and globalised; it also is a contentious position in terms of the specific question that we are interested in, as development is certainly not only determined by national dynamics but also by very local and very regional dynamics. One can only do comparative analysis if the unit of analysis has been surveyed in terms of that unit of analysis. Such data is not available in Southern Africa.

Notes

* The methodology section was written by Hennie Kotzé and Stefanie Schulein
1. Ellis even argues with quite some evidence that the organised crime that plagues the region is based to some extent on networks developed in the anti-apartheid struggle years between elements of the liberation movements, the South African security system and 'ordinary' criminal networks (Ellis 1999).
2. These are many and varied and we point to collections that reflect on issues like democracy activities: Matlosa, 2004; material resource management cooperation: Katerere et al, 2001; possibly the worst case of military intervention: Likoti, 2007, and, lastly, possibly the most important issue of economic policy: Pallotti, 2004.

Section II

Theoretical Reflections

3

Cultural Values and Development in Theory and Practice

Hans Müller (with Tania van Heerden)

Introduction: Value, Culture and Development

The relationship between values, culture and development is seldom investigated, sometimes argued or assumed, often wholly ignored in development literature (Sen 2004a:35). This is an obvious concern in a context where a hidden popular assumption is that culture and values are the real difference between African development paths and development paths in other parts of the world. From a research perspective it is a concern and an opportunity at the same time. The opportunity lies in dealing with a very complex matter in an adequate manner and opening up a field of research in that way. Our aims are presently more limited and specific in that the objective is to elicit the important concepts that are dealt with in existing literature and to describe the state of empirical research on these concepts in our context.

Obviously the field of development draws from almost everything in science that has a bearing on the social and natural features of human existence – which is both commendable and problematic. A most sceptic perspective asks what a field of study aims to achieve if it becomes a site where every concept in social sciences can be deposited and no coherent project can be defined but the nature of the discourses in the field is often such that it is no more than an accumulation of social science sects (Gareau as cited in Hettne 1990:232). Referring back to the Methodenstreit, Hettne responds by organising the development of the field in an interesting and fruitful manner when he distinguishes two axes of difference, namely the positive-normative axis and the formal-substantive axis (even though one may not agree with Hettne's placement of some theoretical perspectives on these axes) (Hettne 1990).

The first axis deals with the position of the theory regarding the desirability of development theory being normative or positive. With Hettne, one has to conclude that all theories depend on certain values, but some theorists do not want to acknowledge that and think of their theories as being objective (Hettne 1990:235-236; Bernstein 1980). The second axis categorises theories in terms of how they define the goals and indicators of development and a formal approach would then work with abstract and finite indicators and goals while a substantive approach would tend to define development in more holistic and inclusive terms. The difference is not particularism versus universalism but, really an economistic definition versus a more comprehensive social and culturally inclusive approach. Obviously, an attempt to discuss and understand the cultural and social dimension of development will tend to find itself in the substantive half of the four quadrants that Hettne uses to categorise theoretical approaches to development as we also subscribe to Adelman's denouncement of the fallacy that 'underdevelopment (or development for that matter) has but a single cause', whether that be 'physical capital', 'entrepreneurship', 'incorrect prices', 'international trade', 'hyperactive government', 'human capital', or 'ineffective government' (Adelman 2001:104-117).

Figure 3.1 (adapted from Hettne 1990:240)

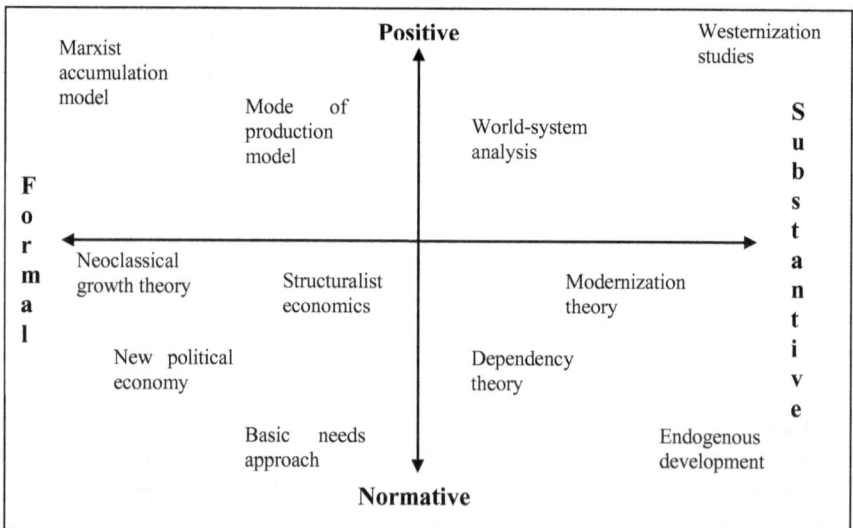

A full survey of research on attempts to relate values and culture to development is a major task. We limited ourselves to broad theoretical themes, to empirical research in the social sciences, to material directly relevant to African conditions and, mostly, to studies on a larger scale than anthropological and specific studies of particular communities or small groups.

The theoretical themes are discussed, firstly, in terms of classic utilitarianism and its most recent and influential critique in capability thought. This provides a useful backdrop for the discussion of alternative views of development that go beyond an economistic approach. Our discussion of utilitarianism and the capability critique will rely significantly on Clark's interpretation of Rawls, Sen and Nussbaum's critique of utilitarianism. Our discussion of alternative development theory will range more widely. Where the debate about utilitarianism is a debate about the nature of a universalist view of development, the debate about alternative development theory is a debate about a type of universalism versus particularism in principle.

The theoretical discussions are followed by an overview of more specific attempts at relating values and cultural aspects to development in empirical research – often a direct attempt at reflecting on theory from empirical research. In an overview of the cultural-social complex of explanations for development, we take a look at Fedderke and Klitgard's discussion of the interrelatedness of social aspects that impact on development, Odiambo's critique of cultural explanations for underdevelopment, and Oyeshile's discussion of the role of 'moral probity' in development. We go back to follow Ruttan's (1988) overview of twentieth century economists who tried to integrate social factors in their economic analyses before relating the results of analyses by Granato and others, Marini and Inglehart when actually combining social and economic data in modelling development. These studies are bound to modernisation theory. We then consider some of the results in Noland and Tyndale's work respectively of the even more specific arguments that attempt to correlate religion and development. We then briefly discuss Lian and Oneal's review of analyses of the role of cultural diversity, as well as a number of other studies on the importance of local culture, trust, group membership and gender in order to give some indication of how these themes are dealt with in empirical research.

A survey of relevant empirical research in political science and sociology makes clear at least one important deficiency in our knowledge about the relationship between values, culture and development in Sub-Saharan Africa. No extensive research has been undertaken that was initiated in terms of African development as a point of departure and that would provide an adequate basis for comparative understanding of the role of values and culture in African societies. However, much that is relevant to such an undertaking has been done, and this will be discussed in more detail below.

Reviewing Relevant Development Theory

Choosing Universals: Classical Utilitarianism and the Capability Critique

Utilitarianism

Central to dialogues about human development is the question of what constitutes a good life, what the exact meaning of development is and what the goals thereof are. 'Modern conceptions of development concerned themselves with growth, capital accumulation, technological change, structural transformation of the economy, and the modernisation of the social, cultural and political institutions necessary to facilitate economic development' (Clark 2002a:1). Thus, traditional development theory has, in many respects, a utilitarian backbone. Within the utilitarian ethical framework, 'actions are right or just in proportion to the extent to which they tend to promote happiness, pleasure or the absence of pain' (Perman et al. 1996:28). More specifically, the framework has three key components: firstly, decisions can only be judged in terms of the extent to which they contribute to the social good; secondly, a criterion for the constitution of the social good is developed; and finally, social good can be measured and compared across persons, time and geographical space (Perman et al. 1996:28). Individual good (utility) is seen to be a function of a person's happiness, where happiness is determined by the attainment of goods and services, and social good is seen to be a function of individual utilities added together (Perman et al. 1996:28). The measurability and comparability of this classical framework allows one to address issues of the distribution of income, wealth and welfare across generations, countries and population groups within countries. This characteristic of utility theory explains why the approach remains enduringly popular.

Utilitarianism has, however, suffered from strong criticism. Criticisms of the classical utilitarian ethic have centred on the view that 'utility, in the usual sense in which the term is used, is defined too narrowly to be an adequate description of human economic behaviour' (Perman et al. 1996:33). In short, critics claim that individuals are motivated by far more than mere personal happiness as determined by the attainment of goods and services.

The Capability Critique

Capability theories are concerned with 'the development of people rather than the development of things'. Furthermore, unlike approaches based on narrow concepts of utility (or basic needs), the capability framework readily accommodates the entire range of "beings" and "doings" that contribute to a good life' (Clark 2002a:162). In other words, the capability approach is concerned with what people are actually able to do rather than with utility or welfare type happiness and income. In terms of the categories of Hettne as discussed above, this means that the capability critique is a substantive theory of development rather than a theory that leads to the definition of formal criteria of development as would utilitarianism. A key component of the capability approach is the distinction between means and ends, where means are considered to be of only instrumental importance in achieving ends and thus only ends have intrinsic value. It is further important to clarify the distinction between capabilities and "functionings": capabilities constitute everything that is possible, whereas functionings constitute everything that has actually been realized (Robeyns 2005:95). Bearing these distinctions in mind, 'what is ultimately important is that people have the freedoms or valuable opportunities (capabilities) to lead the kind of lives they want to lead, to do what they want to do and be the person they want to be' (Robeyns 2005:95). Within this context, policies are to be evaluated in terms of the extent to which they impact upon human capabilities. Importantly, the inputs into capabilities include the social context, within which an individual is situated, the institutions within which an individual has to function, as well as the personal characteristics of the individual. Thus, the capability approach is clearly a multi-dimensional approach accounting for the impact on capabilities of the individual, institutions and groups (via the social context).

Stewart (2005), however, argues that insufficient attention is being given to groups within initial versions of the capability approach. Groups, whether the group is the family, neighbourhood, school, club, institution, association or even country, can serve to constrain the possibilities (capabilities) of individuals: 'the quality of groups with which individuals identify forms an important direct contribution on their well-being is instrumental to other capabilities, and influences people's choices and values' (Stewart 2005:185). Group membership can also increase the well-being of an individual given possible functional gains of group membership or simply by belonging, where belonging increases self-respect and can even bestow identity upon the member (Stewart 2005:187). Individual well-being and capability will increase or decrease depending on how well the group is functioning and on the extent to which the group is influencing individual values, preferences, behaviour and choices (Stewart 2005:188-189). Thus, the concept of an autonomous individual is clearly misleading.

A further important point is that conflict within or among groups can also decrease individual capabilities and increase inequalities (Stewart 2005:190). In the context of the poor, group membership is of particular importance: the poor have little economic or political power, and therefore, they are able to increase their capabilities by joining groups (Stewart 2005:195). Group membership thus facilitates collective action and empowerment – the formation of Stokvels in South Africa is a good example of empowerment via group membership.

One capability type criticism of classical utilitarianism relates to the possibility of unjust consequences: the context within which a classical utilitarian ethic calls for the judgement of actions based on their outcomes creates space for unbridled self-interest where the sacrifices of a few may be justified on the basis of the good of society as a whole.

One advocate for a critique of this ethic is John Rawls, whose critique contends that the self-interest inherent in utilitarianism may infringe upon fundamental freedoms and basic rights, and thus capabilities, of individuals which have an inherent worth that should be protected (Perman et al. 1996:34). Rawls subsequently makes the argument that if all people were entirely impartial and asked to determine the fundamental principles of social justice, all people would unanimously, firstly, identify equal rights and basic civil liberties as being of key importance to social justice, and would, secondly, decide to arrange society in a manner in which economic inequalities would be permitted only to the extent that such inequalities are to the advantage of all and attached to positions open to all (Perman et al. 1996:35). From another angle, this could be interpreted as stating that inequalities and actions are just, only if they benefit even the worst off person in society. Hence, the capabilities of all individuals need to be advanced in order for a policy to be acceptable in development terms. The capability approach, therefore, places the person back into the spotlight of development (Perman et al. 1996).

Rawls, however, is credited with having developed a "thin" theory of the good rather than a "thick" theory of the good, where the "thin" theory of the good leaves the final ends of human existence unspecified and the "thick" theory of the good sets out to identify important ends of human life (Clark 2002a:65). Rawls' theory is also considered to be a "thin" theory of the good because he uses primary goods in his analysis, and primary goods are considered to be means to an end and not intrinsic ends in themselves and are thus unable to account for the entire spectrum on human diversity (Robeyns 2005:97).

One of the most influential critics of utilitarianism, and the true pioneer of the capability approach, is Armatya Sen, who believes in the existence of a sharp distinction between the classical notion of utility and true personal well-being. The framework of Sen, whose conceptualisation draws on the work done by Rawls, conceptualises development as 'the expansion of human capabilities......[in which] Sen argues for the necessity of viewing people as ends in themselves and never as only means to other ends' (Clark 2002a:3). More specifically, 'Sen regards well-being as a multi-dimensional quantity, depending not only on what individuals have achieved or attained in the way of goods and services, but also on various attributes they enjoy as citizens' (Perman et al. 1996:34). A person's fundamental freedom and subsequent ability "to do something" is regarded by Sen to be of particular importance and of intrinsic value rather than of instrumental importance.

According to the utilitarian ethic, all goods, services and fundamental freedoms are only valuable in the sense of their instrumental worth in promoting individual utility. Furthermore, Sen argues that well-being is not the only aspect of human existence which is of importance; individuals are not motivated exclusively by personal well-being, rather individuals may pursue goals that do not improve their narrowly defined well-being (Perman et al. 1996:34).

Of course, Sen's critique and quest for broadening the concept of personal well-being heightens the already complex task of measuring utility for the sake of comparison. However, this is the case for all approaches that wish to go beyond an economistic or utilitarian definition of development.

The importance of individual freedoms and basic rights as propagated by both Sen and Rawls relates to a libertarian moral philosophy. Libertarianism 'asserts the primacy of processes, procedures and mechanisms for ensuring that fundamental liberties and rights of individual human beings are respected and sustained' (Perman et al. 1996:36).

Osmani (2005) also highlights the critical importance of human rights in enhancing capabilities hence alleviating poverty. He argues that the denial of human rights is an important aspect of poverty given that rights are of undeniable instrumental importance to the poor and that true development goes beyond economic progress (2005:206). He emphasizes the importance of individual freedoms and attempts to create a direct link between human rights and the capability approach, stating that 'any human rights can be seen as "capability rights"' (2005:207). Osmani then proceeds to identify two types of human rights – constraint rights and goal rights. Constraint rights involve constraining the behaviour of others such that individuals are granted the ability to engage in the just acquisition of assets as well as the ability to transfer and own assets unhindered (2005:209). Such entitlement to assets and the accompanying command of resources it allows is of critical importance for the poor to be able to develop. Goal rights, on the other hand, requires that human rights be incorporated into the goals of society and this implies that these rights have to be both promoted and protected (2005:211). An example of this would be a society's realisation that people have a right to freedom and consequently incorporating this right to freedom into the society's goals. Within this libertarian framework of an individual's right to capabilities, the maintenance of institutions is also critical for development, as institutions maintain individual freedoms and allow for the just acquisition of resources via contracts and thus develop individual capabilities. Hence, the scope for interventionist government policies such as redistribution is severely limited.

The capability critique has been developed further by Martha Nussbaum, whose work differs from that of Sen mainly in terms of the goals they wish to achieve via their work. Sen's goal is to develop a loosely defined evaluative paradigm, and hence does not attempt to aggregate his results for the purposes of universal applicability; Nussbaum, on the other hand, aims to develop an aggregate theory of social justice 'by arguing for the political principles that should underlie each constitution... To perform this task, Nussbaum develops and argues for a well-defined but general list of "central human capabilities" that should be incorporated in all constitutions' (Robeyns 2005:103). In other words, Nussbaum attempts to determine what is common across cultures. 'In the end Nussbaum effectively concludes that we should design a system that permits "each and every" manual labourer, farm worker and poor person to "live well"' (Clark 2002a:140). Her strategy thus considers local traditions and circumstances and the elements of the strategy 'chosen in consultation with those most deeply immersed in those traditions' (Clark 2002a:68). However, her reference to local cultures remains problematic at least in the sense that she does not reflect on the impact of modern Western society on local cultures.

Nonetheless, it remains useful to mention the basic human capabilities identified by Nussbaum as being applicable to all human life. The list includes a concern for issues related to mortality, a concern for the welfare of the human body, a desire for pleasure and avoidance of pain, an ability for cognition (both sensually and in terms of thinking), infant dependency, the ability to reason, an affiliation to other humans, a relation to other species and nature, the desire for humour and play, the need for individual separateness and finally the need for a strong sense of separateness related to personal liberties (Clark 2002a:68-69). According to Nussbaum, this list refers only to the bare minimum requirements of a decent human life. Therefore, one would want to move beyond this list for true development. Nussbaum then proceeds to further expound the list to include virtues such as such as self-respect, human flourishing, ecology, compassion and friendship and community (Clark 2002a:71-73). Significantly, Nussbaum fails to incorporate the importance of security and access to economic resources. Furthermore, one can certainly argue that essential goods such as food, water and shelter have intrinsic value in their own right and are not merely of value as a means to an end (Clark 2002a:82-83). Moreover, Nussbaum's list is severely criticized given that she provides no direct evidence for the inclusion of the components of her list, and, in addition, the true universality of her list certainly remains questionable. For example, given the inclusion of sensual and thinking cognition as a requirement for decent human living, the blind, deaf and mentally disabled could be considered as living indecent human lives and this is most certainly not the case (Clark 2002a:74). The problematic nature of developing a universal list has given rise to criticisms as regards whether such a list should be developed at all. Despite problems and criticisms, it is undeniable that 'Nussbaum and Sen's capability approach helps to facilitate our understanding of human development by directing attention towards the ultimate ends of life' (Clark 2002a:144).

We now have some perspectives on how we would know *if* development is taking place, but only implicit perspective on *how* culture and values play a role in successful development. The capabilities approach actually makes it more difficult to define effective processes of development as the goals of development are more complex and diverse. A utilitarian approach to development has an almost pre-defined method of achieving successful development incorporated in the definition of development itself. If the aim is the "attainment of goods and services" then development is simply the optimal use of resources and technology to encourage growth in the economy. Every aspect of society, especially government, is defined in terms of its supporting role in the quest for growth. If development is, however, defined in the capabilities mode, it is clear that much more needs to be done to facilitate development and the role of various aspects of society towards the multi-dimensional goal of enhancing capabilities will, of necessity, also be multi-dimensional and complex. However, the role of social and cultural values clearly now become more relevant and multi-dimensional as well as much more coming into play than the simple question of how growth is to be attained and supported by all aspects of society.

Universalism in Practice Versus Particularism in Principle: Mainstream Development versus Alternative Development

Having illustrated the importance of human development above and beyond income and material well-being, it is important to examine to what extent such principles are to be found in mainstream development practice. It is useful to begin the discussion of mainstream poverty assessment with an examination of the World Bank's assessment of poverty in Sub-Saharan Africa. For this purpose, one can refer to the study conducted by Hanmer, Pyatt and White which engages in an analysis of twenty-five World Bank poverty assessments of twenty-two Sub-Saharan countries (Hanmer et al. 1999:795). When assessing poverty, three central questions need to be addressed: Who are the poor? Where are the poor? And, what can be done about poverty? The World Bank's definition of poverty stated that 'people are considered poor if their standard of living falls below the poverty line, that is, the amount of income (or consumption) associated with a minimum acceptable level of nutrition and other necessities of everyday life' (Hanmer et al. 1999:795). According to this definition either income or consumption is the measure used to decide who the poor are, where a critical poverty line is drawn at a critical income level (Hanmer et al. 1999:797). Such an income-based assessment of poverty constitutes the key element of mainstream development analysis and has dominated research in the field for decades.

It is important, then, to determine to what extent and in what way such an assessment is subjective or objective; in other words, 'are the dimensions of poverty to be analysed chosen with reference to those things held to be most important in this regard by either the society under study or the poor themselves, or is some external, objective standard to be applied?' (Hanmer et al. 1999:797-798). In the case of World Bank assessments, despite recognizing and briefly mentioning other indicators and their importance, twenty-two of the twenty-five assessments distinguish the poor from the non-poor based on the setting of an "objective" income-based poverty line (Hanmer et al. 1999:798). The use of income as an indicator raises concerns as regards the nature of indicators adopted: for as our discussion of the capability critique has revealed, income is simply 'one of several dimensions of poverty, which range from basic needs to political rights' (Hanmer et al. 1999:798). Furthermore, the relative importance of indicators may also vary depending on the social context or groups, which may vary by gender or ethnicity, for example (Hanmer et al.., 1999:798). Income-based poverty analysis can therefore not facilitate true social analysis and the only relation to social reality that income-based poverty has is that poverty is also broadly correlated with the characteristics of households, such as size and location; and heads of households, such as gender and education (Hanmer et al. 1999:805). A further important point to note when examining poverty assessments is whether an absolute or a relative poverty line was employed; 'an absolute poverty line can be set with respect to minimum consumption needs... .whereas relative poverty takes into account societal norms so that the definition of the socially acceptable level of consumption tends to rise with a country's overall standard of living' (Hanmer et al. 1999:799).

According to Hanmer et al., there are nonetheless a number of useful results to be drawn from the World Bank poverty assessments. The two most important results are that income poverty in Sub-Saharan Africa is continuing to increase with little indication of an imminent turn-around of this trend, and that Sub-Saharan Africa is recording insufficient growth with a deteriorating distribution of the benefits of the little growth attained (Hanmer et al. 1999:818). Yet, though useful, this information does not truly add to either our understanding of poverty or insights as to what can be done about poverty (Hanmer et al. 1999:819). There is a multitude of important considerations as regards the nature of economic growth and poverty that is not addressed by the World Bank assessments. In terms of growth itself, it is also important to examine not only whether there is growth, but what the pattern thereof is; in other words, it is important to ask whether growth is pro-poor such that the incomes of the poor grow faster than the incomes of the rich, and whether growth is labour-intensive or capital-intensive (Hanmer et al. 1999:814). In terms of poverty, it is also important to examine the key linkages between poverty and the society and the economy more closely, to examine the nature of gender relations and their impact on household welfare and to accordingly examine the nature of intra-household dynamics (Hanmer et al. 1999:819). Moreover, macroeconomic issues, such as low growth and the debt crisis, and political instability should also be considered in terms of their effect on poverty. Finally, the cultural and ethnic context of the society being analyzed also warrants attention.

When considering all the crucial factors not considered by the World Bank assessments, it is not surprising that its simplistic three-pronged strategy of investment in human capital formation, represented by investment in education and health, broad-based growth and the creation of social safety nets has experienced limited success (Hanmer et al. 1999:814). Poor quality of public facilities, especially health and education, and poor access to both public facilities and government transfers reveals that the problem in Sub-Saharan Africa is not merely one of resource provision, but one of access, exclusion and inefficiency, while 'traditional support systems are being worn away by rising population, political violence, AIDS and the increasing scarcity of environmental and other resources' (Hanmer et al. 1999:819). Furthermore, at the micro (household and community) level, gender relations and labour market discrimination hinder resource and asset accumulation and limit the ability of women to generate income, which results in a misallocation of resources and decreased household investment – all of which, in turn, lowers economic growth (Hanmer et al. 1999:812).

Pieterse (1998) takes this discussion further and discusses both what mainstream and alternative approaches can teach us. Given the limitations of traditional income-based poverty measures, there has been scope for alternative development paradigms to take shape. But, it is critical to examine what format such alternative development theories should take (Pieterse 1998:344). Alternative development theories have attempted to redefine the goals of development in order to bring the individual and the community back into development practice. Alternative approaches are also critical of mainstream development theories, being constantly in search of alternatives (Pieterse 1998:350). The two key distinctive aspects of alternative development approaches is their emphasis on the local and their support for de-modernisation given that modernisation is perceived to be incompatible with human development (Pieterse 1998:347). Such approaches can at times even demonstrate anti-capitalist tendencies and a 'valorization of indigenous knowledge' (Pieterse 1998:357). Alternative approaches are, however, criticized on the grounds that they merely represent a loose set of ideas given that all the elements of the approach are not linked by a unifying theory. Indeed, the various elements of the approach can often even be contradictory (Pieterse 1998:348, 357). This point is highlighted when considering the statement that 'if the people are the principle actors in the alternative development paradigm, the relevant reality must be the people's own, constructed by them only' (Rahman in Pieterse 1998:357), which implies that there cannot be a single paradigm of alternative development, but only a collection of a multitude of local development perspectives (Pieterse 1998:357). Such a theory of development is termed to be an endogenous theory in terms of Hettne's classification above and is categorised as both substantive and normative in that it rejects universal definitions of development that reduce development to a limited number of criteria and does not believe that development is simply the unfolding of objective historical processes.

Mainstream development, on the other hand, places greater emphasis on international institutions, international cooperation and institutional change, and when analysing poverty employs variables such as GDP per capita, economic growth, health, literacy, education, housing and some degree of local participation (Pieterse 1998:358). Thus, the mainstream approach can be considered to be to some degree people-centred. Many aspects of alternative theories are consequently beginning to enter mainstream development practice, especially as regards the increased recognition of the importance of community participation in development, and thus the boundaries between mainstream and alternative development approaches are becoming increasingly vague (Pieterse 1998:344). In short then, a definitive shift in development thinking is beginning to take shape: 'development is now more anchored in people's subjectivity, rather than in overarching structures and institutions' (Pieterse 1998:369). However, an important distinction between alternative and mainstream development approaches must be made: mainstream development is people-centred from the top-down, whereas alternative development is people-centred from the bottom-up. Thus, even though mainstream development does support the local participatory principles of alternative development, it 'remains on the whole state-centred, top-down social engineering, in which the state is viewed as the main agent for implementing human development policies' (Pieterse 1998:370). Hence, Pieterse continues to advocate that there should be an enduring distinction between alternative development, newly termed popular development by Pieterse, and more human or mainstream development, but emphasizes also that these two approaches are no longer entirely opposed to each other as the boundaries separating them become gradually more vague (Pieterse 1998:370).

Pieterse also mentions two further development perspectives, namely post-development and reflexive development. Post-development is situated at a far extreme opposite mainstream development, opting for the complete rejection of the concept of development as such, and is consequently anti-imperialist, anti-capitalist and anti-productivist (Pieterse 1998:362). Accordingly, this approach rather advocates the supremacy of indigenous knowledge, cultural diversity and self-reliance: 'post-development parallels dependency theory in seeking to disengage the local from external dependency, taking it further to development as a power/knowledge regime. While dependency theory privileges the nation state, post-development privileges the local, the grassroots' (Pieterse 1998:362). Reflexive development, on the other hand, advocates a constantly reflexive approach to development given past failures and continuing development crises. In the context of this approach, new development policies should be 'increasingly concerned with managing the hazards, risks, unintended consequences and side-effects brought about by development itself' (Pieterse 1998:367-368).

Robins (2003) argues against the complete rejection of mainstream development and its conception as an expansion of Western imperialism, arguing that 'development packages are resisted, embraced and reshaped or accommodated depending on the specific content and context' (Robins 2003:265). Robins, thus, argues that modernity is often indigenised and, therefore, the sharp dichotomy between tradition and modernity is steadily dissipating: 'responses to development are usually neither wholesale endorsements nor radical rejections of modernity. Even when resisting and subverting development ideas and practices, people do not generally do so on the basis of either radical populist politics or in defence of pristine and authentic local cultural traditions' (Robins 2003:265). In order to demonstrate this point, Robins discusses three case studies of post-Apartheid land claims which reveal the incorporation of tradition, cultural rights and the modern legal system in land claim strategies. Robins also draws attention to the fact that benefits of Western modernity and development can be extremely attractive for resource-poor communities, while 'there may be very little that is romantic about their experiences of the local' (Robins 2003:283).

Participatory approaches, both from mainstream and alternative perspectives, to analysing poverty are becoming increasingly widespread in order to obtain the poor's perspective of poverty. Such a study was, for instance, conducted by Lwanga-Ntale and McClean (2004) in order to gain a clearer understanding of how chronic poverty is perceived by the poor in Uganda. Despite having decreased the number of people living below the poverty line from 56 per cent in 1992 to 35 per cent in 2000, chronic poverty remains severe in Uganda (Lwanga-Ntale and McClean 2004:177). Ugandan chronic poverty is mainly a rural phenomenon, and is particularly severe in the Northern Region and among women, children, the elderly and large households (Lwanga-Ntale and McClean 2004:178). Lwange-Ntale and Mclean used this information as well as qualitative data form Ugandan Participatory Poverty Assessments to shed light on the perspectives of the chronically poor on poverty (Lwanga-Ntale and McClean 2004:178-179).

What the study reveals is that the three key aspects of poverty, as defined by the poor, are: a persistent lack of basic necessities such as food, water, shelter, clothes and means of production; a lack of social support or networks, which increases both vulnerability and social exclusion; and feelings of negativity such as hopelessness, resignation, defencelessness and worthlessness (Lwanga-Ntale and McClean 2004:180). The poor also identified five factors which they perceived to cause and increase the duration of poverty. Firstly, the intergenerational nature of poverty transmission was perceived to breed resignation and feelings of inevitability, which often leads to a 'production of poverty' (Lwanga-Ntale and McClean 2004:181). Secondly, insecurity and conflict results in the loss of already limited resources and property as well as in both physical and mental distress and restricted labour mobility (Lwanga-Ntale and McClean 2004:182). Thirdly, drought also results in the loss of resources, and as men are forced to migrate in search of alternative income, women, children and the elderly are plunged into even greater poverty (Lwanga-Ntale and McClean 2004:184). Fifthly, poverty is also often linked to the seasons, where weather and agricultural patterns result in some of the poor being rendered even poorer at specific times of the year. Finally, HIV/ AIDS is resulting in the loss of both the lives and productivity of young men. In conclusion, 'three inter-linked factors causing and maintaining poverty that were often cited by poor men, women, male youth, the elderly and the disabled alike were lack of education, illiteracy, and disempowerment' (Lwanga-Ntale and McClean 2004:185). Importantly, these results reveal that poverty as such, and consequently the task of development, is far more complex than merely economic growth, increasing income and resource and service provision.

A study was also conducted by Allison Goebel (1998) based on a participatory study of a Zimbabwean Resettlement Area. The aim of the first part of the study was to reveal that participatory research both reveal and conceal power relations in communities, whereas the second part of the study attempted to demonstrate that local knowledge and social reality itself can oftentimes be highly challenged and disputed and at times can even be contradictory (Goebel 1998:280). Goebel warns that participation is continually in danger of coming 'to mean "a way to get people to do what we want", rather than a means fundamentally to change the project idea or construction, or a way to involve and respect local knowledge on an equal footing with foreign, particularly scientific, expertise' (Goebel 1998:279). A second danger relates to the adoption of the principles of Participatory Rural Appraisal (PRA) 'without adequately acknowledging the complexity of social realities, or properly practicing the intended notions of "participation"' (Goebel 1998:279).

PRA studies aim to encourage local information sharing and collection and often involve visualizations and the employment of local materials given that local people are often illiterate and, therefore, 'the use of survey questionnaires and other formal methods involving paper and pens that are controlled by researchers, are thought to be alienating, and afford little opportunity for people to express ideas in their own terms' (Goebel 1998:281). Despite PRA group discussions and information sharing activities being able to afford researches the 'opportunity to observe some power relations in action, as people interact during the exercises' (Goebel 1998:284), the Zimbabwean assessments also reveal that the emphasis on group work and consensus when presenting responses can serve to silence 'marginal or dissident views' (Goebel 1998:284). The marginalisation of women in such discussions becomes especially evident. This highlights the importance of investigating the perspectives of different groups rather than viewing the community as a unified whole. Many researches, thus, divide communities into different observable groups based on characteristics such as gender and clan. In the case of Zimbabwe, important clusters of power were observable based on gender, 'totem or clan, wealth, relationship to the ruling party, and witchcraft' (Goebel 1998:285).

Goebel further notes that 'there is no one "indigenous" or "local" knowledge, but competing perspectives. Some dominate while others are marginalized' (Goebel 1998:284). Therefore, it is dangerous to apply Western paradigms on societies when "local" knowledge is treated as a unified whole. Local "knowledges" always have to be investigated 'within their changing historical contexts, contested belief systems, local power dynamics and struggles over the control of resources' (Goebel 1998:294). According to Goebel, what the Zimbabwean participatory assessment also reveals is that Zimbabwean traditional practices have been continually altered under pressures of Western-indigenous interactions and Christianity, 'hence there is very little called "indigenous" that does not have something "Western" implicated in it' (Goebel 1998:294). Therefore, it is essential that indigenous people be allowed to provide their own categorization of what constitutes the traditional and what aspects of this tradition they perceive as being or having been influenced by either the West or Christianity (Goebel 1998:294).

Taylor (2002), in studying the rural livelihoods of the hunter-gatherer Basarwa peoples of Botswana, similarly warns that livelihood components such as money, livestock and wildlife which, in the Western perspective, can be viewed as merely sources of income or food, in actual fact 'exist in a socio-political environment in which each of them signifies a different way of living and a different set of values' (Taylor 2002:470). Money, livestock and wildlife are interconnected in Basarwa communities and represent the essential components in the construction of Basarwa livelihood strategies (Taylor 2002:486). Thus, mainstream development practices cannot successfully introduce development programmes that aim to replace one of these elements of Basarwa livelihood with another. Given their remoteness, the Basarwa people are already facing enormous challenges to obtaining entitlement to resources. For example, they are far from education and employment opportunities, they feel stigmatised given their ethnic identity and are, therefore, reluctant to attempt to gain employment. They are situated in wildlife areas and, therefore, their crops and livestock are prone to be destroyed by wildlife, while hunting legislation denies them their traditional practice of hunting for food

(Taylor 2002:487). This is significant when considering 'Sen's influential work *Poverty and Famine* (1981), which brought to the fore the importance of "entitlements", or the ability to control commodities, in understanding the relationship between people and resources in maintaining their livelihoods' (Taylor 2002:470).

Taylor also proceeds to briefly discuss the value and importance attached by the Basarwa to money, livestock and wildlife. Taylor finds that even in the remote Basarwa communities, money as a source of life is of critical importance. Therefore, employment is important for the Basarwa ,but given their location and ethnicity, employment is unpredictable. Livestock has a very distinct cultural relevance for the Basarwa. Cattle are strongly desired by the Basarwa because they represent symbols of wealth, power and proper humanity (Taylor 2002:477). Cattle have also come to have a wider meaning as a source of food, income and ceremony (Taylor 2002:477). Importantly, these values of cattle were previously applied to wildlife, but given the new legislation the Basarwa culture has gradually transformed into a cattle culture (Taylor 2002:477). However, the substitution of a wildlife culture for a cattle culture cannot be complete. Given drought, the tsetse fly, attack by wild predators and the fact that cattle can be divested given the subordinate ethnic status of the Basarwa and the reduction of their hunting rights, this source of food for the communities has been drastically reduced (Taylor 2002:474, 478). Moreover, even though they do receive food handouts as compensation, the handouts contain limited proteins and therefore, proteins are still highly sought after by the Basarwa (Taylor 2002:478). In addition to the nutritional need for meat, it is also important to note that the Basarwa 'consider game meat to be an essential part of their diet' (Taylor 2002:479), and therefore, of their identity. The combination of cultural and nutritional needs, the "meat culture" of the Basarwa cannot simply be entirely replaced by a "cattle culture" with the imposition of development programmes and legislation and therefore, the Basarwa continue to lay claim to game meat, even if this implies illegally hunting more game than is allowed by their community quota (Taylor 2002:479). Indeed, the question of wildlife rights has become symbolic of the conflict between the Basarwa and the law (Taylor 2002:479). In conclusion, the study highlights that development programmes cannot simply replace traditional livelihoods without affecting community welfare or giving rise to some measure of conflict.

It is clear that a universalist perspective tends to lose sight of particular combinations and a particularist perspective will not be able to provide direction on anything but a local and limited level. The key seems to be in finding studies that look for combinations of a range of universals in particular combinations. Empirical research that has an interpretative sensitivity for different meanings and different relationships between universal categories tends to do that implicitly and sometimes explicitly. These are the basic principles of good comparative methodology and they are explored further in the next sections.

Empirical Analyses of Relationships Between Culture and Development

Modernisation Theory

The first line of analysis of the impact of specific cultures on economic development would always be modernisation theory as the approach has had such a dominant influence on development studies and practice as a whole. This theory attempts to link broad cultural characteristics to both the process of modernisation and economic development. A comprehensive series of studies were done in this regard by Ronald Inglehart and other colleagues (for an overview of the critique against Inglehart that is relevant to African issues see: Müller 2004). Seeing that Inglehart has been publishing on these matters for decades we will only discuss some of the arguments.

The first study conducted in this line of thought relevant to us was conducted in 1995. According to Inglehart, two dominant schools of modernisation theory can be identified: the first school is represented by a Marxist mode of thinking 'which claims that economics, politics and culture are closely linked because economic development determines the political and cultural characteristics of a society' (Inglehart 1995:379); and the second school of thought is represented by a Weberian mode of thinking 'which claims that culture shapes economic and political life' (Inglehart 1995:379). Even though Marxists claim that the mode of economic development determines a society's cultural characteristics whereas Weberians claim that a society's cultural characteristics determine its mode of economic development, the two schools do agree on the important point that there is a close and significant relationship between cultural characteristics and development. Given this purported close link, it is suggested that 'from knowledge of one such trait, one can predict the presence of other key traits with far better than random success' (Inglehart 1995:379). Inglehart, then, attempts to examine the validity of modernisation theory using the World Values Survey of 43 nations, conducted in the period 1990 to 1991 (Inglehart 1995:380). More specifically, the aim of the study is to determine whether coherent cultural patterns exist and whether such patterns are related to economic development. The existence of coherent cultural patterns and their accompanying link to economic development represent the two central assumptions of both the concept of modernisation and the concept of post-modernisation (Inglehart 1995:380-381).

The process of modernisation is accompanied by a shift from religious authority to state authority involving a process of secularisation in which a scientific worldview gradually replaces the worldview based on the mystical components of religion (Inglehart 1995:384). A second component of the process of modernisation is the rise of bureaucratic organisation as accompanied by rules, efficiency, explicit goals and achievement values (Inglehart 1995:384). The shift to postmodernism, on the other hand, involves a movement 'away from both religion and the state to the individual, with an increasing focus on individual concerns such as friends and leisure' (Inglehart 1995:384). Five key components of this shift can be identified: firstly, there is a shift from scarcity values to security values; secondly, the acceptability of modern bureaucratic authority diminishes; thirdly, the western model is rejected while socialism is rejected as a workable alternative at the same time; fourthly, authority is rejected in favour of individual freedom as conducive to democracy; and finally, despite continued secularisation in terms of the lessening need for the security of religion, the importance of science and rationality gradually diminishes as concern for a greater purpose in life increases (Inglehart 1995:385-387).

The first question the study attempts to answer 'is whether the various religious, social, economic and political components of given cultures are more or less randomly related; or whether they go together, with a few coherent combinations being far more probable than others' (Inglehart 1995:388). The study identifies the dimensions of modernisation and post-modernisation. Forty-seven variables were classified according to four dimensions, namely the polarisation between traditional authority and rational-legal authority, and the polarisation between scarcity values and postmodern values. The forty-seven variables were selected from the World Values survey to reflect and encompass a multitude of questions and related entries that demonstrate similar patterns (Inglehart 1995:388). In other words, in order to unearth and convey what Inglehart considers the fundamental cultural patterns, the most sensitive variables of each cluster were selected for the purposes of the study. The selected variables were then classified according to the two dimensions, and consequently the study found that 'there is a great deal of constraint among cultural systems. The pattern found here is anything but random" (Inglehar 1995:388). There is a particular predictable cluster of values that accompanies the transition from traditional society to modernisation and the transition from modernisation to post-modernisation. Hence, as traditional societies move towards modernisation, the shift is accompanied by increased mass mobilisation as well as a move from traditional authority to rational legal authority (Inglehart 1995:402). Secondly, a society's movement from modernisation to post-modernisation is predictably accompanied by 'the emergence of advanced industrial society, with an increasing share of the public having higher education, being employed in the service sector, and feeling assured that their survival needs will be met, gives rise to a process in which high levels of subjective well-being and postmodern values emerge, and in which a variety of attributes, from equal rights for women to democratic political institutions, become increasingly likely' (Inglehart 1995:402).

The study does, indeed, find constrained coherent cultural patterns (given that one has to accept the construction of the categories for the sake of the argument), but these patterns hold over regions rather than over individual countries. Furthermore, the study shows that these cultural patterns are related to a society's level of development. Thus, given these two results, significant support is lent to a general modernisation theory which argues not only that 'coherent cultural patterns exist, but that these patterns are linked with a given society's level of economic development' (Inglehart 1995:397). However, Inglehart concludes that further studies are necessary in order to determine the direction of causality of the revealed linkages. In other words, simply because a linkage exists between postmodern values and development, one does not know whether development will result in spreading these values or whether the spreading of these values results in development. Yet, what is clear is that the cultural changes linked with the shift to postmodern values are conducive to the development of democracy (Inglehart 1995:400). Hence, one of the most important findings of the study is that 'the linkage between culture and democracy found here is even stronger than the linkage between economic development and democracy… This finding suggests that economic development by itself does not automatically produce democracy; it may do so in so far as it gives rise to a specific syndrome of cultural changes' (Inglehart 1995. For how this line of reasoning has been taken further, see Inglehart and Welzel, 2005). Finally, Inglehart speculates on why it is that cultural change follows predictable patterns, and then claims that change is predictable given that it follows a process of rational choice in the long-run: in the gradual shift to modernisation, focus is shifted in order to gain a "better" economic outcome and thus focus is firmly placed on maximising economic growth; the shift to postmodernism, on the other hand, takes place in more advanced industrialised nations where economic gains begin to demonstrate diminishing returns and, in response, a rational choice is made to shift focus to improving subjective well-being and quality of life (Inglehart 1995:401).

In 2000, Inglehart and Baker examined modernisation in terms of two recent schools of thought: the first school of thought argues that in the face of modernisation all values converge, where traditional values are gradually replaced by "modern" values; and, the second school of thought argues that, regardless of modernisation, traditional values persist, and therefore, this approach regards values to be 'relatively independent of economic condition' (Inglehart and Baker 2000:20). As the twentieth century continued, and the West continued to develop while the rest of the world was lagging far behind, modernisation theorists argued that for lagging countries to "catch up" with the West, they would have to relinquish their traditional practices and values in favour of the Western model proliferated. However, towards the end of the century, and in the wake of the East Asian development miracle that occurred within the context of non-western cultures, values and development models, 'few observers would attribute moral superiority to the West, and Western economies are no longer assumed to be the model for the world' (Inglehart and Baker 2000:20-21). As a consequence, it becomes important to empirically investigate whether modernisation is leading to a convergence of values as propagated by earlier theorists, or whether traditional values continue to have a significant effect. Inglehart and Baker again highlight the change in values expected to accompany a move from a traditional society characterised by traditional values to an industrial society characterised by modern values, and again from an industrial society to a post-industrial society characterised by postmodern values (Inglehart and Baker 2000:21).

Inglehart and Baker begin their investigation by using World Values Survey data for sixty-five societies for the period 1995 to 1998 and Huntington's (Huntington 1993; Huntington 1996) eight cultural zones to plot the sixty-five societies on a two dimensional global map of cross-cultural variation. The 'two dimensions reflect cross-national polarization between traditional versus secular-rational orientations toward authority; and survival versus self-expression values' (Inglehart and Baker 2000:23). The zones identified by Huntington are 'Western Christianity, the Orthodox world, the Islamic world, and the Confucian, Japanese, Hindu, African, and Latin American zones' (Inglehart and Baker 2000:22). Using these dimensions, the first significant finding is that economic development has a definite impact on cultural values. The traditional versus secular-rational dimension is related to a movement from a traditional society to an industrial society, whereas the survival versus self-expression values is related to the movement from an industrial society to a post-industrial society (Inglehart and Baker 2000:30-31). Furthermore, the countries in each cultural zone also demonstrate similar cultural and value patterns (Inglehart and Baker 2000:31). This relation between countries in cultural clusters persists even when controlling for per capita income and labour force structure, and, accordingly, all Protestant European countries, for instance, do not merely have similar values because they are wealthy (Inglehart and Baker 2000:34). A further important finding is that 'interpersonal trust is significantly correlated with a society's level of GDP per capita' (Inglehart and Baker 2000:35), a finding which reiterates the importance of the creation of trust for economic development given its role in creating the social structures inherent in democracy and facilitating the establishment of the complex social organisation required for large-scale economic activity (Inglehart and Baker 2000:34). Interestingly, both an orthodox religious heritage and a communist historical legacy has a damaging impact on the formation of not only interpersonal trust, but also on tolerance, well-being and postmaterialism, all of which form part of self-expression values (Inglehart and Baker 2000:35, 39-40). In contrast, Protestantism was found to have a positive impact on the formation of self-expression values (Inglehart and Baker 2000:39). Finally, the study finds that secular-rational values do become more pervasive as a country industrialises (Inglehart and Baker 2000:41-42).

Similar to the earlier Inglehart (1995) study, it was found that as countries industrialise, the emphasis on survival lessens as feelings of security increase, and increased security is accompanied by a move towards postmodern values. As a result of this decreased concern for survival and security, modernisation theory predicts that the pervasiveness of religious faith should decline. However, this is not the case as evidence suggests that religious cleavages remain strong given that, even though institutional religious attendance has declined, spirituality has increased (Inglehart and Baker 2000:46). This trend effectively reveals that 'the need for security is not the only attraction of religion' (Inglehart and Baker 2000:47). As countries move beyond industrialisation into the realm of post-industrialism, people 'are less attached to traditional forms of religion ... but they are more likely to spend time thinking about the meaning and purpose of life' (Inglehart and Baker 2000:47).

The study thus finds that there is a two-fold dynamic occurring which encompasses both a convergence to modern values and a persistence of traditional values. Thus, 'modernization theorists are partly right. The rise of industrial society is linked with coherent cultural shifts away from traditional values. ... But values seem to be path dependent: a history of Protestant or Orthodox or Islamic or Confucian traditions gives rise to cultural zones with distinctive value systems that persist after controlling for the effects of economic development' (Inglehart and Baker 2000:49). This seems to be an important finding and leads Inglehart and Baker to re-conceptualise modernisation theory to account for the fact that the process of modernisation is not linear in nature, that it is deceptive to equate cultural change with Americanisation and that even though 'economic development tends to transform a given society in a predictable direction ... the process and path are not inevitable' (Inglehart and Baker 2000:49).

Generic Social Structures and Goods that Influence Development

Culture and Development in Africa

Modern theorists attempting to explain why the growth and development of lagging regions such as Africa and Latin America has been so low have been unable to uncover any comprehensively convincing explanation. The issues are complex and we discuss a few findings in order to point to some of the important dynamics.

For instance, Barro (1991), and Easterly and Levine (1994) 'find that even after controlling for a wide range of variables, the weak growth performance of Latin America and Sub-Saharan Africa remains unexplained' (Fedderke and Klitgaard 1998:456). Fedderke and Klitgaard argue that the reason why no clear causal linkages can be found lies in the possibility of webs of association existing between growth, political and civil rights, political stability and the efficiency of public institutions; in other words, there may be 'distinct groupings of social indicators with differentiated impacts on economic growth' (1998:455, echoing Adelman's insistence on the complexity of development processes, 2001:117). There may thus be interactions between political and social institutions, and consequently it is not either political or social institutions impacting on growth, but rather a joint impact on economic growth (Fedderke and Klitgaard 1998:456). The Fedderke and Klitgaard study then attempts to test this claim by considering the interactions among a number of variables that include 'instability, violence, political and civil rights, corruption, inequality, political and ethnic fractionalization, separatist and discriminatory pressures, family stability, and an array of cultural characteristics' (Fedderke and Klitgaard 1998:458).

The results of the study reveal that there are, indeed, correlations between rights, instability and institutional efficiency, between regime-threatening instability measures, between non-regime-threatening instability measures and between institutional efficiency and fractionalisation and separatist pressure (Fedderke and Klitgaard 1998:464-471). However, Fedderke and Klitgaard also highlight the possibility that the common use of proxies for social indicators may also distort results as it is often not entirely clear what precisely is being measured (1998:458). It is, therefore, important that interactions among variables be examined when attempting to explain growth performance rather than investigating variables in isolation. This is precisely what the literature on culture and economic growth and development attempts to achieve, where culture as a variable consists of a variety of social indicators, all of which interact with each other and with economic growth.

Given the inexplicable poor growth performance in Africa, there has been a resurgence of theories propagating that African culture inhibits growth (Odhiambo 2002:1). A study conducted by Odhiambo criticizes this theory and rather calls for further investigations into the realities of African cultures today such that development practices would be able to build 'on the indigenous roots of African culture as a way forward' (Odhiambo 2002:1). Some of the ostensible features of African culture believed to inhibit growth include apathy, fatalism, a lack of individualism, a poor conception of time, irrationality, a lack of encouragement of individual merit and traditional religious orientations (Odhiambo 2002:2). Odhiambo does not deny the existence of these cultural aspects in Africa, but argues that such aspects should not be viewed as an inhibitor to growth but should rather 'be considered as the point of departure for dynamic development' (Odhiambo 2002:7). This implies a conception of African cultures as dynamic rather than static phenomena, 'and therefore can be and ought to be evaluated internally by their practitioners, the Africans themselves' (Odhiambo 2002:7). Thus, by refocusing attention on what Africans have to say about both their culture and development, the study again highlights the importance of conceptualising development from the bottom-up rather than from the top-down.

Oyeshile (2003), on the other hand, criticises the popular literature that often seeks to explain Africa's poor growth performance by referring on the inhibiting roles of colonialism and ethnicity. Oyeshile argues that colonialism and ethnicity alone cannot be blamed for Africa's troubles, and that one should rather examine the impact on economic performance of the 'lack of moral probity' (Oyeshile 2003:83). Therefore, the link between morality and governance is reemphasised. One of the dominant features of Africa is the continuing prevalence of instability in the context of democratisation, and political, social and economic theories have failed to account for this (Oyeshile 2003:81). Oyeshile thus considers whether a re-examination of traditional social-ethical values may enhance stability and, accordingly, economic development (Oyeshile 2003:81). In this regard, Oyeshile specifically examines the values of the traditional Yoruba society, which include values such as selflessness, truthfulness, covenant keeping, condemnation of stealing, character, tolerance, sharing, solidarity, support, cooperation, independence, religious tolerance, reciprocal obligation, rectitude and an opposition to hypocrisy (Oyeshile 2003:83). Furthermore, a person is considered to have a good character if his or her actions are good for the community; in other words, the individual and community are integrally linked, where communal well-being is of utmost importance (Oyeshile 2003:84-85). Individuals are not allowed to exist in isolation and therefore have to be able to sacrifice self-interest for the good of the community, and, in return, the community is required to recognise the rights of individuals (Oyeshile 2003:86). Importantly, this principle is also applied in the case of leadership: 'in cases where any leader becomes deaf and blind to public opinion, such a leader soon loses his position' (Oyeshile 2003:86). In Oyeshile's view, the mentioned values and communal cultural legacies are almost entirely lacking in modern African governance, and therefore, he argues that these values should be reapplied to contemporary African governance, institutions and economics (Oyeshile 2003:86). Of critical importance in this regard is a renewal on the part of government and institutions of a sense of responsibility to the community (Oyeshile 2003:85).

The study conducted by Oyeshile in 2004 revisits the issue of Africa's development crisis and the possible role of communal values and cultural identity in alleviating the crisis. Again, Oyeshile asserts 'that the traditional African emphasis on communal values needs to be reinvigorated while remembering that African leaders need to be more ready to adopt new values and ideas such as will promote future development' (Oyeshile 2004:291). In this study, Oyeshile highlights the importance of HIV/Aids, corruption, multi-ethnicity, religious conflict and the alienation of government from its people as important stumbling blocks to economic progress (Oyeshile 2004:292). However, in addition to the reiteration of the need to return to communal values in order to improve governance and institutions, the 2004 study also recognizes that 'instead of trying to defend African identity at all cost, we should preoccupy ourselves with the benefits that can accrue to us from indigenous and foreign cultures in order to improve the current situation' (Oyeshile 2004:301).

In conclusion, despite specifics, what these studies on African development and culture reveal is the increasing importance of recognising the impact of culture on economic and social development as well as recognising the incredible complexity involved in capturing this cultural effect. Development cannot simply be imposed from "above" by an alien culture, but must rather be rooted in a society's culture so as to embrace both the local and the universal. Thus, it is important to examine more broadly the relationship between culture and economic growth in order to gain new insights into the relationship between culture and development in the African context.

Culture and Economic Development

An early study conducted by Vernon W. Ruttan (1988) represents an attempt to more broadly examine the relationship between culture and development. The study introduces a general conceptual model which identifies resource endowments, cultural endowments, technology and institutions as important factors that may influence economic growth. The study also attempts to investigate the relationship among these variables, where the relationship of cultural endowments in promoting or preventing institutional innovation is of particular interest: 'cultural endowments make some forms of institutional change less costly to establish and impose severe costs on others' (Ruttan 1988:250). Within the context of considering these variables, the study proceeds to provide a useful overview of post-war development theorists acknowledging some role for culture in economic development. Importantly, all of these theorists purport that institutional change away from the traditional and towards the modern is required for economic progress and the dawn of modern society.

The first of these theorists is Bert F. Hoselitz (1952), who argues that 'value systems offer special resistance to change (...) their change is facilitated if the market economic environment in which they can flourish is destroyed or weakened' (Hoselitz in Ruttan 1988:252). Hoselitz argues such change in the economic environment is spearheaded by the emergence of minorities, which encourages increased social mobility and aids in the generation of an economic environment conducive to the emergence of a modern society and weakens commitment to traditional production and organisational systems (Ruttan 1988:251).

A second theorist, Everett E. Hagen (1962), attempts to combine the fields of anthropology, sociology, psychology and economics, arguing 'that the interrelations between personality formation and social structure are such that social change could not occur without prior or concurrent personality change' (Ruttan 1988:252). For instance, Hagen argues that traditional societies can be said to be characterised by an "authoritarian personality" and thus requires a personality change before development and democratisation is possible (Ruttan 1988:252). Irma Adelman and Cynthia T. Morris (1965, 1967, 1973), on the other hand, 'use factor analysis to compress a large set of indicators into groups of closely associated socio-cultural, political, and economic indicators of the development process' (Ruttan 1988:253). Two sets of studies were conducted: the first study was performed on seventy-four countries, and the second study was performed on three sub-sets of countries as determined by the countries' level of development (Ruttan 1988:253). The results of their studies are said to reveal that in the earliest phases of development, both cultural and social constraints inhibit development, suggesting that the enhancement of economic activity requires a transformation of the socio-cultural aspects of a society (Ruttan 1988:253). Therefore, the study reflects 'the interaction of an organic system of institutional and behavioural change which underlies the process of economic development' (Adelman & Morris in Ruttan 1988:252).

Myrdal (1968) also argued that traditional values inhibit growth, and consequently juxtaposed Western elitist modernisation ideals with traditional values, where the Western ideals include rationality, efficiency, diligence, innovation, independence, democracy, honesty and equity (Ruttan 1988:253). Thus, according to Myrdal, the South Asian people 'have lived for a long time under conditions very different from those in the Western world. And this has left its mark upon their bodies and minds. Religion has, then, become the emotional container of this whole way of life and work and, by its sanction, has rendered it rigid and resistant to change' (Myrdal in Ruttan 1988:254). Ironically, Myrdal thus argued that a strong state is necessary in order to enforce the social change and discipline needed for economic progress, and he was thus critical of South Asia's "soft state": 'planning for development requires a readiness to place obligations on people in all social strata to a much greater extent than is done in any of the South Asian countries (…) development cannot be achieved without much more social discipline than the prevailing interpretation of democracy in the region permits' (Myrdal in Ruttan 1988:254).

The works of P.T. Bauer (1984) focus on the impact on output of ethnic groups with different cultural endowments (Ruttan 1988:255). His views of the possibility of cultural constraints on development resemble those of Myrdal, except that Bauer favours market forces above the strong state (Ruttan 1988:255).

Bauer examined Chinese and Indian output, observing that even with the same inputs and equipment, Chinese output more than doubled Indian output. In response to this observation, Bauer made the claim that since 'the great majority of both Indians and Chinese were uneducated coolies [sic]... the differences in their performances could not be explained in terms of differences in human capital formation (...) [and] was to encounter similar phenomena in West Africa, in the Levant, in India and elsewhere (...) [emphasizing the] differences in economic performance among different cultural groups as a feature of much of economic history' (Bauer in Ruttan 1988:255).

A study conducted by Granato, Inglehart and Leblang in 1996 also broadly examines the impact of culture on economic development, arguing for a complementary relationship between economic and cultural factors (Granato et al. 1996:607). In their study, they use as a base the standard endogenous growth model and then include two cultural variables perceived to represent motivational factors that may encourage or discourage economic growth; the two variables are achievement motivation and post-materialist values (Granato et al. 1996:607). As regards achievement motivation, the study draws on the Weberian line of analysis which argues that the Protestant reform of Christianity played a key role in the rise of capitalism in Europe given a new found support for education and achievement (Granato et al. 1996:608). Yet, the study also attempts to shift attention beyond the limited scope of Weberian theories of the rise of capitalism, arguing that the Protestant role in the rise of capitalism is merely one case in a more general phenomenon. For example, a similar argument applies to the positive impact of "modern" Confucian values on economic growth; early Confucian values, as was the case with early Christian values, stigmatised profit and entrepreneurship, but again its eventual reform was instrumental in the rise of capitalism (Granato et al. 1996:608). Post-materialist values, on the other hand, no longer place emphasis on economic growth, but rather focus on factors such as the environment and quality of life.

The first segment of the quantitative analysis of the study used the World Values Survey to construct an achievement motivation index based on the summation of the percentage of people in each country studied that emphasised the values of thrift and determination, where these values were considered to reflect the importance of autonomy and achievement, minus the percentage of people that emphasised obedience and religious faith, where these values were considered to reflect the relative importance of conformity to traditional norms (Granato et al. 1996:611). In constructing the index, the level of emphasis of the values was not as important as the relative priority attributed to them (Granato et al. 1996:613). East Asia was revealed to occupy the highest position on the motivational index and also had the highest per capita growth, with the two

African countries in the study (Nigeria and South Africa) occupying the lowest position in the index accompanied by the lowest per capita growth (Granato et al. 1996:612). Finally, the European and New World countries were placed in the middle of the index, and the per capita growth of these countries was also placed between that of East Asia and Africa (Granato et al. 1996:612).

In the second segment of the quantitative analysis, three growth models were estimated. In the first model, mean per capita economic growth for the period 1960 to 1989 was regressed on the initial level of per capita GDP, on investment in human capital and on the rate of capital accumulation (Granato et al. 1996:616). The results of the model reveal that the initial per capita GDP coefficient is negative, indicating the presence of conditional convergence – meaning that poor countries grow faster than rich countries (Granato et al. 1996:616). Furthermore, both investment in human capital and capital accumulation were revealed to have a positive impact on economic growth (Granato et al. 1996:616). In the second model, mean per capita economic growth for selected countries for the period 1960 to 1989 was regressed on the achievement motivation and post-materialist values. The results of the model revealed that achievement motivation was positively related to economic growth, whereas post-materialism is negatively related to economic growth (Granato et al. 1996:616). In the final model, models one and two were combined and this model again revealed that achievement motivation was positively related to economic growth, but post-materialism was now revealed to be insignificant (Granato et al. 1996:620). Thus, the importance of motivational factors in encouraging economic growth can be recognised. What these three models reveal is that both economic and cultural models are important in explaining economic growth and therefore the results lend support for the argument that economic and cultural factors play complementary roles in encouraging economic growth.

Marini (2004) also considers the relationship between culture and economic growth and argues that there are two opposing drives in the theory regarding the relationship between culture and development; the first drive emphasises achievement motivation as being crucial for economic growth, and the second drive emphasises "trust syndrome" as being crucial for economic growth (Marini 2004:765). The first school of thought focuses on individual values and the need for achievement. McClelland (1967), for example, found a positive correlation between economic growth and cultures emphasising a need for achievement, but no such growth correlation was found in countries emphasising values relating to social relationships (Marini 2004:769). These results are supported by the Granato et al. (1996) study which also finds a positive relationship between achievement and economic growth, but similarly, finds a negative relationship between social relationship values, such as obedience and religious faith, and economic growth.

The second school of thought, in contrast, highlights the importance of social relationships and culture as a whole, and emphasises the importance of the creation of trust between impersonal agents (Marini 2004:769). The creation of trust is argued to be particularly abundant within the context of the limited institutional framework of traditional scenarios, stimulating arguments for the importance of traditional cultures (Marini 2004:769). This line of thought has been revived given the recent East Asian development boom. In this regard, the best-selling novels of Putman (1993) and Fukuyama (1995) set out to prove 'that cultural factors play an important if not crucial role in explaining economic growth around the world' (Marini 2004:767). However, empirical evidence for both schools has at best been confusing and at worst entirely contradictory, and hardly ever have studies been conducted that combine the two schools of thought. One possible reason for the persistent lack of consensus may be 'the multidimensionality of the values system, a realm too vast to be mastered by the human mind' (Marini 2004:770).

According to Marini, achievement and trust are complementary because achievement motivation, and thus the enhancement of competition, led to the industrial revolution, whereas trust facilitates market transactions and lowers transaction costs, and thus leads to the enlargement of market size (Marini 2004:774-775). Therefore, achievement and trust are two complementary and necessary requirements for economic growth and the attainment of basic materialist goals. Finally, when society reaches the threshold where basic needs have been met, secondary needs such as spiritual goals (…) can be pursued by the vast majority of the population (Marini 2004:775). This movement relates to the move towards post-materialist values. In short then, Marini's model argues that following limited growth in the traditional society, the encouragement of achievement motivation and trust creation will stimulate growth and propel the society into an era of industrialisation and modernisation, and as growth continues to increase and materialist goals are met, the society will move into a post-materialist phase of development. Following the conceptualisation of this model, Marini engages in a brief empirical study using the World Values Survey and finds that the variables associated with traditional society, such as obedience, religious faith and tolerance, are negatively correlated with economic growth, the values associated with achievement and trust, such as independence, thrift, determination and responsibility, are positively correlated with economic growth and post-materialist values, such as imagination and unselfishness, are uncorrelated with economic growth (Marini 2004:776). It is clear that religion has to be discussed as part of culture and it has also been investigated somewhat as an explanatory variable – even if always in terms that originated in Europe rather than in the African religious experience.

Religion and Economic Development

A widespread feature of the studies discussed thus far is that religious faith, except in its Protestant work ethic formulation, is either found or expected to be negatively related to economic growth given its association with values such as obedience and tradition. However, given the immense impact of the various religions on the cultures of the world, it is important to examine whether this negative relationship is as dominant and prevalent as it seems.

A recent study in this regard is that by Marcus Noland (2005) which empirically investigates the relationship between religion and economic performance. Noland argues for a positive relationship between religion and economic growth: 'Abundant evidence affirms that religious beliefs affects a wide range of behavioural outcomes, and religious activity can affect economic performance at the level of the individual group, or country through at least two channels' (Noland 2005:1215). These two channels, or two economic advantages, were argued to exist by Adam Smith in the *Wealth of Nations*: the first channel identified by Adam Smith is that of reputation, where membership to a so-called "good" sect could lend the individual a "good" reputation by association, and thus reduce the risk associated with that individual; the second channel is that of trust and discipline outside of the formal legal system such that uncertainty and transaction costs are reduced and transaction efficiency is increased (Noland 2005:1215). The argument of Adams is applicable to a wider conception of group associations than religion only.

Max Weber also contended that there is a strong link between religion and economic performance: according to Weber, 'the Protestant Reformation was critical to the rise of capitalism through its impact on belief systems' (Noland 2005:1215). In the process of the development of the so-called Protestant work-ethic, attitudes towards achievement, economic activity and wealth accumulation were revolutionised. In addition, the values of diligence, efficiency and thrift were cultivated, which were seen to be essential building blocks of capitalism (Noland 2005:1215). However, Weber's argument focuses only on Protestantism and does not broaden its discussion to include the impact of religion, in all its manifestations, on economic growth.

The Noland Study attempts to test the Weberian line of argumentation with particular consideration of the purported negative impact of Islam on economic performance, drawing attention to the possibility that 'intermediate institutions may be the mechanism through which religious belief affects economic performance at the aggregate level' (Noland 2005:1216). In this quest, Noland employs three sets of evidence; firstly, a cross-country analysis was conducted, secondly, a smaller cross-country analysis was conducted covering nearly a century, and, thirdly, Noland conducted 'analyses of subnational data for three multireligious, multiethnic countries' (Noland 2005:1216). Seven religious categories are identified by Noland, namely Catholic, Protestant, Orthodox, Christians, Muslims, Jews, Hindus, and Buddhists (Noland 2005:1217). The results of the regressions reveal that although it is evident that religious affiliation is correlated with growth and factor productivity performance, 'the regressions do not yield a robust pattern of coefficients with respect to particular religions' (Noland 2005:1227). The long-run results yield a positive relationship between the Buddhist and Christian variables and growth and factor productivity performance, whereas the relationship between other religious variables and performance proved to be insignificant (Noland 2005:1219). The medium-run results, however, yielded a negative relationship between the Jewish, Protestant and Catholic variables (Noland 2005:1217-1218). This result of a negative correlation in the medium-run and a positive correlation in the long-run of especially the Christian variable certainly warrants further investigation and explanation. Noland hazards no theoretical explanation for the nature of his results. However, what is certain is that there is a statistically significant relationship between religious affiliation and performance even though no coherent pattern of this relationship emerges (Noland 2005:1227).

Islam is commonly associated with values and attitudes that are negatively associated with economic growth and is considered to be generally anti-market. The first problem with these theories is that it is not even clear whether Islamic countries have in fact been underperforming economically in the past number of decades (Noland 2005:1220). Indeed, 'Indonesia, the world's largest Muslim country, has grown far more rapidly than the world average for the past four decades' (Noland 2005:1220). The growth of Middle Eastern countries, on the other hand, has outperformed Sub-Saharan Africa, and though worse than East Asia, has been similar to that of South Asia and Latin America (Noland 2005:1220). A further complication here is to what extent the Middle Eastern growth performance merely reflects the growth impact of oil. Furthermore, 'it could be that the negative interpretations of Islam's historical legacy are correct, but that enough convergence in institutions has occurred that the effects have dissipated in the contemporary world, or that other positive characteristics in Islamic societies overwhelm the negative influence of Islam, or it could be that received wisdom is simply wrong' (Noland 2005:1220; Sala-i-Martin et al. 2004 seems to have produced the same results). In all the regressions attempting to analyse the relationship between Islam and either growth performance or factor productivity performance, the coefficients revealed either a positive or an insignificant relation with performance (Noland 2005:1221-1222). The only negative coefficient found on Islam was in the sub-national regression for Malaysia, where Islam is the state religion (Noland 2005:1228). This empirical result seems to counteract popular claims that Islam inhibits economic performance. However, the contradictory results of different studies suggests that results may be dependent on the manner in which models are estimated or the samples used, and thus further investigation into this relationship will be necessary in order to clarify results (for a sustained attempt at teasing out the detail of the argument see: Kuran 1997; Kuran 1998; Kuran 2001; Kuran 2003; Kuran 2004a; Kuran 2004c; Kuran 2004b; Kuran 2005. For an opposing argument, see: Lewis 2003).

Wendy Tyndale (2000) also conducted an interesting study with normative dimensions that investigates the importance of religion in development. Her study aims to place the individual back into the concept of development by highlighting the importance of individual faith in shaping individuals and their concept of development and the importance of religious institutions given their close contact with individuals, and thus to the grassroots of development. Tyndale draws on the argument that in the absence of spiritual advancement, there can be no true physical development, but that such spiritual considerations have been given little or no attention in mainstream development economic theories and practices (Tyndale 2000:9). In consequence, "development", widely defined as the process by which non-industrialised countries would catch up with the more "advanced" nations, has not traditionally been understood in the context of the spirituality, values, and cultural heritage, either of the developers or of those supposedly being developed' (Tyndale 2000:9). Thus, there is an ever-increasing need to clarify the "true" meaning of development and to adjust interpretations thereof to account for local conditions, cultures and religious beliefs; and, accordingly, international institutions need to acquire a 'more intimate knowledge of the people whose poverty [they wish] to eradicate' (Tyndale 2000:10).

In short, religion, and its accompanying priorities, should not be perceived to be stumbling blocks to either development or efficient capitalistic economic functioning, but rather as an integral part of the advancement of development and economic production (Tyndale 2000:10). Tyndale then proceeds to discuss the various manners in which the majority of religions in the world are conducive and not contrary to development. Firstly, it is in its ability to empower individuals and provide a vision that religion is most powerful in stimulating development: 'for the faiths, "empowerment" involves the concept of personal dignity, of self-worth, of a kind of contentedness, which does not depend either on the opinion of others or on fulfilling immediate desires. This sort of empowerment brings hope and vision with it" (Tyndale 2000:11). In the end, for a people to develop, they firstly need the hope that they are able to rise above their circumstances and secondly need a vision towards which they can develop. The remaining elements of religion conducive to development are the encouragement of a sharing of wealth, the recognised importance of equity and inclusion, the relationship between people and the environment, the encouragement of personal transformation and the provision of education and leadership.

In terms of sharing wealth, the majority of faiths condemn greed and exploitation, while encouraging equity, compassion, generosity, solidarity and self-sacrifice. This suggests that the developmental models that religions may propagate may be far more in tune with a conception of the welfare state than with the current liberal models. However, 'economists warn that a move towards self-sacrifice – the reduction of consumption – in the rich countries would slow down global growth and lead to more hardship for the poor; but, even if one accepts that growth is the prerequisite for poverty reduction, the *way* we consume should be scrutinized' (Tyndale 2000:12). Within the sharing context the emphasis on equity is also highlighted, where the majority of religions contain some conception of all peoples having been created by God and consequently have an element of God within them, and are thus worthy of respect. However, despite this theological conception of equity, true equity is not necessarily exercised in practice. Inequitable practices are particularly evident in gender relations, and it is therefore important that the religions clarify 'how much of the male domination which is practiced within many of their communities is practiced within many of their communities has to do with cultural traditions which could now be considered "out of date"' (Tyndale 2000:14). This is an important point given that women and children are some of the poorest people in the world, and thus improved gender relations are crucial for "true" development and optimal economic growth (Tyndale 2000:14).

Religions also contain precepts on the relationship between man and the environment, where people are seen as either stewards of the environment or merely a part of creation's whole (Tyndale 2000:14). In short, people have a duty to care for the environment and maintain a harmonious balance between man and nature. This stands in contrast to the exploitative view – which now needs to be reversed – taken of the environment in past decades. Thus, in our quest to "save" the environment, the religions may have an important role to play.

Finally, Tyndale argues that religions have an important role to play in terms of bringing about change. The first manner in which religions can bring about change is by personal transformation: 'any strategy for change must be based on an analysis of the causes of the ills we want to change. For the faiths, these causes lie first and foremost with the individual human being. They are then to be found structurally within the societies which human beings construct' (Tyndale 2000:15). Religions can thus alter societal structures by transforming individuals from being generally self-interested to being generally selfless (Tyndale 2000:15). This role of religion is closely related to its role as educator: 'In some countries of the world – Tanzania is an example – the education system would be almost non-existent if it were not for schools run by religious bodies' (Tyndale 2000:16). Religious bodies are able to teach literacy, basic health care, self-reliance, basic organisational skills and leadership skills, all of which is important for development (Tyndale 2000:16). Thus, religious bodies have the potential to be agents of change and deliver individuals who can also be agents of change. Lastly, and in many ways in summary, religious bodies as organisations closely connected to communities are also able to aid international institutions in the setting of criteria for development. Religious criteria can highlight the importance of hope and dignity, of equity, of personal transformation and of education, all of which are critical to development.

The problem with analyses like that of Tyndale is, of course, that it mixes normative semi-theological statements with the sociological analysis of a particular facet of society in a way that a scientific analysis should not ignore but often does – exactly because it does not know how to deal with statements that seem to be theological. It is quite difficult to explain the content of religious motivation without dealing with the theological claims that structure the meaning of any variety of religion. In this case, there are a number of critical perspectives built into the analysis. Furthermore, the basic point is that the motivation to attempt to go beyond the desperate situation of poverty and exclusion comes from a sense of direction or meaning that religion could provide. This meaningful content of religious beliefs also creates institutional and social realities that should not be ignored. On the other hand, there have often been structural relationships between what was asked in the name of religion and the economic and political exploitation of a group. The nature of the Methodist attempt at converting the Barolong Bo-Ratsidi in colonial and early industrial South Africa is as good an example as any (Comaroff and Comaroff 1992). Any argument about the value of religion in society has to be tempered with a very clear understanding of how religions of all types have been a camouflage for ideological and political-economic projects of the worst kind.

The problem with the standard method of inquiry about the impact of religion and especially different religious traditions on development is the neatness of the categories. African religion is always a mixture of different facets (if European religious denominations can be categorised neatly). It is only a result of significant fading of a variety of different influences that were standardised in the formation of the European nation-state system. African Islam is African, and Muslim and East African Islam is very different from West African Islam (Brenner 1993; Westerlund and Rosannder 1997). Methodism in South Africa (Comaroff and Comaroff 1991, 1997, 1992) and in Zimbabwe (Ranger 1995, 2003) had very different trajectories and occupy very different religious spaces in that the other denominations that make up the landscape and the cultural, political and social context within which Methodism found itself differs significantly. The combination of local cultural specificity, broader political-economic and social dynamics and the manner in which non-traditional religion was imported and received makes a comparison in the standard form very difficult. This will also be an issue later on when we attempt to put forward our own Southern African analysis of the Protestant Ethic theme.

Cultural Diversity and Economic Development

One approach to examine the effect of culture on economic development is to suggest that the specifics of individual cultures are not as crucial as the number of cultures in any one country. In other words, the diversity of cultures is what is important in determining the level of economic development. One such study on the economic relevance of cultural diversity was conducted by Lian and Oneal in 1997, whose study aimed to determine whether cultural diversity has a negative impact on economic development given that 'there is a long line of thought suggesting that culturally diverse states are apt to have relatively slow rates of economic development' (Lian 1997:62). The study made use of the GDP growth per capita of a total of 98 countries for the time period 1960 to 1985, as this is the time period for which the most complete data was available (1997:62).

In their introduction, Lian and Oneal provide a brief overview of previous research in this regard. Previous research generally attributes a negative relationship between diversity and development 'to the variety of competing demands on political and economic capital that must be met or the difficulty disparate groups have in communicating or cooperating' (Lian 1997:62). One such study was conducted by Adelman and Cynthia Morris (1967), whose study involved ranking 74 less developed countries for the period 1957 to 1962 in terms of a 10-point ordinal scale of diversity (Lian 1997:63). Their results revealed that the more homogenous a less developed country, the less their development is hampered. Indeed, homogeneity encourages both social and political integration as well as continuous growth (Lian 1997:62). A second study was conducted by Marie Haug for 114 countries (1967). Haug identified sectionalism, race, language and religion as variables, of which language was afforded the greatest weight. Her results seemed to indicate that cultural diversity is negatively related to economic growth (Lian 1997:63). A further study was conducted by Lloyd Reynolds (1985), who investigated thirty-seven less developed countries for the period 1950 to 1980, and his results also seem to suggest that there is a negative relationship between diversity and economic growth (Lian 1997:63). However, the widespread applicability of these results remains suspect given the limited scope of these early studies.

Hence, given the limited scope of these early studies, the Lian and Oneal study attempts to reinvestigate the relationship between cultural diversity and economic development. The authors firstly compile a cultural diversity variable that contains three different cultural characteristics, namely ethnic composition, religion and language (Lian 1997:64). According to the authors, 'these characteristics are important because they compete with and often precede attachments, not just to a particular government but to the state itself' (Lian 1997:64). This cultural variable is then controlled for using political and economic factors as based on Barro's 1991 cross-national study (Barro 1991). In other words, the Lian and Oneal cultural diversity variable is added to Barro's general model that draws on both exogenous and endogenous growth models (Lian 1997:65). The reason for their choice of model lies in the fact that Barro's general model supports the Lian and Oneal hypothesis in that it finds that the 'geometric mean rate of growth in GDP per capita is an inverse function of the initial level of per capita GDP and is positively associated with primary and secondary school enrollment rates and with political stability' (Lian 1997:65).

In contrast to earlier studies, the study found no significant relationship between the cultural diversity variable and economic growth, and as a result the authors attempted to examine whether the purported cultural diversity effect may be indirect via political stability or fragmentation (Lian 1997:72). In consequence, two further intervening factors were added to the model, namely political stability and political fragmentation (a measure of the number of political parties and their share of votes) (Lian 1997:62). However, no relationship was found between political instability and cultural diversity, neither was a relationship found between political fragmentation and economic development and neither was 'high levels of both cultural diversity and political fragmentation, which might indicate that a nation's politics were rooted in cultural differences, associated with slower rates of development' (Lian 1997:73). Therefore, Lian and Oneal did not prove an indirect inverse relationship between cultural diversity and economic development. It is still important to note that this result can by no means be taken as revealing that cultural diversity benefits economic growth – no evidence for such a positive association was found (Lian 1997:73). In short, what the study does reveal is that far more research needs to be conducted in this regard in order to clarify the effect of cultural diversity on economic growth.

Global Culture Versus Local Culture

Another important direction of research attempts to examine the importance of interactions between global and local cultures in the context of including culture as a variable in development research. In terms of Jan Nederveen Pieterse's arguments (1995), it is important for researchers to avoid both the chauvinism of global culture and the chauvinism of local culture. In other words, research needs to ensure that a balance is maintained between the two extremes of globalism and localism (Tucker 1996:2). Lehman (1990), on the other hand, addresses the issue of modernity, and claims that all discussions on post-modernism, post-colonialism and globalisation represent expressions of cultural approaches to development, but more specifically represent a discussion on how global cultures impact upon local cultures (Tucker 1996:1). The point is that globalisation is not an a-cultural phenomenon and it hybridises local cultures. Such discussions raise caution in terms of where boundaries are drawn between local and global cultures given the historical and ever-increasing interconnectedness of the cultures of the world – what type of entities can be characterised as "local"? Does local refer to villages, towns, cities, provinces, nations or regions, and, moreover, who decides where "local" boundaries are drawn and what is the reason for the chosen boundaries (Tucker 1996:11)? In other words, the possibility exists to investigate local and global cultures and processes not as two entirely separate entities, but rather as two complementary perspectives and two entities that continuously impact upon each other (Tucker 1996:14). Hence, this line of research attempts to move away from both the ethnocentrism and westernisation of analytical approaches.

Studies conducted by Fagan et al. and Skelton (1996, 1996), similar to the capability approaches, have aided in refocusing attention to the acknowledgement of the "voices" of the recipients of development, thus reemphasising that it is the perspectives of local peoples that is of critical importance and not foreign analysis (Tucker 1996:2). This raises the issue of the concept of development being criticised as being in essence based on Western knowledge and values which, by its widespread propagation, is inadvertently heralded as superior to marginalised local knowledge. However, such "Western" knowledge is often equated to "global" knowledge in popular literature, and thus globalisation receives a large proportion of the criticism aimed at Westernisation. Consequently there is an increasing need for relevant literature to begin to clearly differentiate between the two concepts in order to aid in clarifying research results. Yet, in counteraction, Collins and Tucker caution such studies in identifying local peoples as the location of "authentic" development, pointing to the importance of factors such as class differentiation, gender, external economic, political and cultural forces and the ever important interaction between local and global actors in impacting upon local peoples to effectively act as the source of development (Tucker 1996:2-3). It makes sense therefore, to see what can be gained from a study that is local, but that also investigates the classical categories of social analysis.

Group Membership, Class and Gender

Barbara Thomas-Slayter (1992) provides an interesting study of the important interaction between resources, class and gender in Kenya. Her study is based on data collected in July and August in 1987 in conjunction with Kenya's National Environment Secretariat (Thomas-Slayter 1992:810). Thomas-Slayter finds that 'in the context of declining per capita food production, severe drought, and famine, African resource degradation has received considerable attention [but] analysts… have not explored the relationship between gender and resource access, use, and management' (Thomas-Slayter 1992:809-810). This is a conclusion which any attempt at understanding development from a cultural and social side should be taking seriously. Thomas-Slayter found that gender interacts with class to determine internal village management structures and, therefore, access to resources. Rural women are poor and uneducated and accordingly, have little status in their village or broader social and political arenas, but bear the majority of the burden for the viability of their households. Although women have to maintain the viability of their households, they have no power to impact on resource, assets or land use practices. For example, women have no ability to intervene in poor soil usage practices even though they generally have strong soil management skills and as a result soil degradation continues to increase, plunging households and villages further into poverty (1992:825). Thus, it becomes evident how the interaction between gender relations and status has a significant impact on poverty, and though 'the specific resource issues may varry, ... the interactions of class and gender with respect to resource management at the local level are pertinent considerations across rural Africa' (1992:826).

If the kind of insights that can be found in a closer and more local analysis of the lives of the poor can offer are so important as the above on gender, it makes sense to investigate other studies on that level. A study conducted by Warner, Al-Hassan and Kydd (1997) attempts to reveal the importance of understanding the true complexity of the lives of the poor. The general gender and household targeted development measures have had some success in reducing poverty and therefore should not be entirely dismissed, but what should be noted is the need to examine aspects of poverty such as rights, resources, obligations and the work load of women in more detail (Warner et al. 1997:163). All of these aspects accompany the distinction between married and unmarried women, given that marital status significantly impacts upon the ability of women to engage in productive activities and accumulate assets (Warner et al. 1997:146-153). Therefore, by engaging in more detailed analyses, development practitioners and theorists would be better able to reflect actual circumstances of the poor, and thus allow for the creation of more targeted policies (Warner et al. 1997:164). For example, 'by taking account of basic and widely-recognized differences which exist between senior and junior women in all African societies..., projects could be structured in such a way that they aim at least to meet the needs of the majority of intended beneficiaries, while endeavoring not to worsen the position of other categories of women and men' (Warner et al. 1997:164). Furthermore, 'any approach needs to be flexible enough to take account of diversity rather than attempting to impose a single "universal truth" onto all rural peoples' (Warner et al. 1997:160). The Warner et al. study, for instance, finds that in the Dagomba society, cooking status is of particular importance in determining the status of women, but 'in other parts of Africa, other social constructs may be even more important in determining the social and economic position of women and men' (Warner et al.

1997:160). Thus, the study reveals the importance of accounting for the full complexity of the characteristics of the lives of the poor in Africa in order to create both culturally sensitive and effectively target development policies (Warner et al. 1997:159).

Trust

With the increasing interest in social capital themes and the association between social capital and trust, many studies on trust are being done. Haddad, Maluccio and May (2000, 2003) conducted typical studies which focus on the importance of social capital. Even though there is no clear definition of social capital, there is an increasing recognition in the literature that social capital is a central characteristic of social interactions (Haddad 2003:573). In their view, there are currently two broad directions of research on social capital. The first direction of research is interested in examining the sites of social interaction such as groups and networks, whereas the second direction of research is concerned with the 'underlying mechanisms through which social capital is thought to work' (2003:573). Examples of such underlying mechanisms include transaction costs, trust, norms and rules. The second direction of research is understood far more poorly than the first direction of research. In other words, significant evidence has been found to suggest that participation in groups and networks offers economic benefits. However the mechanism that allows for the achievement of these benefits is poorly understood (2003:573).

Haddad and Maluccio attempt to combine the two approaches by examining the precise relationship between group membership and trust (2003:574). More specifically, employing longitudinal data from KwaZulu-Natal Province in South Africa, three variables were considered: the impact trust has on deciding whether or not to join a group; the extent to which groups are able to create trust; and, the extent to which membership and trust contribute well-being as measured in terms of per capita household income (2003:574). Previous literature predicts that trust should have a positive impact on group membership, although previous literature has been unable to determine whether group membership creates trust (2003:577-578). In terms of the literature on the relationship between group membership and household welfare, research tends to reveal that group membership has a positive effect on household welfare. The Haddad and Maluccio study divides the groups under study into financial groups, which tend to be relatively more formalised, and non-financial groups.

The results of their study indicate that the two measures of trust are unrelated with general group membership and with non-financial group membership 'but are significant determinants of participation in financial groups' (2003:588). However, membership in both financial and non-financial groups has a positive impact on per capita income (2003:593). Given that group membership is treated as a proxy for social capital, it is possible to begin 'to understand how returns to social capital by way of groups are generated: it all seems to start with high levels of trust in local agents' (2003:596).

The issue may be developed further by an even finer definition of trust where a distinction is made between "bridging" and "bonding" trust (Beugelsdijk and Smulders 2003). This distinction is intended to enable investigation of the role of different types of trust in business and other relations that are increasingly dependent on the ability and willingness to trust people that are not known personally. Beugelsdijk and Smulders anticipate the bridging trust would be important in economic success in any given society, but the application of this notion would be different in a situation where rule of law and well developed civil and public institutions bolster trust across boundaries. It is no surprise that Haddad and Maluccio find that, given that the positive impact on income of group membership is not solely the result of trust, it is not possible to conclude that trust has a positive impact on income (Haddad 2003:593, 596). The trust notion itself is vague and an explanation for the mechanism through which trust is created remains elusive in general terms and in particularly African terms.

Conclusion

The results are not altogether encouraging. Although significant work has been done and important initiatives have been undertaken, the issue of the role of values and culture in development is far from being an established feature or a settled body of knowledge in development research. The obvious culprit in this regard is development economics. In fact, the economistic mode of thought still fixes almost all attention on capital, technology and labour (even when this is done with broader definitions of capital and labour than the classic model allows). The lack of comparative empirical material that allows one to form an informed and rounded perspective on the role of values and culture in development in Africa, results in limited possibilities for informed policy-making and successful implementation strategies – even when the policy-makers are so inclined.

A case in point is the recent Sachs report (UN 2005), *Investing in Development, A practical plan to achieve the Millennium Development Goals,* to the UN Secretary General. Although there are many important observations and analyses in this specific document – also for African development, the fact that reference to culture and values is almost entirely absent in the report (other than in agriculture and less than in ten other references) is shocking. This can be seen as a consequence of the content of the Millennium Development Goals (Sachs is indeed critical of the MDGs and calls for attention to the investment in human and social capital, among other things (UN 2005:28-29). But it is an example of the diffuse and inadequate way in which culture and values are considered in much of development economics.

One might compare this document to the so-called Blair document (2005), *Our Common Interest, Report of the Commission for Africa*, as this was published with similar aims and in the same time-frame. This report was not bound to the MDGs and wanted to reflect more on the internal African processes of change and did so with significantly more African participation in the process of drafting the document. It exhibits a sophisticated understanding of the role of values and culture in development and makes it an integral part of its view of African development. It actively propagates this approach as the only appropriate one: 'At the outset, our recommendation is that the international community should recognise the need for greater efforts to understand the values, norms and allegiances of the cultures of Africa, and in their policy-making display a greater flexibility, open-minded willingness to learn, and humility. Such an approach will pay respect to the Africans who must be partners in this enterprise' (2005:132). However, even though one cannot but support a nuanced and strong voice for the integration of a cultural perspective on development in every aspect of development, the report acknowledges that empirical research on the matter in African terms is limited: 'It is… noticeable that the role of culture in development is relatively less studied in Africa than, for example, in much of Asia' (2005:131). This is the crux of the matter. Even with the resources available to the Commission for Africa, they had to rely on expert submissions to the Commission and a smattering of empirical studies to be able to support the basic theoretical approach of the Commission on the matter of the relevance of values and culture in development. When one compares the supporting evidence for a particular view in the chapter on the role of values in development with the evidence supporting claims in the other chapters of health, politics, agriculture, trade and economic development in general, the results clearly show that there is a lack of useful empirical material on a scale that makes sense in development planning and development theorising respectively.

4

Cosmology, Power, Human Relationships and Human Qualities

Hans Müller (with van Heerden)

Introduction

We argue that any analysis of the role of values in development in Africa would have to incorporate investigation into four areas. These are cosmology, power, human relationships and human qualities. Under these categories, we consider many different aspects to be worthy of investigation. Many of these aspects are multi-faceted and relate to more than one of the areas. We relate and enumerate the aspects and the areas in Figure 4.1.

The first area is cosmology. We are interested in seeing how deep-seated cultural and social views on the composition of the world and how change in that world happens affect development. Cosmology is associated with religion and metaphysics, but one should not lose sight of the connection between cosmology and social patterns. In many ways, cosmology and general social patterns are two sides of the same coin (Asad 1983, in his critique of Geertz, is quite correct in relating power and meaning). However, we would argue that an analysis that focuses on cosmology would tend to open up other insights than the ordinary social analyses. As the explicit focus is on meaning and not function or behaviour, we may be able to grasp dimensions of African values and culture that would not be as visible in a different kind of analysis. For example, there is some literature pointing to the significance of a type of social capital that makes trust across boundaries important for development; while strangers and foreigners and, for that matter, the unknown, are often incorporated in a cosmological scheme as

Figure 4.1: Values in Development

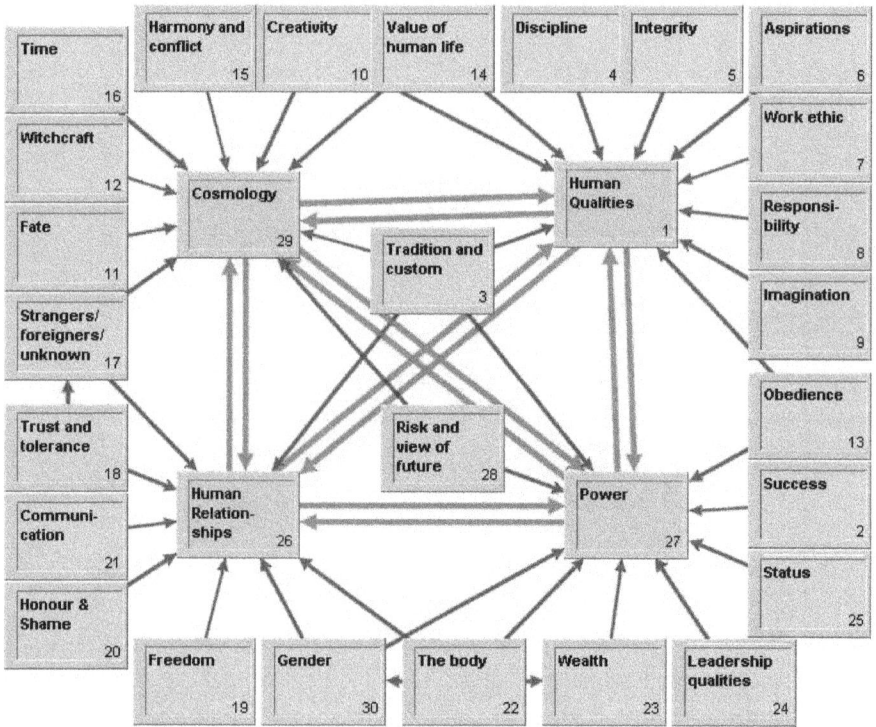

non-human. Does such a scheme exist in African cosmologies and how important is it in the lives of African communities facing continuous change often driven from outside? We list conceptions of fate, witchcraft, time, harmony and conflict, the value of human life, creativity and views of the future as dimensions of cosmology that could be important and require some conceptual explanation first and then empirical investigation. The reasons for this selection of aspects are set out below.

The second area of aspects for investigation is that of power. In a sense, questions of power need to be discussed as a countervailing argument to the cosmology interest. Even though one could argue that power is just a sub-dimension of cosmology, posing power as an area of concentrated attention enables one to focus attention on activities and balance the world of ideas with the world of actions, relationships and structures. We consider power to be the ability to make a difference that may not necessarily be negative or positive, but will depend on what difference is made and how that difference is made. We also consider different "faces of power", including not only the ability to directly influence and coerce others, but also the so-called "structural bias" that determines the context within which decisions are taken and the power of ideology that determines the way in which reality is defined. The set of aspects that we would like to consider in this area include, leadership conceptions and qualities, gender, the body, success, wealth, tradition and custom, obedience, risk and view of the future.

The third area of aspects deals with human relationships. Again, one should say immediately that human relationships are encompassed by cosmology, or the other way round, and power is obviously always present in human relationships. However, we want to focus attention of human relationships specifically because the social nature of development has been the emphasis of the project and this publication from the beginning. Development is not adequately described in economic terms and any attempt at unravelling the social dimension of development has to include a full analysis of the nature of relationships as limiting and enabling factors in development processes of whatever kind. We have a limited number of aspects that we consider important to highlight. These include some that also occur in the list dealing with power – as can be expected. They are gender and the body. We also consider relationships with strangers and foreigners, and the unknown in general, as important human relationships and these were also noted in the cosmology area. The other aspects are trust and tolerance (closely related, but not the same as the interest in strangers), honour and shame and communication.

The last area which we are interested in is more of a collection of aspects than a clearly defined category; but it is a set of aspects that always seems to make its way to the table of analyses of the role of values in any social process and to the role of values in development in particular. Many of the items here have some relation to notions like moral economy and social capital. From a different perspective, the list includes some aspects that can properly be understood as terminal values in the psychological sense. Terminal values are values defined in terms of the Rokeach framework (1970, 1973) and are end states that are highly desirable for their own sake and not for some instrumental reason. Of course, the definition of anything as a terminal value instead of an instrumental value is wholly in the eye of the beholder – in this case, the beholder is African discourses on these values. These values can also be understood as moral virtues but then, obviously, in a double-edged way, as some of these virtues are sometimes considered to be the very social barrier that limits development. These include notions like obedience, discipline, integrity, work ethic, responsibility and imagination. The content and strength of individual and collective aspirations are also considered under this rubric and the perceived importance of tradition and custom is also relevant here, not just as a dimension of power, but also as a definition of a type of human quality.

The substantive claims made in this chapter are the result of our literature survey of cultural and social explanations of relative development patterns. However, there is an ambiguity in our approach here. On the one hand, we do believe that the general categorisation of the aspects discussed is appropriate. These categories do constitute a theoretical claim on our part. However, under the categories, there are aspects that have been collected from development literature, common perceptions and discourses about development and values and very particular and limited studies of specific cases of development that we do not know to be useful explanations or dimensions of the role of values in development. Therefore, the aspects presented under the categories incorporated are not all argued to be good explanations for relative development trends in Africa. These aspects are discussed and explained so as to develop exploratory hypotheses that can be tested if the data that we investigate in the next section allows that.

At the same time, the categorisation presented here will seem odd to some readers in that it does not deal directly with some aspects of what has become standard fare in many analyses of African culture – especially those that are inclined to describing Africa as the opposite of Europe or modern Western society. For example, we do not specifically lift out the individualism-collectivism scale that so many have deemed to be a fundamental way of explaining the difference between 'Africa' and 'the rest' (Hofstede 2001; Inglehart 1997; Triandis 1988; Schwartz 1994). Although there are many of the aspects that we discuss that are relevant to that theme (harmony and conflict, discipline, obedience, tradition and custom, wealth, etc.), we do not find the broad notion of individualism as the opposite of collectivism to be terribly interesting if divorced from these aspects that we do discuss.

The aim of this chapter is thus to develop an overarching framework for the claim that social and cultural values do, indeed, impact on development, and to set the scene for an engagement with African culture and values in development. In the process, we also explain aspects that others have claimed to be critical in the cultural explanation of development. The aim of being inclusive in this manner is to facilitate the dialogue rather than to impose a theoretical point of view.

There are serious methodological issues that emanate from the range of issues and material that we will be dealing with. The best we can do is to limit our claims to the extent that the issue here is conceptual development of issues that should be considered and that are not necessarily considered in current comparative values research. Our selection of material is necessarily eclectic and the theoretical discussions of the selected concepts are wide-ranging but not comprehensive or definitive. It is not the 'Malinowskian doctrine that the only true knowledge of a society is that of the ethnographer him or herself' (Kuper 1983:196)! In fact, we often find ourselves in a situation where we would prefer to speak in first person terms, but use objectifying language and references in order to anchor the argument in published academic literature. This only serves to underscore the need for more African research on these matters.

We are also not able to indicate how the concepts relate to current issues in any great detail. It is tempting to develop perspectives on the relationships between corruption, clientilism and matrilineal social solidarity or the relationships between power, harmony and actual peaceful resolution of conflicts; but such discussions will have to be informed by much more detailed analysis of data than what is available to us.

Methodologically, it is important to note that this chapter is based on a review of literature on issues and themes that we have framed and chosen. It means that we try to stay close to the specific points made by quoted authors, but weave this into a larger framework of our own.

The Complexity of Cultural and Social Aspects and Dimensions

As argued in the first chapter, culture is a notion of relatively recent origin. It relates directly to the development of the idea that society; and human differences are acquired and not predetermined in nature. It has also been tied to the idea of social engineering (or civilising gardening a la Baumann) for a considerable and, for Africa, an especially significant length of time. Even when the modern notion of culture can be stripped of the instrumentalist assumptions of gardening or engineering and presented as a way of life that encompasses symbols, rituals, practices and resultant social institutions and structures, one still has to have respect for the complexity that is at stake. All the so-called cultural notions that we listed under the areas of interest in Figure 4.1 above are related to broader structural tensions that are incredibly complex. This is not the place to develop a full argument about the various levels of complexity, but one should at least state the broad terms of the matter as we see it and take a position on the major issues.

The first level of complexity has to deal with the incorporation of an action-perspective and a structure perspective in a holistic and adequate social theoretical view of culture and society. Because we are interested in values and culture, the expectation may be that we would tend to prefer an analysis of development that privileges meaning in contrast to structure and function and that we would tend to focus on subjective experience rather than objective explanation. We do not take this dualism to be a useful categorisation of options for a values perspective on development, but would rather argue that we need to move beyond objectivism and subjectivism (Bernstein 1980). This implies an integration of action and structure perspectives where structure is seen as existing by virtue of the continuous flow of actions and action is constrained and framed by these very patterns that we call institutions and structures (Giddens 1986:5-40). One could also use the language of Habermas (1981) to make more or less the same point and argue for an integrated social theory that has an eye on systems, while at the same time understanding that all systems emanate from the lifeworld of shared meanings dealing with truth, rightness and beauty – to use Kantian categories.

One could argue that the basic thrust behind the moral economy approach is correct if this is understood to be 'a call for an economic science that takes as its center the location of the economy in the architecture of society – its institutions and values – and a new normative theory, one guided by the question of what end or good the economy ought to serve' (Booth 1993b:953). We know that the moral economy approach leads us to an often reified and essentialist set of traditional values that may "require" enforcement, and thus further division in society (Booth 1994:658)[1]

In contrast to the moral economy approach, one might consider the social capital approach. We do not consider this a viable approach primarily because the notion of social capital is silent on the notion of capital and because Fine's argument that "all capital is social" is taken as persuasive (Fine 2001). Whereas moral economy approaches want a return to traditional values, social capital theorists are in favour of the cultivation of the "right" values for development: if they are present in the traditional, traditional values must be rehabilitated; if not, community values need to be adapted so as to include values conducive to collective action and development. Social capital is not concerned with the traditional per se, but is rather concerned with values of collective action which are perceived as good for development and which are by chance often to be found in the context of the traditional.

Our approach to the areas and the aspects that we regard significant enough to consider as part of the values dimension of development is not to only focus on meaning and the subjective experience of individuals and communities, but to position these meanings in their social context of structural constraints and institutional frameworks. We do not find it moral or feasible to attempt to manipulate society by cultivating the "right" values. We are much more interested establishing how values function and interpreting and making a dialogue possible that goes beyond the abstractions of both the moral economy and social capital theorists.

The second level of complexity deals with the choice of working at the elucidation of culture through the means of values analysis. We take this approach because, as is indicated in the introduction, values are not as fluctuating as beliefs and opinions and constitute the most general life-orientation that one can conceptualise. However, this means that the level of analysis is complex. Values do not present themselves in packaged format but are latent variables that are constructed in a process of interpretation. It may be that extensive data is available that is sufficiently coherent and systematic and that one is thus able to do the interpretation with the help of data reduction techniques like factor analysis. This is done in subsequent chapters where possible. However, we are quite clear about it that such an analysis is as much dependent on interpretation as is qualitative analyses of specific events or experiences. This matter has been discussed in the introduction, but it is relevant here as well, as this chapter is dependent on a lot of conceptual argumentation that is related to anthropological – and thus mostly qualitative work – while some quantitative work is also presented as supporting argumentation.

The third level of complexity has to deal with the historical situatedness of culture in our time. Culture has been manipulated and distorted, first by colonial administrative systems (Lord Lugard arrived in Africa in 1888) and more recently by modernist assumptions about civilisation and modernisation. Culture is now also more reflexive than ever in the sense that the awareness of culture, cultural difference and cultural choice is almost universal. Values are talked about, formulated and used to define difference and identity also by politicians and business people. In the popular parlance about values a number of confusing dimensions arise. Purported values may not be the same as the underlying constructs of a sophisticated factor analysis or conceptual interpretation of opinions, beliefs, ethical positions and religious ideas. This adds another aspect of interaction to the mix.

The fourth level of complexity is possibly most difficult to deal with and is really the heart of the matter. The object of the investigation into values and culture in African societies is the interaction between culture and social and economic development. Not only is development itself a cultural artefact, but the interaction between culture and development has numerous feedback loops that make any attempt at causal conclusions fraught with real and statistical complexities.

Cosmology

Cosmology is defined as the world of ideas holding the governing principles that form a meaningful horizon of the world as we experience it. Cosmology is often associated with religion and metaphysics. This is because cosmology deals with ideas about the origins of the world and the essential nature of the world. Of course, one does not have to take a position on particular religious or metaphysical perspectives or this class of truth claims in general to accept that metaphysical and religious views play a role in society. However, the tendency in social science has been to discount cosmology and metaphysics as these kinds of truth claims cannot be verified in a scientific manner and are, therefore, not open to interrogation in scientific procedures. It is not without significance that the notion of cosmology itself is not really found in political science or sociology. The association between superstition, religion and cosmology is strong. The opposition between cosmology and science is equally strong. However, cosmologies are often discussed and researched in anthropology and in some traditions in sociology. What needs to happen for this to take place is that the particular methodology has to have room for and an interest in the study of meaning and symbols for their own sake. Cosmologies work with symbolic narratives, places, events and rituals and quite often require a specific vocabulary to articulate what it is that they claim about the world and how it developed.

The Notion of "Traditional Society"

The first aspect that we discuss is that of tradition and custom and its role in a values perspective on development. This aspect is discussed first as it relates to all four areas and is quite central to the enterprise of proving arguments for a historically informed and socially aware perspective on the role of values in development in Southern Africa.

A typical description of traditional societies is Rostow's view on the cosmology of the traditional world. It is set in a larger and famous argument about the stages of development and includes reference to other factors in development. However, Meier argues that a 'traditional society is one whose structure is developed within limited production functions, based on pre-Newtonian science and technology, and on pre-Newtonian attitudes towards the physical world. Newton is here used as a symbol for that watershed in history when men came widely to believe that the external world was subject to a few knowable laws, and was systematically capable of productive manipulation' (Meier 1964:13).

According to Meier, Cairncross argues tangentially and says that '[n]o one doubts – least of all Rostow – that innovation is a social process and that its acceleration in the eighteenth century was associated with what he calls for short 'Newtonian science': a new way of looking at the world and a new ambition to change it. The self-sustaining character of development derives from this outlook and ambition, which issue in a continuous effort of technological improvement' (1964:34).

Meier proceeds to offer a summary of the classical economic view of traditional societies and because we take this summary as paradigmatic for the classical view, we quote at length. This particularly negative view of the general impact of the traditional on economic growth is a view that should be contextualised and, therefore, can be debated:

[T]he social structure and value patterns in many poor countries are still inimical to development. The structure of social relations tends to be hierarchical, social cleavages remain pronounced, and mobility among group is limited. Instead of allowing an individual to achieve status by his own efforts and performance, his status may be simply ascribed to him, according to his position in a system of social classification by age, lineage clan, or caste (Meier 1964:44).

Note that the notion of traditional societies seems to be dependent on a structural definition of society and that the role of individual or collective sense-making is discounted.

A value system that remains 'tradition-oriented' also tends to minimize the importance of economic incentives, material rewards, independence, and rational calculation. When the emphasis is on an established pattern of economic life, family obligations and traditional religious beliefs, the individual may simply adopt the attitude of accepting what happens to exist rather than attempting to alter it – an attitude of resignation rather than innovation. Within an extended family system or a village community, the individual may resign himself to accepting group loyalties and personal relationships which remain in a stable and tradition dominated pattern, assigning little importance to material accomplishments and change (Meier 1964:44).

Here, it becomes clear that the classical view also holds that the structures of traditional societies are internalised to such an extent that they structure attitudes and values.

Even though they may have latent abilities, individuals may lack the motivations and stimulations to introduce change; there may not be sufficiently large groups in the society who are 'achievement-oriented', concerned with the future, and believers in the rational mastery of nature (Meier 1964:44-45).

It now becomes clear that the definition of the traditional is quite dependent on a definition of the modern and that the definition of the one is a mirror image of the other.[2]

This is as good a summary of the list of typical issues that crop up in descriptions of cultural reasons for lack of development as any. However, this description is so clearly predisposed to an ideal-type of Western modernity that it may be a fruitful exercise to take into account Horton's comments on likeminded analyses of rationality in so-called "traditional societies".

When someone in a pre-literate society answers questions about the cause of an event by making a statement concerning the activities of invisible personal beings, the neo-Tylorian takes the statement concerning the activities of invisible beings at its face value. He accepts it is an attempt at explanation, and goes on to ask why members of the culture in question should try to explain things in this unfamiliar way (Horton 1993:53).

Note that the Meier argument takes a particular view of rationality (one which is no longer as easily defended fifty year later) as part of a package of social structures and value patterns. If we take Horton's critique of the assumptions of the outside analyst of rationality in such poor countries to be correct, the question is how much of the rest of the analysis is correct or at all relevant. We will have to reserve judgement on the matters relating to human relationships and power until later in this chapter, but at least, it is clear that the kind of rationality that is at stake in an analysis of the role of cosmology in development is needed. In that regard, Horton's caution is a first step:

> In the sort of pre-literate cultures that social anthropologists study, there has been little development of that ideal of objective understanding of the world which is so central to the modern Western ethos. Hence, intellectualist interpretations of the ideas of such cultures is out of order (Horton 1993:54).

The next level of the problem is that we are not primarily interested in pre-literate societies, but in societies that seem to have significant imprint of what is called traditional society, but is in interaction with the rest of the globe. As Giddens points out more than once (1991:174-176, 1994), it makes very little sense to think that any society in contemporary times would not have been deeply affected by modernity through the process of globalisation. This is echoed by people who have studied traditional societies over many years starting with luminaries like Worsley (1957), Hobsbawm and Ranger (1983) and Anderson (1983) and more recently the Comaroffs (1997), Appadurai (1996) and Hannerz (1996) van Binsbergen et al., make the point rather succinctly.

> [M]uch of what is presented as being traditional in character could be shown upon closer inspection, to be shot through with aspects of the modern world – indeed the globalizing world – to such an extent that it would be better to refer to these allegedly traditional identities as pseudo-traditional identities (van Binsbergen et al. 2004:7).

Although the above authors have mostly not been interested in the traditionality of such societies from the same point of view as was Rostow and Meier, their conclusions are salient in that the notion of traditionality is fundamentally questionable. It does make some difference to the question of development that only the notion of a traditional identity is no longer sustainable and that that does not mean that some aspects of traditional social structures and value patterns (to use Meier's terms) no longer exist. However, the idea that these structures and patterns can exist in any "pure" form must be rejected.

What this means for empirical research on large data-sets like the World Values Survey or thick descriptions of the detail of developmental dynamics in a particular community of group of people is that one should not longer be thinking in opposites, but in continuums and grades; and one might do well to look for very modern phenomena and dynamics exactly there where the traditional is invoked or ordinarily expected. Even the idea of a continuum as the proper way of capturing a more nuanced perspective in the place of African societies on these dimensions assumes that there is an existing polarity. This dualistic frame may be a misconception (Wiredu 1997).

It is exactly in the notions of secrecy and witchcraft that we can see this dynamic at play. If there were any set of aspects of African tradition and culture that one would expect to be closest to tradition it would be these notions. Work has been industrialised since the imposition of Western slavery and subsequent proletarisation of African communities under colonial and post-colonial economic relations. Politics has been imprinted with the logic of the nation-state even if this has found its own, sometimes perverted, forms in Africa. But one would expect that the secret societies and witchcraft notions would be least touched by globalisation and all its associated notions.

Secrecy and Rites

In general one can say that '[s]ecrecy serves to establish boundaries' (De Jong 2004:258). Furthermore, '[d]eeper truths are understood to constitute the core of culture. Indeed, when ethnographers talk about male initiation, secrecy and secret societies, they assume they are dealing with the hard core of culture'. In fact, secrets 'constitute an essential part of their identity, even a sacred force inherited from the past' (De Jong 2004:263).

If the core of culture is secrets, change cannot be an intervention of that culture, but must rather come from outside, from "our" world. Cultures depend on this core of secrecy to withstand turmoil and change. Therefore, it is possible to posit that culture will not fare well if change is pursued from outside – change will be regarded with suspicion and prohibited from penetrating this "core of culture" (De Jong 2004). However, what is most interesting about De Jong's experiences of secrecy and his role as an anthropologist in "keeping the secrets" and letting the cat out of the bag at the same time, is the reception of his position in the particular community. There is significant reflexivity about his position as an outsider and therefore a limited threat to the significance of the secrets of initiation. It means that certain core aspects of the secrets of initiation could even be commoditised and sold due an implicit understanding that there are different positions possible in how the core of the secret initiation is understood and taken up by insiders and outsiders.

If we continue the discussion from the same edited book and look at Rasing's analysis of female initiation rites in Zambia we see that these are portrayed as 'an intrinsic part of traditional culture and society' (2004:278).

Initiation rites remain important for women today despite the many social, religious, political and economic changes that have significantly altered Zambian society. Initially, the slave trade, pre-colonial state formation, the introduction of Christianity and colonization brought about changes in society, predominantly in the sense of a shift in power – from locals to westerners – and between men and women, centralizing men and marginalizing women. More recently, urbanization and economic problems such as massive unemployment, reduced household incomes, a lack of medical care, and the rapid spread of diseases such as HIV/ AIDS have brought about changes predominantly in the economic and health spheres (Rasing 2004:278).

However, it is exactly here that initiation rites become interesting to us as it becomes a basis for power and plays a role in human relationships while still based on a cosmology that gives it meaning in contemporary society. 'The rites remain important for women as a means of constructing their identity and celebrating their culture' (2004:305). This can be viewed as a representation of continuity with the cosmologies of the past but it has a role in the present.

The performance of initiation rites in today's urban Zambia should not be seen as a longing for the past that is forcibly being maintained in a globalized world, but as a local institution that is part of a religion... In this religion, woman's power is shown in the sense of continuing life, giving birth, having contact with spirits that have power over fertility and life and death (2004:305).'... Initiation rites emphasise traditional knowledge, mainly about procreation, human relationships and relationships with spirits, topics remain important in a globalized formal economy (2004:305). ...Women's power and autonomy are also related to procreation. Fertility is a person's most important gift – particularly for women – according to matrilineal cosmological ideas (2004:306). ...Women show reflexivity and resilience in their performance of the rites in adapting them to modern urban life (2004:306).

Together, these perspectives on tradition, secrecy and initiation can be understood as reflections on cosmology. Initiation represents a form of religious teaching, imparting cosmological knowledge on initiates. Secrecy, on the other hand, represents a source of empowerment, protection, stability, harmony, community and solidarity but this is based in cosmology. Initiation, and the secrecy that accompanies this, serves to define interpersonal relations.

In the face of globalisation, societies need to adopt strategies to deal with new reality. This leads to questions on 'modes of selection, appropriation [and the] creation and transgression of boundaries' (van Binsbergen et al. 2004:18).

Witchcraft

The theme of witchcraft has been used to contain and frame African societies in colonial and neo-colonial terms whereby Africa is seen as the ultimate other and where barbarism is to be researched in order to counter and contain it (Pels 1998). This is not the point of our interest in witchcraft. We would rather point out that witchcraft is a very current and modern theme in African societies and the obsession with witchcraft in many parts of present-day Africa is not to be viewed as some sort of traditional residue. On the contrary, it is particularly present in the more modern spheres of society. In the comparative, global perspective, this linking of modernity and witchcraft is not peculiar to Africa and Geschiere notes that in other parts of the world modern developments coincide with a proliferation of what have aptly been designated as "economies of the occult" (van Binsbergen et al. 2004:32).

The question is why so many of the aspects of modernity have been interpreted by Africans as emanating from witchcraft (Geschiere 1998:811). The Comaroff answer is that witchcraft has become a finely calibrated gauge of the impact of global culture and economic forces on local relations, on perceptions of money and markets, on the abstraction and alienation of "indigenous" values and meanings. Witches are modernity's prototypical malcontents. They provide – like grotesques of a previous age – disconcertingly full-bodied images of a world in which humans seem in constant danger of turning into commodities, of losing their life blood to the market and to the destructive desires it evokes... They embody all the contradictions of the experience of modernity itself, of its inescapable enticements, its self-consuming passions, its discriminatory tactics, its devastating social costs (Comaroff and Comaroff 1993:xxix).

But why is there this link between witchcraft and modernity? Africa is also not unique the construction of this link. As in other times of tumultuous change, a fascination with witches and liminality are a product of social instability for a variety of possible reasons.[3] An argument in modern terms is made by a number of anthropologists.

The power of contemporary African discourses on occult forces, according to Geschiere, is that they relate people's fascination with the open-endedness of global flows to the search for fixed orientation points and identities. Both witchcraft and spirit cults exhibit a surprising capacity for combining the local and the global. Both also have specific implications for the ways in which people try to deal with modernity's challenges (van Binsbergen et al. 2004:34).

To gain insight in the complexities at play, it makes sense to consider the detail of a particular situation. New types of witchcraft seem to develop and the connection to new forms of wealth is striking (Geschiere 1998:820-821). In western and southern Cameroon. one name for this new type of witchcraft is *ekong*.

[E]kong is explicitly contrasted with older forms of witchcraft that make people eat their victims. Instead, ekong witches turn their victims into some sort of zombies which are put to work on "invisible plantations". Ekong witches are to be recognized by their possession of the much coveted new items of wealth: sumptuous houses with tin roofs, refrigerators and other electronic equipment, cars. Indeed, it is ekong which makes these witches so rich through the illicit exploitation of the labour of their zombie-victims (1998:822).

According to Geschiere, one has to take note of the fact that 'the spread of the same set of ideas on new forms of witchcraft and wealth has had very different effects in the Grasslands in the West and Northwest Provinces of Cameroon'. His explanation is that it is from these areas that 'a new bourgeoisie of successful entrepreneurs emerged who are now supposed to play a dominant role in the national economy of Cameroon... The new forms of wealth are, apparently, as suspect in the Grassfields as in the forest areas... The difference is that in the Grassfields, this novel witchcraft threat seems to be under control, at least to a certain degree' (1998:828). In conclusion, he argues that '[t]he general use of [Western] notions like "witchcraft" now reduces older cosmologies in which all men's surroundings are animated to an ugly core: the horrible image of the witches feasting on each other's relatives. In this sense, the resilience of "witchcraft" in postcolonial Africa, despite all "modern" changes, can be seen as the very effect of globalization and the impact of modernity' (Geschiere 1998:831-832).

These conclusions regarding the social role of witchcraft are remarkably similar to those of the Comaroffs in South Africa when they try to explain the sudden upsurge of witch-hunting in the post-apartheid era with terminology and concepts that are not at all indigenous to the particular community – zombies seem to have come to the North-West Province via Hollywood rather than from local cosmologies. The upsurge in witch-hunting and even killings seems to have been a response to the vagaries and distant dynamics of global business and national policy rather than some local dynamic or tradition, even though they would not discount the facilitating role of local cosmological schemes of explanation (Comaroff & Comaroff 2002). Similar patterns feature in Niehaus' discussion and analysis of a different province in South Africa (Niehaus et al. 2001). Although the material discussed does not prove that all witchcraft-accusations in all African societies follow exactly the same pattern it does give us enough insight into mechanisms that seem to be at work in different African societies. Witchcraft-accusations or even individuals identifying themselves as being witches are as present in modern African contexts as in a traditional setting; but although they rely on elements of traditional cosmologies, the dynamics are geared to deal with modern problems and often do so with a mixture of contemporary and traditional means. Witchcraft-accusations are not employed as items of nostalgia or as an attempt to sustain traditional society but as mechanisms of protection, explanation, manipulation and meaning in contemporary society. They also signal a distinct lack of feeling of control in the normal operations of political and economic processes 'at a distance' (Giddens 1991).

In Western thought, the opposite of witchcraft, magic and secret rituals has to be rational processes of explanation. In the standard version of empirically informed rational explanation, these processes are supposed to be open, deliberate and dependent on observation and ordinary logic. We now discuss rational explanation as an element of African cosmologies that attempt to deal with the human need to make sense of events and sequences, causes and effects.

Religion, Reason and Explanation

One of the classic (rooted in the rationality debate started by Evans-Pritchard 1937) if controversial arguments about African cosmologies is that 'religious ritual and religious mythology do sometimes get used as symbols of social relationships and social alignments' (Horton 1993:21). For instance, initiation rites define the roles of men versus women as well as power arrangements and the 'included' versus the 'excluded'. Horton argues that generally, the type of cosmological scheme depends on the social aims of the communities involved. 'If what the participants want to do involves disintegrative competition, then the world of their gods is likely to include some who are defined as helping their human partners in such competition; or if what they want to do involves little competition, their world of gods is likely to be more concerned with the collective welfare and harmony of all' (1993:37). Therefore, he argues that in West and North Africa, 'religious relationships between a god and an individual are considered to essential instruments of [their] competitive and even anti-social aspirations' (1993:41).

The problem with this picture is obviously the inherent functionalism and therefore reductionism that underlies the argument.[4] Moreover, Horton's functionalism not only reduces beliefs to objectified needs, but also takes away the historical context within which these beliefs are articulated and re-interpreted. It is this point that Levinson makes quite convincingly when he discusses Horton's ideas and says that, 'traditional religious thought, on the one hand, and scientifically oriented thought, on the other, loom so large as single frames that the very fact they are abstracted from historiographic material is obscured' (Levinson 1981:54). This has been borne out by many subsequent critiques of Horton's depiction of the openness of Western science (Barnes 1968; Skorupski 1976) and the closed character of African traditional thought (Bauer and Hinnant 1987).[5]

However, Levinson and others take Horton's point that important similarities do exist between Western science and African religion. The confusion that he wanted to address was that of thinking about African cosmology and religion as the African version of Western theologies and religion. If one takes Luhmann's point that modern Western religion is primarily about the ultimate epistemological problem of the foundation of any knowledge at all (Luhmann 1982, 1985), it means that modern religion is relevant to ontology, but not terribly practical. In contrast '[m]embers of pre-literate cultures tend to be of a practical rather than a theoretical bent. Hence, analyses that treat the religious ideas of such cultures as explanatory theories are beside the point' (Horton 1993:55). 'Religious ideas do not 'really' attempt to explain the events in the space-time world. They are concerned with other things' (Horton 1993:57). These "other things" do deal with explanation, but only the type of explanation that leads to prediction and control (Kopytoff 1987:207 agrees that this seems valid in terms of empirical evidence), i.e. one that has the same instrumental interest in knowledge than that of modern science. Of course, the issues that need to be controlled are social and not so much chemical, biological or physical – as can be seen from the above.

Horton was interested in a somewhat different issue than that which interests us. He wanted to describe and understand traditional African thought. We do not consider such a quest useful as the very notion of 'traditional African thought" is problematic – as has been indicated earlier. Not only is the notion of a singular pattern of thought problematic, but the idea that tradition continues unchanged anywhere cannot be sustained – at least not in the continent that has been in intense and extended conflict, exchange and accommodation with modern Western society for three centuries and with the forces of globalisation and internationalisation for the past four or five decades.[6] We, therefore, need to draw out the lines of argumentation to the present situation. There are still a few things one could learn from Horton.

African cosmologies may conceivably be employed in the same pattern as before, i.e. in order to explain with the aim of prediction and control of social and associated processes. At the same time, African cosmologies may continue to sustain the idea that more than one explanation can be found for events[7] and circumstances, and that events that go unexplained are potentially dangerous (Horton 1993:244-248, 332).

If we take a look at the religious form that signals the interaction with the West most clearly, namely, new religious movements, we see some of these patterns repeating. '[I]t is often pointed out that Africans have developed strands of reasoning that seek to explain and provide solutions to the confrontation with global systems and the feelings of exclusion that commonly result from such an experience' (van Binsbergen et al. 2004:32). In the endeavour to explain and solve, 'Africans hit on explanations that seek to deal with the world, and which to observers may appear to be absurd, fantastic and beyond the bounds of the rational' (2004:32). Our interpretation is that it is not a case of not understanding or grasping the kinds of explanation that would be used in the West, i.e. political and economic and social explanations.

The point is not that Africans do not always find Western explanations useful. Pretorius has found that more than 60 per cent of trained African nursing staff in hospitals in Bloemfontein hospitals in South Africa use both clinical Western medicine and solutions to illness and traditional African medicine and solutions (Pretorius 1989, 1994) and do not in practical use find it contradictory to do so (this finding can be supported with a very refined explanation of the changing structure of an African cosmology itself and in its relationship with the West: Comaroff 1980). The point could be that Africans are able to argue in the terms that Horton and most Western science find unscientific.

Here Horton's perspective is again instructive. The West tends to use impersonal models to explain the cosmos (Horton 1993:62) while African explanations may wish to include (at least) personal explanations. The religious cosmologies of most African communities are intensely personal, as they deal with divine personalities and/or family connections of the remembered past. Traditional medicine and divination, traditional cosmologies, etc. are all dependent on the personal relationships of the living and the world beyond that of the living.

When reading the Pretorius findings with the Horton arguments, it seems to imply that we can make sense of the actual use of cosmologies that seem to be traditional and cosmologies that seem to be modern or scientific by means of a practical approach to problems of understanding and explanation where more than one type of explanation is not considered to be cognitively dissonant. In fact, more than one possible explanation may even be preferred if it would allow the accommodation of both a personal and an impersonal mode of explanation. Therefore, we are implying that the possibility of more than one, but practically (if not theoretically) complementary cosmologies, is to be considered. This argument becomes stronger when we consider the material conditions of most African people.

Many African people have two continental points of reference for forming an identity. Of course, all of humanity has more than one point of reference for the continuous formation of an identity as we are all differentiated in terms of gender, age, social status, personal history, language, culture, etc. However, the impact of the forces of colonialism and globalisation has been tremendous in Africa. That has meant that many Africans, even in the most rural of places have made something of the Western and Arab-Muslim socio-cultural and ideological influences. Of course, this is a most dynamic and changing picture. However, the main current challenge in Africa south of the Sahara stays the relationship between African images and Western images.

We can see this in something as mundane as approaches to consumption. Consumption deals with the value of and relationship with food, clothes, household items and other items that are consumed in some way. Friedman sums up the different approaches to consumption as argued by Appadurai, Kopytoff and Bloch and Parry by saying that they are alike in one key dimension. 'They all represent substantial critiques of the opposition between traditional and modern exchange, arguing for a more nuanced view in which features of gift and commodity are combined in various ways in all transactional schemes' (Friedman 1994a:15). Gift is a code word for a communally oriented (personal) transaction scheme and commodity is per definition an impersonal feature of modern capitalist exchange.

At the same time, Friedman shows with his analysis of what he calls the 'political economy of elegance' of Congolese youth that try to remake their identities in Parisian terms (or what they consider to be Parisian). Poverty, marginalisation and exclusion call forth a process of identity construction that is oriented at finding new bases of power – at a cost. '[T]hese symbols, *la haute couture*, were not expressions but definitions of power, of the life force whose form is wealth, health, whiteness and status, all encompassed in an image of beauty... The state-class became great men of elegance by means of political violence and maintain that elegance by means of the theft of the state treasury, and even this can only ultimately be understood in terms of witchcraft and the magic of evil' (Friedman 1994b:185). In the process of taking up Western symbols, they sometimes take on a logic that belongs in a personalised relational definition of society and individuality, i.e. some aspects of a traditional cosmology are married to a modern cosmology in such a way that the modern is given meaning and creates power from an African cosmological scheme.

Fate and Coincidence

We have indicated above Horton argument that African cosmologies do not allow for chance events. This was also alluded to in the arguments of Leatt his study of migrant mine-workers in South African mines. Mining is the sphere of the South African economy in which black South Africans (and non-South Africans) have had the longest and most sustained exposure to the influences on consciousness and social relations of the modern capitalist system and its imperatives. Leatt argues that religion functions as a mediating force in the miners' attempts to come to grips with the 'clash of cultures' encountered when entering the modern industrial environment, but it also functions as a medium of resistance to what Leatt calls 'total assimilation into the culture of the mine' (Leatt 1982:82). The miners seem to be quite pragmatic with regard to accepting the basic rules providing for continued access to the economic benefits provided by employment and advancement in the industrial sector (Leatt 1982:81), but they find religion (specifically churches in this section of the survey) to be valuable with regard to social needs not provided for by the mines (Leatt 1982:87). Contact with the ancestors seems to be of significant importance to many miners as well and although many may deny contact with the ancestors (not willing to speak of such matters to any outsiders) about 70 per cent say that the ancestors are powerful (Leatt 1982:75-77).

The study shows that religion (defined in the way Leatt does) does not explain everything to the African miners, nor does it govern their cosmology in any total sense. Between 72 per cent and 77 per cent of miners surveyed explain accidents in the mines by reference to concepts like carelessness and chance in preference to religious explanations (Leatt 1982:79). Particularly the reference to chance (37%)

is significant because this type of explanation is unthinkable in 'classic traditional societies' as defined by Horton. In addition, the acceptance of rules governing access and advancement in the industrial arena is a clear indication of the ability of the Africa miners surveyed to appropriate aspects of a non-traditional cosmology (with regard to time, social status, the future, etc.).

The survey done by Leatt is, of course, dated, but the assumptions are typical of the problematic view of African cosmology that we would like to counter. The assumption that African cosmologies are not affected and have not come to a new understanding of aspects of capitalist production processes and conditions is just wrong. Africans have lived in interaction with the West for years and the mines have specifically been a place of industrial production regimes for more than 150 years (Sharp and West 1982).

The critique of dualism of the Sharp and West poses an important question as to the appropriateness of what has been gospel in so much of Western economic perceptions of African culture. The notion of fatalism that is understood to be pervasive in traditional communities may be quite wrong. Long-run fatalism is 'the assumption that the range of possibilities open to one's grandchildren would be just about what it had been for one's grandparents' (Rostow in Meier 1964:14). For economists of Rostow's generation to even consider cultural explanations in an evaluation of the potential for development in African and other non-Western countries is strange. Classical economics does not do so. It seems clear that even those who did consider culture and cosmology as a factor within the framework of classical economics operate with unsophisticated or possibly even ideological frames for their understanding of African cosmologies.

The question that is interesting to us now is what we can expect to discover in a more nuanced and open exploration of African societies when it comes to notions like creativity and invention, risk, time, and the future and harmony and conflict. If tradition, secrecy, "witchcraft", rational explanation and fate are not what they seemed to be to traditional descriptions of African culture, and if the notions of difference, hybridity and fluidity are more important in understanding African culture than dualism and stability, we would suspect that the same would be true for the other notions that we are interested in and which we would like to explore under the heading of cosmological aspects.

Creativity and Invention

The issue of African creativity is no longer a matter that is discussed with the assumption that it has to be proven. The mere fact that Africans have survived colonialism and imperialism and continue to survive currently is a testimony to inventiveness. The ways in which combinations, re-combinations and adaptations have been made on a cosmological level has been demonstrated above. However, the question that may still be posed is whether Africans cannot do better than survive and whether particular values are a resource or a hindrance to development that will provide a decent human life for Africans. As indicated in previous sections, the question is also not simply whether African creativity and innovation can deliver better growth figures.

Gyekye is correct in saying that the question is not whether Africans can adapt to modernity, but how we are doing it. Borrowing is a fact of cultural existence but 'practical wisdom dictates that what is borrowed or taken or received from alien cultures be such that it will enrich the lives of the recipients, rather than confuse and deracinate them culturally... African modernity must be a self-created modernity if it is to be realistic and meaningful, sensitive, enduring, self-sustaining' (Gyekye 1997:296). In his mind it is not a question of whether Africa is inventive and creative but how. We know from the brief reference to consumption that some African inventions are not to the benefit of African people. However, as long as normative arguments are not purely romantic wishes, and as long as there is a realistic possibility or actual realisation, of these possibilities African agency is not denied. A discussion of creativity in Africa cannot simply be a statement and proofs of creativity. What is required is a more comprehensive theoretical position that makes room for a systematic and fundamental understanding of the creation of new ideas in terms African world-views.

Guyer discusses the need for a theory of knowledge production, i.e. the development of new knowledge, in her attempts to deal with what she even calls "traditions of invention".

I simply began to find the central issues of my own work in social and economic anthropology impossible to address adequately without a social theory (or theories) of knowledge production and mobilization. The production and management of money, the volatile valuation of people and things against currencies, the creation of skills in the informal sector, the adoption patterns for new cultigen; all risked being consigned either to the operation of a kind of "response to" rationality (coping, etc.) or to the radical contingencies of a basic theoretical indeterminacy (Guyer 1996:2).

As long as the discussion of difference in African philosophy remains oriented to race and what are assumed to be the major differences of being "alien", it eclipses the profound question of how difference has worked within African communities, networks, diasporas and other organizational contexts... Diagne ridicules the political result of an ethnophilosophical standpoint – a "Cultural Charter" – and argues that cultural history "is not a unilineal chronicle of foreign values getting precipitated, layer after layer, onto a single cultural matrix... (but) several processes of evaluation... working constantly to re-establish cultural balances evolving in the face of repeated challenges" (Quoting Diagne 1993:271, Guyer 1996:18).

African creativity, is therefore, not an issue in itself. The question is the mechanism and context within which Africans create meaning. We have shown that the notion of a fixed tradition and complementary notion of a cosmology that cannot accommodate change or newness cannot be sustained.

Ritual, Risk and Danger

The next aspect that we have to consider is the notion of risk behaviour and the effect of African cosmological schemes in the estimation of risk. The "resignation" to the vagaries of life that Meier mentions when listing the issues that are seen to hold traditional societies back, cited above, means that risks are not seen as risks but as dangers. This distinction between risk and danger is critical as risk is a quantified guess that allows the risk-taker to estimate probabilities and consequences of failure in new undertakings while danger is to be avoided and fenced off with reference to known categories of acceptable and foreign, good and evil (Bernstein 1998; Luhmann 1993). The question is now how we evaluate and understand the place of ritual and taboo in the context of African cosmologies. Are rituals, taboos and purification rites about protection against dangers that lurk and that cannot be estimated or are they in some cases also about estimating risk and therefore attempting to wrest control of the future from the gods – to use the imagery of Bernstein (1998)?

In Douglas' famous book, *Purity and Danger: an Analysis of Concepts of Pollution and Taboo* (1966), Mary Douglas focuses on the notion of impurity (pollution) and its relation to rules of protection against that which is considered to be impure. Dirt represents disorder. Rituals of pollution create a unity of experience – it makes the world conform to an idea, rather than avoiding real dangers of dirt (e.g., disease). Such rituals also create boundaries, hence reordering society politically, economically and socially; ritual 'creates harmonious worlds with ranked and ordered population playing their appointed part' (Douglas 1966:72). 'For I believe that ideas about separating, purifying, demarcating and punishing transgressions have as their main function to impose system on an inherently untidy experience. It is only by exaggerating the difference between within and without, above and below, male and female, with and against, that a semblance of order is created' (Douglas 1966:74).

The main point to us is that Douglas argues for the universality of such ritual pollution: 'The difference between pollution behaviour in one part of the world and another is only a matter of detail' (1966:35). Pollution control serves to create boundaries between good and evil in order to protect the physical and social body from contamination, while also ensuring the maintenance of order and thus managing risks. In short, our pollution behaviour is the reaction which condemns any object or idea likely to confuse or contradict cherished classifications (1966:36). ...If uncleanness is matter out of place, we must approach it through

order. Uncleanness or dirt is that which must not be included if a pattern is to be maintained. To recognise this is the first step towards insight into pollution. It involves us in no clear-cut distinction between sacred and secular. The same principle applies throughout. Furthermore, it involves no special distinction between primitives and moderns: we are all subject to the same rules' (1966:40)....
Disorder leads to risk, where risk is both dangerous and powerful: 'though we seek to create order, we do not simply condemn disorder. We recognize that it is destructive to existing patterns; also that it has potentiality. It symbolises both danger and power (1966:94).

Gausset argues that Douglas is not correct when saying that dirt and untidiness constitutes the universal problem. He argues for the more fundamental and important category of *transition* being the universal problem – at least in his area of study, namely Sub-Saharan Africa (Gausset 2002:628-30). '[W]herever something is seen as operating a transition or being in a transitional state, and is characterised by some uncertainty or risk of failure/misfortune, it is likely to be seen as threatened by the conjunction with other things sharing the same transitional characteristic' (Gausset 2002:646). Without going into the detail of the arguments, Douglas and Gausset provide interesting arguments about the notion of risk and how it is viewed in conjunction with ritual and taboos.

A central theme of the work of Mary Douglas is the perception and interpretation of risk, which in her view should be based in cultural theory. In her book, *Risk and Blame: Essays in Cultural Theory,*[8] she conceptualises risk as 'not only the probability of an event but also the probable magnitude of its outcome, and everything depends on the value that is set on this outcome. The evaluation is a political, aesthetic, and moral matter' (Douglas 1992:31). Risk is essentially about uncertainty and the perception thereof. She then argues that 'cultural theory starts by assuming that a culture is a system of persons holding one another mutually accountable... From this angle, culture is fraught with the political implications of mutual accountability' (1992:31). '[E]very choice we make is beset with uncertainty. That is the basic condition of human knowledge. A great deal of risk analysis is concerned with trying to turn uncertainties into probabilities' (Douglas 1985:42). 'One of the functions of the cultural process is to provide ready-made categories for storing and retrieving information; social pressures ensure that the various separate responsibilities will be remembered... A shared culture tells them where they stand in the table of life's chances, without elaborate calculations' (1985:80-81).

The definition of risk in terms of probability and outcome estimation is in line with standard definitions. The cultural slant is new and important. What we see here is a confusing picture. On the one hand, Douglas argues that ritual pollution and purification is a universal pattern of human existence. It serves to create moral order and contain the power that is located in the evil. She also gives a standard definition of risk as the turning of uncertainty into probabilities. On the other hand, risk is understood to mean the threat of disorder and pollution – which is to be countered by keeping to the known classifications and reinforcing the boundaries of good and evil. Is risk and danger, therefore, the same in her view? Is risk quantified and engaged with in order to deal with it in an assertive manner and take control or is risk more or less the same as danger and therefore to be avoided through reference to known categories of order and exclusion?

The answer to this question can only come from a less abstract and more contextualised reading of her work. She provides that in the grid-group analysis – still quite abstract, but with an intention of being able to deal with historical difference.

The grid-group analysis is meant to 'express the [cultural] character of social relations' (Douglas 1970:59). Douglas hypothesises that 'when social relations are not finely ascribed, when they are easily broken off and carry little in the way of obligation or privilege, the formal aspect of wrong-doing is disregarded. The more fluid and formless are social relations the more internalised the idea of wrong-doing' (1970:102). She argues that 'the relation of self to society varies with the constraints of grid and group: the stronger these are, the more developed the idea of formal transgression and its dangerous consequences, and the less regard is felt for the right of the inner self to be freely expressed. The more that social relations are differentiated by grid and group, the more the private individual is exhorted to power his passions into prescribed channels or to control them altogether' (1970:102). Group refers to the extent of boundaries between insiders and outsiders, whereas grid refers to the rules that determine the nature of individual relations.

Douglas' grid-group typology is presented in Figure 2 below. At the one extreme, societies in quadrant B are characterised by low grid and group. Their citizens are free of social constraints, and social relations are interpersonal and optional (1970:59). In this case, the individual takes precedence over the group. Therefore, social structures and relations are fluid and there is a high incidence of social mobility. At the other extreme, societies in quadrant C are characterised by strong grid and group and are thus 'dominated by ancestral figures, but also energised by other powers, by witchcraft and evil eye, and the automatic dangers of pollution. It is a complex world, dangerous for the rebel, good for the conformist' (1970:105). In this case, the maintenance of order and boundaries (pollution control) is crucial. The group is thus most important in social relations – the individual is regulated for the sake of the good of the group. Ritual is important and all individuals have specialised roles to fulfil for the good of the whole society. Role definition is highest and most complex in quadrant C and weakest in quadrant B. We do not go into the rest of the detail here.

Figure 4.2 (Douglas 1970:105)

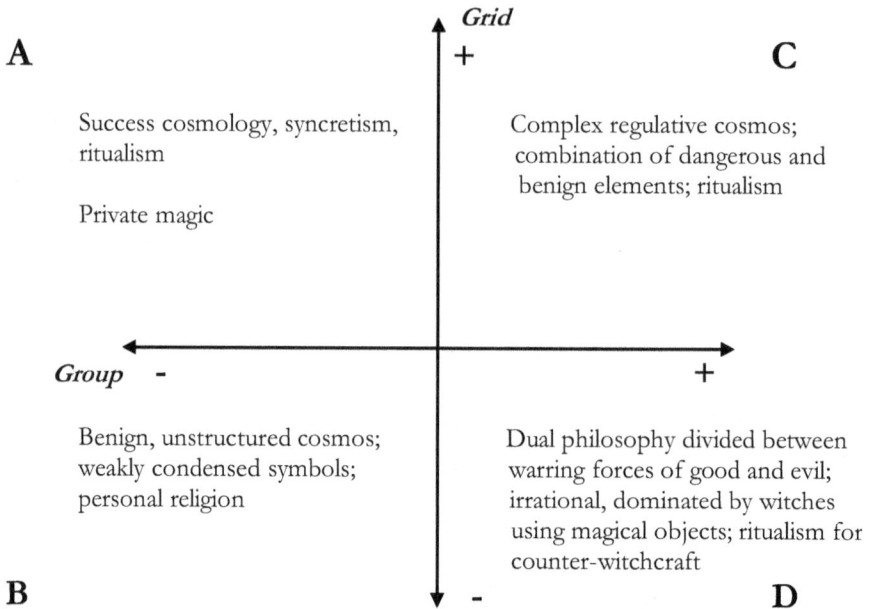

	Grid	
A	**+**	**C**
Success cosmology, syncretism, ritualism Private magic		Complex regulative cosmos; combination of dangerous and benign elements; ritualism
Group **-**		**+**
Benign, unstructured cosmos; weakly condensed symbols; personal religion		Dual philosophy divided between warring forces of good and evil; irrational, dominated by witches using magical objects; ritualism for counter-witchcraft
B	**-**	**D**

The conclusion that we can reach here is that new uncertainty is converted to probabilities best in a weak group and weak grid society. When societies face known uncertainties and deal with social problems that seem universal and timeless, they can get away with ritualism and a regulative cosmos. In the light of the critique of conservatism (Beidelman 1993), and misconstrued empirical data (Gausset 2002), we need to be cautious about taking Douglas' views on face value. What does seem to be useful is the idea of thinking about risk when estimating the effect of culture and values in development in Southern Africa. In such a process, one would have to take into account various possible ways in which individuals and communities interpret change, newness, disorder, transition and combinations of transition. This cannot be done on the level of simple behavioural analysis, but has to be related to cultural constructs and cosmological schemes. We would propose that the result of such analyses would produce a complex picture in which 'grid and group' would play a role and in which ritual and taboo would count; but in which, if our previous discussions are anything to go by, these terms would be hybridised and mixed with patterns that would not fit into the conceptions of ethnography.

Harmony and Conflict

We argue that one cannot understand the variety of reactions to conflict situations without reference to African cosmologies and to the specific frames provided by notions of personhood in these cosmologies. In spite of romantic depictions, Africa is full of conflict. In spite of extreme social stress, African communities sometimes find it possible to develop harmonious solutions to serious problems. What is the relationship between cosmology and harmony and conflict? We argue that the question raises serious problems for much of what is said about African communal orientations. Individualism and communalism are often set up as the opposites in a dimension that forms a fundamental social tension between Western world-views and African worldviews.

Respect for the interest of cultural groups involves a fundamentally different orientation of humans to life itself from that which seeks to protect individual self-determination. This tension is irreconcilable, because it involves contradictory views of the human situation, human life, and the purposes for which humans have been created. What is truly at stake in the process of globalization is the basic question about the purpose of humanity itself (Sijuwade 2006:136).

Sijuwade does not provide any empirical support for his analysis whatsoever. It is, however, the overdrawn and abstract picture that one often gets in African reflections on the difference between Africa and the West (Lassiter 1999b) and a mirror image of what one also sees in Western depictions of an African communal orientation. Sijuwade is correct to cite the ancestors as being of fundamental importance in the self-construction of most Africans in Southern Africa. It has long been recognised that the ancestors are a fundamental part of construction and identity of most African communities (Fortes and Dieterlen 1965). Sijuwade is also correct to identify a difference between Western individualism and African identity construction but the reality is much more complex than it seems from the outside. Competitiveness would seem to be out of the question in his abstract version of African communal harmony cosmologies. Social solidarity in Western societies would be a derivative or residual category in the same dualistic framework. Clearly both these notions are too unsophisticated to deal with real situations. We are not interested so much in the Western self, but the African self and idea of personhood is fundamental to a good understanding of African cosmology.

Gyekye argues, contrary to many, that the African self is defined in both communal and individual terms and that 'it manifests features of both communality and individuality… African social thought seeks to avoid the excesses of the two exaggerated systems, while allowing for a meaningful, albeit uneasy, interaction between the individual and the society' (Gyekye 1988:31-32).

Given some of the arguments that we have put forward above on the hybridity of African cosmological schemes, it seems obvious that contemporary African selves would exhibit aspects and integration of both individualist and communal orientations. That is too easy though. We argue that the Gyekye argument is correct in more fundamental terms. It is not a recent development that leads to the combination of individualist and communal orientations. It is part and parcel of traditional African society to work with a much more complex idea of personhood. In order to gather the appropriate categories for such an argument, we need to go back in history somewhat and gain an empirically informed understanding of why competitive relationships are not foreign to the "African psyche".

The Comaroff studies of the Barolong boo Ratshidi lead them to claim that the reality of social identity is considerably more complex than the reductionist notion of collective identity as the only form of identity that is of significance in African societies. Not only is there a complex interplay between different aspects of identity but this interplay is dynamic and constructed.

The Tswana world of the time was at once highly communal and highly individuated. From within, it was perceived as a rule-governed, hierarchical, and ordered universe, and yet as an enigmatical, shifting, contentious one: a universe in which people, especially men, had to "build themselves up" – to constitute their person, position, rank – by acquiring "wealth in people", orchestrating ties of alliance and opposition... "the person" was a constant work-in-progress; indeed, a highly complex fabrication, whose complexity was further enhanced by gender, generation, class, race ethnicity, and religious ideology' (Comaroff and Comaroff 2001:268-269).

> ...Given the workings of the Southern Tswana social universe, initiative lay with individuals for "building themselves up". The emphasis on self-construction was embodied.... in the idea of tiro, labour. Go Dirain the vernacular, meant "to make", "to do", or "to cause to happen"... It yielded value in the form of persons, things, and relations, although it might be undone by sorcery and other malign forces (Comaroff and Comaroff 2001:273, Also referring to wider studies of the Tswana people: Alverson, 1978).

This means that African conceptions of personhood or identity are not all that different from other socio-cultural constructs that may be considered and that the supposed opposites are not quite what they seem.

> ...The Southern Tswana conception of personhood, in sum, was part and parcel of a distinct, historically-wrought universe of meaning and action; an Afro-modernist universe in which labour, the self, and the social were mutually constituting... the antinomy between Euro-individualism and African communitarianism, past and present, is profoundly misleading. For one thing, as anthropologists never tire of pointing out, personhood, however it may be culturally formulated, is always a social creation – just as it is always fashioned by the exigencies of history. This is true in Europe and the USA as it is in Africa or Asia; as it is true of the eighteenth century as it is of the twenty-first century (2001:276).

The conclusion is simple and very clear: 'African societies did, in times past, have a place for individuality, personal agency, property, privacy, biography, signature, and authored action upon the world. What differed was their particular substance, the manner of their ontological embeddedness in the social, their ideological formulation' (2001:278). The only empirical part of this argument that has been shown here is the manner in work was defined. We should also, however, refer to the way in which the family relations play a role in both competition and solidarity as this is the base of so many popular arguments for a unique African orientation to the ancestors and, therefore, to communalism and to the exclusion of competitive and individual notions of self.

The different roles and effects of matrilineal and agnatic relationships play a constitutive role. Competitive relations for status and influence were a public phenomenon based on agnatic relations, while relations of solidarity were located and based in the private relations of the household (Comaroff and Comaroff 1992:103). The result of the different types of relations between the Tshidi, depending on the contrasting agnatic and matrilineal discourses embedded in different practices, was a series of 'contradictory tendencies towards aggregation and hierarchy on one hand, and individuation and equality on the other... As a result the concrete shape of Tshidi society varied widely over space and time' (1992:106). The important point is that the type of variation resulted in a very varied role for agnatic and public discourses and matrilineal and private discourses. In situations where the political and public face of Tswana societies is threatened, there is another social network of relations (dispersed households not competing for influence and public space) which will be strengthened and which will take on a more important role in Tshidi life. If opportunities for political and public discourse and practice arise again and stronger leaders are able to counter centripetal forces by connecting households in one hierarchical discourse, a reverse situation could again develop. If we take the quickest possible look at the changing face of African communities in early and pre-colonial Central and Southern Africa, we can see that the variety of types of political and economic structures makes an argument for a continuously changing profile of communal and competitive definitions of personhood viable (Mafeje 1978:26-27).

Time

Contrary to the supposition that Horton portrays, it is not only traditional Africa that has many different time-scales. Giddens elicits interesting information in this regard when he considers the development of the nation-state in Europe, finding for instance that time-convergence in Britain is a strictly new development in nineteenth century industrialisation there (1981:175). Be that as it may, African time is an interesting issue in that Horton claims that, at least in traditional African societies 'the passage of time is seen as something deleterious or at best neutral' and on the major time scale of traditional culture 'things are thought of as having been better in the golden age of the founding heroes than they are today', while on a 'minor time-scale, the annual one, the end of the year is a time when everything in the cosmos is run-down and sluggish, overcome by an accumulation of defilement and pollution' (Horton 1993:247).

> This has an important impact on other matters that we are interested in, namely future orientation and risk estimation. '[T]he new and the strange, in so far as they fail to fit into the established system of classification and theory, are intimations of chaos to be avoided as far as possible. Advancing time, with its inevitable element of non-repetitive change, is the vehicle par excellence of the new and the strange. Hence its affects must be annulled at all costs…the passage of the year is essentially an accumulation of pollutions, which it is the function of renewal rites to remove' (Horton 1993:248).

> This kind of conclusion is behind the position of Kuznets who is famous for his analyses of the ebb and flow of development in economic systems. 'This African aversion to the passage of time, and thus to change, can have significant implications for the process of development: 'stocks of knowledge and social inventions themselves change over time; and that the modern economic growth of different countries is a process of combining the different complexities of historical heritage with the common requirement of the modern "industrial system"' (Kuznets in: Meier 1964:31).

If development does bring about affluence for some but it is not diffused through society until much later (the Kuznets curve), it would of course seem quite correct for some time that the past was indeed better for most. The assumptions of this kind of economics cannot be taken on board without any consideration of the context and the mechanisms with which the "development" takes place but it is clear that time cosmologies do ask important questions to the theme of development as such. We have come to suspect from the other analyses that the Horton depiction of African time may be outdated or skewed in some way, but the point that time cosmologies should be investigated closer in African context has been made.

Power

Power is a fundamental category of any social analysis. However, it is not a simple notion. Not only do we have a whole literature that attempts to define different faces of power; we also have different schools that are implied in those notions (Bachrach and Baratz 1962; Lukes 1974; Martin 1977; Isaac 1987; Bourdieu 1992). The issues have already been raised in chapter 1. We agree that the notion of three faces of power is useful. But that it is to be read from the perspective of Isaac

(1987) who calls for a perspective on power that understands that it is 'socially structured and enduring capacities for action'. This is close to Giddens' view that power implies 'transformative capacity' (Giddens 1986:7, More systematic and theoretically developed in: Giddens 1981) based on the employment of 'allocative' (control over material goods) and 'authoritative' (control over activities of human beings) resources. This view is an explicit attempt to incorporate Foucault's argument that power only exists as 'exercised by some on others' (1994:340) and that power can only be exercised over 'free subjects' (1994:342) who have choices of some kind or another whether the exercise of power functions directly or indirectly through social institutions and structures. Power is also not seen as simply negative and repressive but as creative and productive (Foucault 1990:94, 136).

Therefore, power is present in all relationships and interactions and social structures. 'A society without power can only be an abstraction. Which… makes all the more politically necessary the analysis of power relations in a giver society, their historical formation, the sources of their strength or fragility, the conditions that are necessary to transform some or abolish others' (1994:343).

It is clear that the general terms for the concept of power can be set in such a way that it incorporates the cosmologies and meanings that the preceding discussion refers to. The question is how it relates to more particular aspects of power in African societies. Women are generally in a weaker position than men in all societies. What difference do African values in different African communities make to the picture? The body is clearly a very important component of any ritual and taboo. How are African ideas of the body an inscription of power relationships? How is wealth related to power and to status and success? Some indications are that a personalised and symbolic power may be dependent on ostensive and bodily power. Is this a very particular instance or something that requires more serious investigation? How is obedience understood in African communities? Does it relate to a personalised notion of power and is it dependent on personal relationships? How does it relate to age and gender and familial status? These are almost random questions that we find in the literature and that were interesting to us as alternative questions to the standard dimensions of other value-enquiries. We would like to explore some of these issues in more details to develop some perspective on how these aspects might relate to each other, and how significant they may be to the issue that structures our interest in values, namely import of cultural and social values in development in Southern Africa.

Gender

We need to go beyond the brutal facts of Africa's poor position on the Gender Empowerment Measure of the UNDP (2002:36) and attempt to see how social and cultural values play a role in these figures and in the betterment of the situation. Of course, gender is part of every aspect of social development. For that reason, as well as the fact that gender is an often hidden dimension of power relationships, we found it necessary to focus on the matter. However, because gender is such an important part of just about every aspect of development that one can think of, it very soon becomes a difficult choice of what aspect of gender one has to focus on. To us it seems important to take good notice of general international trends described and tabulated by Castells as comprising a 'crisis of the patriarchal family' (1997:134). At the same time, it seems to be obvious that there are very particular and local dynamics that are relevant to our aims and that may remain hidden in a general discussion.

Manji's analysis of the Policy Research Report on Land Institutions and Land Policy of the World Bank is telling in just how much about power relationships we can hide in seemingly ordinary economic analysis and policy processes regarding development and on what level of significance this can happen:

The assumption [in the report] that non-contractible effort is indeed more efficient needs to be challenged. The important question is not in fact whether such labour is more efficient than hired labour, but whether in fact this is based on the unequal position of non-contractible labour within the wider family and society. The idea that family labour is more "motivated" than wage labour is a central assumption of the Report. In its Orwellian usage of the word, the Report conjures up images of happy women deriving immense personal satisfaction from working in the fields. What the idea of motivation elides is the coercive element in the use of family labour. There is a presumption of the coercive power of the male head of the household, which is hidden by the term "motivation"…[T]he very terms employed in the Report mask the fact that the Report is at the very least taking for granted, and at the most advocating, feudal family relations. The patriarchal power of kinship structures appear to be a prerequisite for the World Bank's plans for increased agricultural productivity in the developing world' (Manji 2003:104).

When institutions do not structure policies in this way or when women take a hand in the definition of their economic efforts, the reality can be quite different from the feudal concerns that Manji raises though. In their analysis of some self-reliance initiatives in South Africa, Binns and Nel demonstrate that women can play a powerful and critical role in development in rural areas – note that in one case women insisted that no men be involved in the running of the project (Binns and Nel 1999). In the interplay between the World Bank report and a local case, one becomes wiser as to the complexity of the dynamics that may be at play here.

On a political level, the role of gender may be overplayed. On the most basic level of support for democracy, Bratton and Mattes pick up an instrumental approach to democracy in new democracies in Africa in their study of new generation democracies in the world. At the same time, it seems that 'African societies do not contain entrenched pockets of generational or gender-based resistance to democratization [and] the prospects for the consolidation of democratic regimes would seem to be slightly brighter than is sometimes thought' (Bratton and Mattes 2001:469). We do not have much information on the assumptions that Bratton and Mattes refer to, but one might hazard a guess that many commentators and researchers would point to a patriarchal power structure that may make it seem in the interest of some men to object to democratisation of society. The surprise is that, at least in their analysis, it cannot be identified – and their analysis is one of the most representative in African comparative research. These findings are interesting but run contrary to gender bias evident in all sorts of other political domains – from citizenship newly increasingly based in patrilineality (Cheater and Gaidzanwa 1996) to post-conflict recognition and participation in developmental projects (Jacobson 1999).

It may be that gender equality increases in general terms under conditions of incorporation in Western and industrial society and with exposure to international dynamics, but at least in some cases the very opposite is true – as Becker proves just about conclusively in her analysis of the development of gender relations in three San communities that have been incorporated in some or other way in broader and more modern society in South Africa and Namibia (Becker 2003).

Gender relations are very often played out on the bodies of women. A range of bodily taboos and rituals clearly support a patriarchal relationship between men and women in African societies. This continues even when a particular community or society becomes fairly developed economically. At the same time, these taboos and rituals and their associated social patterns are not all that simple to assess. Menstrual taboos are not necessarily an indication of female subordination (Kaspin 1996:574), but is quite often a double-edged phenomenon that connotes power and life rather than subjugation (Ben-Amos 1994; d'Azevedo 1994; Kaspin 1996). At the same time, the body is the centre of another power struggle if one considers the association between perceived female infertility and personhood. In this power struggle it seems that, in some communities at least, females that are perceived as being infertile are taken as being a non-person that is not recognised in society. This is the case even in Botswana where marriage and child-bearing has become separated due to changing social, economic and educational patterns. However, not being able to have children still means that a women often becomes invisible (Upton 2001). It is clear that body and gender issues are intricately related in terms of the power relationships that are rooted in these social constructs.

However, '[d]espite the explosion of research on women in the last three decades due to the political impetus of the global, and African, women's movements and the emergence of the women-in-development and gender-and-development paradigms and projects, restrictions on women's and gender research remain widespread because of the historical, cultural, social, and institutional marginalisation of women in many African societies and academies' (Zeleza 2002:15). Therefore, much more needs to be done to examine these specific and local dynamics and we anticipate significant new insight to emanate from such research.

The Body

We find the body to be an important category of power that should feature strongly in African comparative studies that deal with development. The personalised cosmology that we discussed in the section dealing with cosmology already provides a clue as to the importance of bodily notions of power. At the level of general interaction, all societies have certain taboos and patterns of behaviour and meanings attached to bodily functions and relationships. These are varied and specific, but still quite important in many relationships. We would argue that in a context where relationships are defined in terms of personalised cosmological schemes this dimension of power is even more important to study.

We need not agree that the body is used as a 'metaphor for society'. We need not agree that it is universally true that pollution rituals 'enact the form of social relations and in giving these relations expression they enable people to know their own society' (Douglas 1966:128). However, we do need to understand that the body is a medium, a testing ground and a basis for social power. This is clearly the case in gender relationships, but it is also the case in all sorts of other relationships of domination and persuasion.

The rainmaker acquires his power as a magician through acts of mimicry, influencing the cycles of nature through his own physicality. This type of sympathetic magic is possible only because the body is as much a map of the territory as the territory is a map of the body: the land is the feminine source of life, the rain its male inseminator, and the land draws the rain to it as a woman draws a man (Kaspin 1996:568).

It makes sense that in such a bodily definition of power, power does not reside in positional status but in imbibing or 'eating' whatever it is that is being dominated (Fabian 1994). This has obvious implications for definitions of leadership (political, religious, etc.) in African societies as is pointed out by Fabian in his analysis of the dispersed leadership of the Jamaa religious community.

This line of enquiry very quickly leads to the political level and a discussion of neo-patrimonialism where 'real power is primarily exercised via personal networks and patron-client relations, which may be hidden from sight and which are thus tantamount to invisible forces preying on the common man' (Møller 2006:16). These ideas of the bodily inherence of power may be quite valuable to explore further in detailed comparative research.

Wealth

As we are interested in development and the material and other benefits that are to be built up by African communities, we are also interested in the way wealth and its origin and purpose is understood. Again, the Comaroff studies are an excellent background for a larger discussion.

For Tswana in Botswana during the 1970's... itirela [(to make, work, do) for oneself)] still referred to the accretion of riches in family and social relations, in cattle and clients, in position and possessions; all of which was also held, hegemonically, to contribute to the common good. The creation of these forms of value was dubbed 'great work' – the effect of which was to extend the self through ties of interdependence, often by means of objects. Thus, the significance of objects, most notably beasts, was that it both indexed and capitalized leverage over people. By extension, power was taken here to be a measure of command within a complex, labile field of material and signal exchanges. Far from being understood in terms of individual autonomy or self-sufficiency, its signature was control over the social production of reality itself (Comaroff and Comaroff 2001:274).

Not only is wealth a social construction, but it is also consistent with the general definition of power that we employ, an instance of power in social relationships. Self-construction is taking place in the process of building up powerful relationships and the accumulation of signs of wealth.

However, even though it seems to be implied that these processes take place with some ostensive demonstration of wealth, the Comaroffs find that such demonstrations are done with a consciousness that takes into account two fundamental perspectives on the dangers of ostensive wealth:

First, because that self was not confined to the corporal body... anything that acted on its traces might affect it for good or ill; which is why human beings could be attacked through their footprints, immobilized by curses, enabled by ancestral invocation, undermined or strengthened by magical operations on their, houses, their clothes, or their animals. Second, to the degree that anyone was "known" to others she or he became vulnerable to their machinations, to being consumed by them. Conversely, empowerment, protective or predatory, lay in the capacity to conceal: to conceal purposes, possessions, propensities, practices – and, even subtly to conceal concealment, to hide the fact that anything at all was being hidden (Comaroff & Comaroff 2001:275).

The subject of money itself is also interesting as this shows something of the ambivalence and pain of the incorporation of African and capitalist worlds. Money is termed *madi,* but this is also close to "blood" and, therefore, to Jean Comaroff signals that money is associated with the 'circulation of essential vitality in the social world' (Comaroff 1985:175). In another publication, the Comaroffs elaborate by explaining that:

Money… is 'hot'. Like a corrosive acid, it 'burns' the pockets of those who try to hold on to it; like the unpredictable, dangerous fire of female fertility, it is explicitly opposed to the cool stability associated with cattle and male political control… The point, rather, is that virtually all, Tshidi, now at the mercy of the capricious coin, exist in the state of subordination formerly associated with femaleness (Comaroff & Comaroff 1990:209).

This is in opposition to cattle which remains 'a symbol of economic and cultural self-sufficiency' and 'represents the freedom from the labor market of which many Tswana dream' (Comaroff & Comaroff 1990:209).

The question to a comparative study of the importance of wealth in power relationship in Southern Africa is obvious. How much of the dynamics explained by the Comaroffs is found in other communities and how does this dynamic change in circumstances of further and more assertive integration of African communities in the first world economy? Are we to expect a situation where one part of a population will start to supplant cattle with Western consumer products and find identity and power in that while another (larger) part of the population will continue to find that money "burns" them and that wealth in any sense of the term will continue to evade them? These are both questions of socio-economic change in the future and the cultural reaction to such change and it is precisely why we are interested in how wealth is seen in Southern African and how perceptions of wealth change. The consequences of change and the reaction to these consequences are expected to be more complex than simple greed is pure nostalgia. Something of the most recent dynamics can be estimated from discourses in the Pentecostal churches.

There has been a surge in membership of this kind of religion worldwide. Latin America, Africa and East Asia have all seen significant increases in numbers of these churches (2006). These churches also seem to be creating wealth for their members and this has raised the interest in economic analyses as to what the mechanisms are that lead to this. However, Meyer shows that the striving for prosperity is not simply blind greed, nor is it a simple savings orientation.

Despite PCCs' strive for prosperity, the achievement of wealth is moralized by distinguishing between divine and occult sources of wealth, often by referring to traditional ideas concerning the nexus of wealth and morality… Because the modern world is represented as thriving on temptation … PCCs appear to alert believers of being wary not to lose themselves in crude consumptive behavior and to use wisely the money they earn. People should avoid drinking alcohol, leading a loose moral life, and, in the case of men, squandering money with "cheap girls."… The ideal is a moral self, not misled by the glitzy world of consumer capitalism nor misguided by the outmoded world of tradition, but instead filled with the Holy Spirit. Although there is likely much overlap between the Protestant modes of conduct that Max Weber found to be typical of early Protestantism, the strong emphasis on becoming prosperous and showing off wealth distinguishes PCC's from early modern Protestantism (Meyer 2004a:460).

Gifford (1998) shows that some of these churches are purely about consumption and blind prosperity theologies.

Leadership, Obedience and Status

The African Leadership Forum established by Nigerian President Obasanjo is as good a place as any to gather a few ideas about the common perceptions about the importance of leadership in development in Africa: 'The general feeling was that Africa needs strong leaders if it is to acquire an enduring philosophy of government and shake off its vulnerability to external pressures, leaders with "a revolution of perceptions and of approach"' (Aka 1997:213). Such platitudes are common and most probably not incorrect at all. Of course, leadership at the level of national and regional positions is different in important respects to leadership in a community. However, this question is whether communities do not also want "strong" leadership with new ideas and what this means in the social and cultural and political context of African communities.

Western leadership theory is said to be ethnocentric and cannot, therefore, be applied to leadership in African organisations and communities as

In Africa, individual achievements frequently are much less valued than are interpersonal relations. The value of economic transactions lies as much, if not more, in the ritual surrounding them and their capacity to reinforce group ties as it does in their worth to the parties involved. Wealth is, first, extended family or clan wealth, and second ethnic or tribal wealth; often it can be acquired legitimately at the expense of the organization (Blunt and Jones 1997:15).

We know that this picture is an over-simplified depiction of the situation. At the same time, one has to give credit for the sensitivity to know that European assumptions may not work. However, such sensitivity may lead to the posing of opposites in analysis. This is a problem that people like Hofstede (2001) and Schwartz (1994) attempt to deal with in their analyses. Of course, we understand that analyses of data can be facilitated with the creation of dimensions and testing for intensity of responses on those dimensions. The question always has to be what one does when many respondents in a particular population find themselves in the middle range of the dimension. It may be that the theory sets up false dichotomies. That is exactly what we have come to suspect when reviewing the standard positions on many of the other aspects that have already been discussed.

African leadership has to be contextualised in the very varied structures of social organisation in different African communities. Not only is there the difference between matrilineal and patrilineal (and combinations thereof) communities, but also new dialectics that impact on older notions of dependence and status that refer to lineage and kinship. Here, one has to take into consideration the immense impact of what Goheen calls 'national politics and accumulative economics' (Goheen 1992:391) even though this has to be balanced with due consideration of the need for accommodation of local and traditional leadership forms (1992:401). One has to take into account the impact of regime type, with neo-patrimonial regimes not being the only possibility even if Bratton and van der Walle argue that it is the dominant and core type in Africa (1994:459). One has to expect surprises in these analyses if the result of a study hypothesising that ethnicity would play a major role in determining succession and thus leadership power construction is anything to go by (Londregan et al. 1995). Londregan et al. found that the only positive prediction that could be made on the basis of ethnicity was that rulers are most likely to be replaced by members of their own ethnic group, but that leaders from large ethnic groups do not tend to be able to get power or stay in power longer than others (Londregan et al. 1995:23).

The question as to: what the relationship between "real" leadership and political power on whatever level? is has not been settled with these few comments. It is not possible to settle the matter in theoretical terms, as the notion of leadership has to be a contested notion if it is to mean anything. However, it would be good to know whether African people and communities also think that it is no more than natural (as Bratton and van der Walle seem to suggest) for African leaders to exercise leadership only and preferable in the "big man" format of personalised leadership relationships that are network dependent.

Another dimension of leadership is the connection between leadership and intellectuals. Pityana laments that intellectuals in South Africa have become middle class and that this leads to all sorts of social problems (Pityana 2006). Intellectuals have been a central part of the process of liberation in many African countries and the regime type post-liberation has a significant impact on their subsequent place in society. What does it mean to be a critical intellectual in a globalised African society where many states are neo-patrimonial at root? How does this impact on the visionary ability of leadership?

Human Relationships

Human relationships are central to African communities and to their development paths. One does not need to subscribe to social capital views to see this point. The mechanisms that structure these relationships may be much more complex than we assume and there are important theoretical choices to be exercised when thinking about human or social relationships. The choices that are relevant, first and foremost, have to deal with the type of philosophical anthropology one wants to espouse. Individualism has a significant series of choices associated with it. Equally so, communitarianism can be articulated in different ways. The question, however, is how African people articulate their own positions on these abstract frameworks. In a sense, there is an inevitable circularity in this way of framing the matter as one has to take some set of options in mind to be able to define significant dimensions, choices and issues about which African people are asked about. All observation is theory-laden (Popper 1963)!

To state something of a framework for the enquiry into aspects of human relationships we refer to Gyekye's limited communitarianism as this is at least an attempt to provide a critical but African philosophical anthropology that will help us to define some of the important issues. Gyekye does not agree to a full-blown communitarianism, as this would imply that actors do not really have choices in their social relationships because their humanity is fundamentally determined by their communal structure (Gyekye 1997:52). There are various ways of limiting the communitarian argument. Gyekye does so by arguing for relatively independent rational and moral judgement while holding on to the central point (for him) that communities are formed around shared values (Gyekye 1997:52-58). These values are not what Castells has termed primary values of language, religion or ethnicity but substantive values that specify general definitions of humanity and community as being guiding principles. In such a framework, generosity, compassion, reciprocities and mutual sympathies are asserted within a recognition of individual human rights as well as human dignity (Gyekye 1997:62-65). Gyekye's arguments are relevant to us not only because he philosophises about the nature of human relationships, but also because he does so from a critical but African perspective. We will use that to profile the issues that we are interested in.

As indicated in the introduction to the chapter, we identified the aspects of freedom, honour and shame, communication and trust and tolerance as critical aspects that either come to the fore from existing material that deal with key values for development or that we find in empirical of theoretical material to be important aspects of African value conflicts that could impact on development.

Honour and Shame

It is often said that Mediterranean culture is dominated by the paired notions of honour and shame (Peristiany 1974), even though one might have questions about how this actually operates as a frame for understanding the societies (Abu-Lughod 1989). This is tied to the patriarchal definition of maleness. A patriarchal definition of maleness is fairly common on many societies, historically and currently. However, we were interested in seeing whether the notions associated with honour and shame (or honour and modesty – if we follow Abu-Lughod) have any resonance in African communities. The results have been mixed in a literature review. The interesting insight that comes from the literature is the connection between honour and respect. This may be a more immediate connection to the concerns that lead us to think about honour and shame. The issue is whether we can get to a different frame for the moral dimensions of human relationships that will resonate better with ordinary discourse on relationships than notions like sin and individual moral responsibility that are typically associated with western individualism. The connection between honour and shame/modesty and respect seems to exist in some discourses about respect.

According to van der Geest's analysis of Akan society in Ghana (also more generally Green 1983), respect is seen as 'the basic moral value which regulates social behaviour. In its first, superficial, meaning it refers to a type of behaviour that is shown, similar to etiquette or politeness. But "respect" may also refer to an inner quality. The concept then includes admiration, affection and love. Such respect is the basis of the care which elderly people enjoy from their children or other relatives' (van der Geest 1997:535-536). We would consider it a worthwhile enterprise to investigate this notion as a key aspect of human relationships in African communities. The connection with age is important as this poses a challenge for development when seniority is an absolute. The inherent social conservatism that goes with such an emphasis on seniority and the consequent problems of gerontocracy (especially when as male as it often is) poses interesting questions to development. At the same time, the human cost of not caring and of youth that find it important to pose themselves as the opposite of their seniors is a different dimension of the matter.

Morrell cites a number of indications that respect for age and seniority in the Southern African colonial context was already under threat around the end of the nineteenth century and the customary respect practices like *hlonipha* (Nguni) were considered to be under threat (Morrell 1998:621). This problem is complicated by the gender relationships that we also see developing in African communities (in line with the general trends described by Castells 1997).

The following description from Tanzania is telling as it points to a changing gender relationship also among the poor and marginalised communities of Africa. It also specifically uses the term honour:

> The fact that women are becoming increasingly economically independent and leave husbands is a serious threat to the male ego and honor. Many men expressed outright jealousy and fear that when wives have their own business projects outside the home, they may feel attracted to other men... A man's honor, reputation, ego and masculinity are severely affected if he cannot control his wife. The code of honor is associated with an agency for self-defense against encroachment from the outside, and men are projected into an active role, the role of controller and aggressor (Silberschmidt 2001:665).

The description here does make it seem as if men are victims; but this is only true to the extent that migration to the cities and involvement in marginal industrial society has brought about changes which are a threat to their interests.

Honour and shame or modesty functions as a very powerful framework for interaction in the Mediterranean world and also further afield towards the Indian sub-continent. The power of this framework is such that social cohesion and solidarity is fostered, but it seems to be the fount of blood feuds and honour killings as well. The African notion of respect may be associated with the same dynamic but, due to the premium placed on harmony and human dignity, seems not to lead to the same kinds of enforcement in case of a lapse or general disregard of customs showing respect. This axis seems to be worth investigating as a value axis that could be an important facet of African development dynamics.

Communication

Communication in societies that are not dominated by formats that assume literacy, but have a long history and deep practical knowledge of oral communication, coupled with a strongly developing visual dimension dependent on video and television will be complex. Are all the cues that an Africanist oral communication specialist will pick up cues?

We cannot be satisfied with the superficial notion that 'communication is the mechanism through which the flow of acculturation between the modern and the traditional cultures is facilitated and made less discordant' (Nwanko and Nzelibe 1990:263). They argue that with the advent of the mass media, instant communication has become possible not only within communities but also throughout most African nations... mass communication can play a profound role both in the management of conflict between communities and in the creation and maintenance of common ideals, aspirations, and patterns of behaviour that preserve and strengthen both the national and the local communities. Communication promises to be the most effective means of establishing a framework in which effective conflict management can be undertaken. Moreover, communication generally, and mass communication in particular, can help establish the goals and objectives of community development... Communication plays a significant role in limiting the level of diversity and developing broader areas of consensus on which individuals and groups can function properly and productively. Another effective role of communication in the management of conflict in African communities is the provision of awareness of opportunities for enduring compromises which can create suitable environments for effective development planning and implementation (Nwanko & Nzelibe 1990:263-264).

Such a view of the role of communication assumes a number of objectives that require serious consideration and possibly rejection (communication cannot in itself establish goals for development, the level of diversity should not by any means be something that should be limited, control of mass media and the various interests at play are fundamental issues that cannot be glossed over). The main question, however, is how any of these or more limited and less naïve goals are to be reached. How does communication do all of these things when people who communicate do so with different types of signals and different frames of reception? We have seen mention of gender, age, cultural and many more divides and differences. These aspects impact on communication. How will mass communication deal with these differences? Of course, communication is important, but we would like to know more about the values that are associated with good, respectful, efficient and sensitive communication in different groups. This requires detail analyses.

Trust and Tolerance

The trust term has become a huge field of study in anything from economics and management to anthropology. We are interested in trust as a key area of basic human relationships, as we believe that something in the social capital literature is correct. Trust across boundaries as well as within groups does make a difference. The question is how trust is constituted and upheld and denied and lost in different communities and also what that trust allows and enables. The next question about social capital has already been stated and asks whether the social capital construct is not in service of a social engineering ideology.

Whitely defines social capital as 'the extent to which citizens are willing to cooperate with each other on the basis of interpersonal trust' (2000:443). He is concerned with the extent to which interpersonal trust reduces transaction costs, encourages investment, encourages reciprocity and cooperation and minimizes the burden of policing. Trust, therefore, 'plays an important role in explaining both the efficiency of political institutions, and the economic performance of contemporary societies' (2000:443). Trust is conceptualised here as originating within the family and influenced by societal norms and values rather than originating 'in secondary groups such as voluntary organizations' (2000:460). This is the typical definition and framework for trust research in the social capital paradigm (Knack 1997).

From that base, Whitely examines the relationship between trust and growth in a sample of 34 countries. Three variables from the WVS (1990-1993) are used that are consistent with the manner in which Whitely defines social capital, namely, 'questions about trusting members of one's own family, trusting fellow nationals and, finally, trusting people in general' (2000:453). These variables are then included in the neo-classical growth model, and Whitely the finds that 'it is a highly significant predictor of growth in a diverse set of countries, and in the presence of various control variables. Moreover these results are not dependent on the fact that a country has a democratic government or a market-based economy, since a number of authoritarian and communist countries are included in the sample' (2000:460).

The important question posed at the beginning of this section about the elements that make up trust seems to be settled in such international comparisons. However, the picture changes when more specific focus is on African countries themselves. Widner and Mundt (wholly within the standard form of social capital research and after a serious comparative attempt) find that 'norms and behaviour typically included in the concept of social capital do not cohere in the two African contexts studied the way they do elsewhere in the world' (Widner & Mundt 1998:21)

The study by Narayan and Pritchet (1997) examines social capital in the context of generalised trust and voluntary organisations in rural Tanzania. Their data consists of household income and the results of the Tanzanian Social Capital and Poverty Surveys (SCPS) conducted in April and May 1995. The 'econometric estimates show a large (and arguably causative) effect of a village's level of social capital on the incomes of all households in that village' (1997:27). One standard deviation increase in social capital increases each member of a household's expenditure by at least 20 per cent (1997:20). The study further demonstrates that this effect is social and operative at the village level (1997:34). They claim that their results 'suggest that social capital is *capital* and not merely a consumption good' (1997:35). These results cannot, however, be generalised and applied to contexts outside of rural Tanzania.

Carter and Maluccio (2003) examine the potential role of social capital in helping households face risk in Kwazulu-Natal. Given incomplete financial markets in developing countries, especially in rural areas, households may be unable to insure against shocks. The results of the study do seem to suggest 'that households that suffered a loss were better able to absorb it if they were in communities with a larger number of groups in 1993... [and] this capacity is weakened in those communities where the neighbour losses were very large; there is little evidence, then, of the bridging sort of social capital that would allow shocks to be absorbed across communities' (2003:1160).

Maluccio, Haddad and May (2000) attempt to gauge the causal relationship between formal and informal group membership and household welfare, as measured by per capita expenditure, in South Africa. They are particularly interested in the direction of causality. The results suggest that social capital did not provide significant welfare returns for households in 1993, but did 'yield substantial returns in 1998' (2000:77).

When one considers these results, it may be surmised that the notion of social capital sometimes seems to explain something of the dynamic of human relationships and sometimes not. The issue, first of all, is how it is operationalised in research and whether the aspects included in the analysis are relevant and predictive. It seems that this does not always work out if taken in a conventional way as shown by Widner and Mundt. What we can establish, though, is that trust plays a role in economic development. The mechanisms and the elements of that process are not clear yet.

Human Qualities

As indicated in the introduction to this chapter, the aspects discussed here are a collection of items that have come up in discussion, in the literature and in values analyses that have been done by others. Obviously, we have made a selection and we cannot discuss the literature or existing analyses fully. The idea is only to provide a framework and an approach to these items.

If one looks at development projects all over the world, and in Africa as well, one of the main findings has almost consistently been that projects fail. Within a number of years from start-up, most development projects are empty shells. Of course, development cannot be limited or even primarily described and analysed in terms of projects. If we take a step up and have a look at large policy-driven initiatives that were to have driven development on a comprehensive scale in national and regional contexts, it is equally clear that such initiatives have failed grandly. Structural Adjustment Programmes supported or enforced by the World Bank and the IMF make up quite proportion of such failed initiatives. It seems as if something is missing. Obviously, our entire argument is that we should not only be considering whether the SAPs and projects were conceived correctly, but we should also consider more specifically whether the social element has been part and parcel of the conception and subsequent plans.

One of the problems with a first attempt at explaining failure with reference to human and social factors (as opposed to technical or structural factors) is that this is often done so poorly and so superficially. At the same time, some of these issues are relevant if they are considered within a larger cultural and social context and they do not shift blame but attempt to understand. That is our approach to the material as well.

Imagination and Other Qualities

The first point to make about imagination is the one that Sen makes when he argues that culture matters in particular ways in development. One of those ways is the ability to imagine something different as expressed in arts and crafts (Sen 2004a:36-39). Not only does this create work and income, but it also creates a different framework for understanding ourselves and for being understood from outside. There is, therefore, a normative reason for promoting imagination in communities and for promoting all types of activities that will enhance imaginative outputs for the betterment of all.

However, the question is whether there is an interest in newness and whether imagination is prized in African communities. If the traditionalist interpretation of African culture is taken up, it may mean that imagination is suppressed or just not supported. The best place to locate this question is with the youth of a community.

[T]he movement of western discourses on youth through various institutions and personnel, to which youth are framed both as prototypical consumers and as prototypical social problem, condenses many of the critical issues of globalization and historical conjuncture. Moving through these conjunctures, reconfiguring webs of power, reinventing personhood and agency, youth stand at the center of the dynamic imagination of the African social landscape (Durham 2000:114).

In this quote, the problems of imagination become clear. The imaginings that may happen are not pure or without context. So much effort is invested in capturing markets by cultural and media entrepreneurs, and so much happens that could transform imaginative youths to consumers that one wonders whether any imagination is left that is not framed in pre-existing consumer-defined packages. Durham clearly thinks that the youth has much more to offer than a regurgitation of consumer packages.

We would like to investigate this on a comparative scale and also take a look at the very expectations and frames that exist in society at large about the imagination of the youth. In such an investigation, the generational (Comaroff & Comaroff 1999:284) axis of difference in African societies is very pertinent, as it may well be that the youth have much more to offer than the rest believe.

The World Values Survey and the European Values Study have been asking about the values that parents would want to encourage in their children or more precisely 'important qualities to teach a child'. Some of the qualities listed are thrift, working hard, being responsible, aspects of respect, tolerance and imagination. In some of the more recent analyses, Inglehart frames the results of the data analysis on a two-dimensional scale and in terms of basic orientation of a society towards survival or well-being and traditional authority or secular-rational authority (Inglehart 1997:82). These results are the product of a data reduction process on aggregate level and must, therefore, be a reduction of some kind. The question to us is how much of the end result is determined by the selection of items. One can immediately say that other items may have produced a different result. The end result of the analysis seems so perfectly synchronised with the self-image and contrast that the West has been positing as the difference between the West and the rest that one has to be wary of the effect of theory-laden observations. Our interest in the terms that we noted would be to investigate contradictions and mixed forms in order to see whether we can come up with a different framework than the one that Inglehart seems to "find" every time.

Aspirations

The aspirations of African people are different types of aspects than the qualities noted above. Freedom has clearly been an important aspiration in all African countries in the colonial and even in the post-colonial era. However, material aspirations have been important as well and as can be seen from the discussion of consumption and the relationship of, for example, Pentecostal believers with wealth and success, the situation is complex. Bayart poses an interesting and important question with his notion of extraversion (Bayart 2000). According to him, African dependence on the West is an activity. It takes on various forms and the political and economic is no less important than the cultural and the ideological. Bayart is brutally deliberate in his attempt to make clear that Africa is not marginalised in the sense that it is not part of the rest of the world. It is, through emptying itself out to the West, part of the world. However, this is conceived and described mostly on the level of the nation-state and international and corporate economic relations. Although he does make mention of the cultural and social dimensions, the questions of how beneficial and how dependent relationships are on this level is much less sorted out than on the economic and political levels.

Meyer discusses the matter in terms of exchange in religious context and analyses the Pentecostal influence in social and cultural context in Africa. She finds much that is transported from the West and that is even good or acceptable. However, she cautions that [t]here is a danger, though, of overemphasizing the creative and positive aspects of extraversion, which would bring the notion disturbingly close to earlier approaches toward Africanization in the sense of tradition-oriented wholeness and harmony. In many respects, the study of PCCs has little eye for the possibly disorienting, unsettling, and destructive implications of born-again Christianity, the contradictions on which it thrives and the disappointments it generates (Meyer 2004a:463).

The aspirations of Africans are complex and Africans are making and remaking their aspirations every day.

Conclusion

We have trawled through a large territory and found a series of conflicting and confusing perspectives on what may be important values in development. Most of our energy has gone into establishing the nature of the confusion. The point is to define issues that should lead to or connect with an existing dialogue within African communities. Africans make their own future and, in a sense, it is appropriate to close with Bayart's perspectives on the interwoven relationship that Africa has with the rest of the world. Much of that relationship is a continuation of dependency through very dubious means and with dire consequences. At the same time, nostalgia for values that used to regulate and guide life in African communities is not only unproductive but also inconceivable. Africa is not disconnected and has not been on its own for quite some time. The values that will guide African people and communities will be values of the present. We need to know much more about the nature of these values and the confusion that they carry with them.

Notes

1. It is most edifying that a number of African intellectuals are taking a critical position regarding "traditional values" (Hountondji 1996; Wiredu 2001; Appiah 1992; Gyekye 1997.

2. One is reminded of Orientalism as defined by Said (1979).

3. The debate among historians about the causal reasons for an increased interest in witchcraft and especially a sharper interest in witch-hunts still continues. The reasons range from weather changes to structural socio-political reasons (Behringer 2004; Robin, Larsen & Levin 2007), but they all culminate in some from of social instability.

4. Of course, Horton's intellectualism that disregards the other dimensions of religion and its value to believers, is an other reductionism at play here (Meyer 2004b:458).

5. Both types of criticisms have been accepted to some extent by Horton (1993:308).

6. We are closer to Mudimbe in that we argue for a composite and changing characterisation of "Africa" (Masolo 1991:1004).

7. It is interesting that the term equifinality is a key notion in the theory of open system as used in biology and physics and comes close to the African pattern of thought (von Bertalanffy 1968).

Section III

Exploratory Empirical Investigations

5

Linking Values and Development: An Empirical Analysis

Hennie Kotzé and Stefanie Schulein

Introduction

What has loosely been called 'traditional African values' has historically been viewed by scholars as a significant impediment to political and economic development in the twenty-first century. As argued by Mattes and Shin (2005:5-6), those following traditional value patterns have been said to prioritise the collective good of the family and community over procedure and individual rights. Similarly, self-identification as members of sub-national kinship groups rather than modern nation-states is said to prevail. These factors, together with uncritical respect for authority and social hierarchies, are often seen to make traditional societies inhospitable for market economies and democratic consolidation to take root. We have argued against a monolithic and simplistic notion of traditional society. However, the data available is, to some extent, tied to these notions and we will explore it taking these terms into consideration.

The question is: what exactly are these traditional value patterns assumed or argued to be? Is there any consciousness that it may be an oversimplification to merely view values in terms of set 'mental programmes' instead of complex orientations which are constantly in flux? This chapter starts the discussion of these questions by way of an empirical exploration of Afrobarometer survey data in six Sub-Saharan African countries (Botswana, South Africa, Zambia, Zimbabwe, Tanzania and Mozambique).[1] Through linking various value dimensions to the extent of development[2] at the aggregate country level, vital insights are provided into possible relationships between these variables. Although secondary data analysis necessarily brings with it certain limitations,[3] this exploratory study, nevertheless, takes some initial steps towards a better grasp of the often misunderstood concept of African values.

The Link between Values and Development

Kluckhohn, Parsons and Shills (1951:64) have probably provided one of the most used definitions of the values concept as 'a conception, explicit or implicit, distinctive of an individual or characteristic of a group, of the desirable which influences the selection from available modes, means and ends of action'. They also formulated the concept of 'value orientations' which they defined as being organised complexes of values which apply to broad segments of life and are a key factor in cultural integration.[4] There is a significant debate about the role of values in the integration of society and we do not agree with the Parsonian version of this matter. However, the definition is not dependent on that application.

The theory of political culture argues that traditional values result from norms and values embedded in ethnic cultures which are transmitted through socialisation. Scholars such as Almond (1963), Eckstein (1997) and Inglehart (1988) claimed that these values have a profound influence on how individuals order and conduct their lives. By extension, these value patterns were seen to have a direct influence on the country's economic and political regimes.

As noted by Mattes and Shin (2005:7-8), modernisation theorists[5] accepted these premises and advocated policies that would bring about rapid urbanisation, industrialisation, an increase in formal education, and growth of middle classes. It was thought that these factors would in turn change individual values over the course of a lifetime.[6] However, this process should perhaps rather be seen as a circular chain in which a changing environment influences values, which in turn impact on environmental factors (i.e. development or the lack of it) (Van Deth and Scarbrough 1995a:65). Here, the question arises as to where Africa currently finds itself within this circular chain and whether the effect of the forces of globalisation changes the conceptualisation associated with the idea of modernisation. In order to adequately assess this, we are left with the challenging task of 'measuring' the evolution of values and environmental factors over time.

'Measuring' Values

It is clear that when empirically testing the relationship between values and development within given societies, one is presented with various methodological challenges. What is required is cross-national data about individual and collective value structures across a wide range of countries. One such study which potentially provides particularly useful data in this respect is the Afrobarometer survey, with three rounds of the survey having been conducted since 1999 (2007a). In this chapter, we will analyse data from six countries in the Southern African region which participated in the second round of the survey (between 2002 and 2004) - South Africa (2002), Tanzania (2003), Mozambique (2002), Zambia (2003), Zimbabwe[7] (2004) and Botswana (2003). Background information on these six countries with regard to socio-economic trends is given in Appendix A. Although these countries only provide us with a limited number of cases (making significant results highly unlikely), interesting initial insights into the empirical relationship between development and values in the Southern African region will nevertheless be gained.

In each country that participated in Round 2 of the Survey, the Afrobarometer Network trained researchers interviewed a representative sample of the adult (i.e., those over 18 and eligible to vote) population in face-to-face conversations in the language of the respondent's choice. A random sample was developed based on a multi-stage, stratified, clustered area approach, which aimed to give every eligible adult in each country an equal chance of being selected. Across 15 countries, a total of 23,197 respondents were interviewed during Round 2 of the survey. The sample size in each country ranged from 1,200 to 2,400. A sample size of 1,200 is sufficient to yield a margin of sampling error of plus or minus 3 per cent at a confidence level of 95 per cent. In the countries with sample sizes of approximately 2,400, the margin of sampling error decreases to plus or minus 2 per cent (Afrobarometer 2007a).

Table 5.1 Sample Sizes for the Countries Included in this Analysis

Country	Date	N
South Africa	Sep/Oct 2002	2,400
Botswana	Jul/Aug 2003	1,200
Tanzania	Jul/Aug 2003	1,200
Zambia	Jun/Jul 2003	1,200
Mozambique	Aug/Oct 2002	1,400
Zimbabwe	Jun/Jul 2004	1,104

It is important to note that the Afrobarometer results should not be generalised to Sub-Saharan Africa as a whole. The selection of countries is intentionally biased toward liberalising regimes, with authoritarian regimes and countries in conflict therefore being under-represented (Afrobarometer 2007a).

Furthermore, the significance of the fact that this is an opinion survey and not a value survey has to be noted. Value analysis requires significant sets of data on individual level on opinions, beliefs, attitudes, behaviour and cosmology; and this data can only be reduced to the underlying and latent values if the variation and changeability of opinions is cancelled out by the variety and volume of data that is analysed.

While analysing the data, one continually has to remain cognisant of the limitations inherent in aggregating attitudinal data on a country level.[8] Firstly, the survey instrument is of vital importance, in that reliable measures of values need to be developed which have validity across various cultures. Secondly, one may ask how widely these values are, in fact, held across these mass publics (i.e. does the aggregation of data blind us to internal variation?).

Thirdly, the question of causality comes into play. Even if a relationship between development and value systems is found, one may ask to what extent traditional values as such actually preclude development; or whether there are in fact certain environmental factors which are shaping these values. Similarly, it is important to note that survey items often simply provide an uncontextualised snapshot of certain attitudes at a given point in time. In many cases, this does not adequately capture the ever-changing nature of values within a complex social environment.[9] Ideally, longitudinal analysis of changing value patterns should, therefore, be undertaken to draw meaningful conclusions.[10]

Finally, surveying the worldviews of individuals may give us some insights into their systems of beliefs and may help us in developing explanatory theories about individuals and the world they live in. However, these beliefs must find expression in action. As noted by Hammond-Tooke[11] (1974:319), we need to constantly remain aware of the realm of ritual, both religious and magical, which can be defined as 'the techniques man has devised to manage satisfactorily his relations with gods, nature and other men'. He refers to ritual as the 'articulation point between the belief system and the network of day to day interactions between men' (1974:320). Although surveys may tap into broad worldviews of individuals, an understanding of the translation of orientations into concrete action is often neglected.

Despite these limitations, however, findings from surveys such as the Afrobarometer provide a valuable exploratory macro view[12] which then needs to be contextualised within the specific societies.

Conceptualising African Values

Reflecting on the traditional frame of analysis of African values when comparing them to European values, Mattes (2005:7) points out that African values[13] (used as a generic term which naturally requires further interrogation – see chapter 2) are generally seen to be in conflict with the values necessary for sustained development in several ways.[14] First, the emphasis on "communal good" means that producing just outcomes, even if it requires the use of violence, may be valued more than procedure and rule of law.

Similarly, the "history of traditional rule" is said to lead people to think and act as clients dependent on patrimonial relations to provide for their welfare. Individuals are therefore seen as 'passive, deferential subjects of external forces rather than as agents, with some degree of control over their lives[15] or the wider polity' (Mattes and Shin 2005:25).

The patriarchal nature of many African polities is also understood to mean that women are seen as inferior and unequal. In addition, a sustained emphasis on consensus may breed intolerance of dissent, while individuals with strong group-based identities may be more likely to develop antipathies towards others (Owusu 1992:85). Indeed, as Mattes and Shin (2005:12) argue, in many cases the 'lack of national identity may deny young democracies the necessary 'political glue', turning every element of political contestation into a zero-sum, group-based conflict'.

The above identification of certain 'types' of African values quite possible, in terms of our previous discussion of these categories, would merely be an oversimplification, essentially setting them against certain 'ideal' western norms. In the process of conceptualising African values, ethnocentrism necessarily becomes a particular impediment. From the time anthropology emerged in the nineteenth century, controversies have continually arisen regarding how to conceive differences among people, and how to understand where western civilisation fits in relation to other societies. It is clear that what Westerners consider as progress, is not necessarily seen as progress in the eyes of others who have been raised with different cultural preferences. As highlighted by Hatch (1983:64), the standard we use in judging is in many respects determined by the culture in which we were raised.

In order to provide a more nuanced view of African values, we have subdivided this rather broad and nebulous term into various dimensions which seem to have particular applicability in the Southern African region in terms of the previous theoretical discussions.[16] Various items in the Afrobarometer questionnaire have been identified under the following four dimensions: Human qualities (subdivided into "paternalism/dependency,[17] "consensus-seeking[18] and pursuit of justice vs. pursuit of rule of law"[19]); Human relationships "Community vs. Individual Interest[20], "Social Capital"[21] and "Identity"[22] and "Identity"[22]); Power "Gender Equality"[23]; Although the dimension of Cosmology is a crucial one in the Southern African region, no items in the Afrobarometer survey seemed to adequately gauge its complexity. Some cursory comments on this dimension will, however, be given in the concluding section.

Admittedly, the above four dimensions and their subdivisions may in themselves not fully tap the full range and immense diversity of African values, yet this analysis aims to provide a starting point on which future studies may expand. The aspects defined as value dimensions have been discussed in chapter 4, but have had to be reduced to the barest of essentials to create terms that cannot be seen as anything else than broad proxies for the actual intention of the book.

Measuring Development

Scores on the UN Human Development Index (HDI) will be used as an indicator of development in each of the six countries under investigation. In an effort to blend the economic and social approaches to measuring development, the HDI was first introduced in the 1990 *United Nations Human Development Report* and is based on an equal weighting of three factors: purchasing power parity adjusted real per capita GDP, literacy and life expectancy[25] (Lindenberg 2002:304). Table 5.2 shows the scores which the six countries obtained on the HDI in 2003.

Table 5.2: Human Development Index Rank 2003 (UN Development Report, 2005)

Country and Rank	HDI	Score
South Africa	(120)	0.658
Botswana	(131)	0.565
Zimbabwe	(145)	0.505
Tanzania	(164)	0.418
Zambia	(166)	0.394
Mozambique	(168)	0.379

In the data analysis section below, the HDI scores were correlated with various value dimensions within the categories of Human qualities, Human relationships and Power.

Analysis of Data

Human Qualities

The first value dimension to be analysed is that of human qualities, and more specifically the degree of paternalism/dependency[26] prevalent in the given societies. This dimension seems to have particular relevance in Africa, as in pre-colonial times political rule was rarely exercised on the scale of the modern state. As noted above, this may have led people to act as clients dependent on patrimonial relations for their welfare, essentially lacking control over their own lives (Chazan 1993:78).[27]

Figure 5.1: HDI Score vs. Mean Level of Dependency

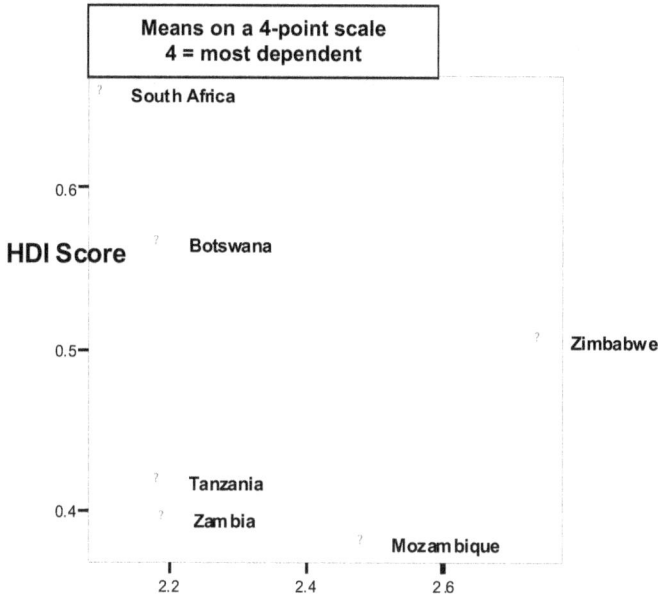

Figure 5.1 seems to indicate a slight negative relationship between level of development and level of dependence prevalent in the six countries. South Africa, which has the highest level of development, also has the highest proportion of individuals who feel they should take responsibility for themselves and not be reliant on government or patronage networks. A weak correlation (Pearson's $r = -.272$) was found, although not significant due to the limited number of cases. For more conclusive arguments to be made, this finding would, therefore, need to be tested amongst a broader array of countries, with adequate controls being applied.

The second value orientation is extent to which individuals feel the need to build consensus within the given societies. In his analysis of value systems of the 'Bantu-speaking peoples of Southern Africa', Hammond-Tooke (1974:318-320) found that basic to traditional cosmological ideas is the great value placed on harmonious social life, the elimination of discord, and the insurance of cooperation and mutual good-will between individuals. By extension, illness and misfortune are almost inevitably interpreted in human terms, with a failure in health or fortune typically seen as the result of some failure in social relations. The nature of traditional societies, with their small-scale relationships, meant that even stronger pressures operated to eliminate conflict that may have disrupted the group than is the case in modern industrialised society. With regard to development, an excessive emphasis on reaching agreement/consensus on certain issues may lead towards an intolerance of dissent, thereby preventing diverse voices from being heard.

It is, however, not only within the field of development where this notion has relevance. As noted by Owusu (1992), this emphasis placed on consensus has had a crucial impact on democratisation on the African continent. In fact, the desire to agree, which is supposed to safeguard the rights and opinions of individuals and minorities, is often exploited to enforce group solidarity and oppressive group conformity. In this way, it may, therefore, be used to legitimize what Sono (1994, quoted in Louw 1998) refers to as 'totalitarian communalism' which 'frowns upon elevating one beyond the community'.[28]

Figure 5.2: HDI Score vs. Mean Level of Consensus-seeking

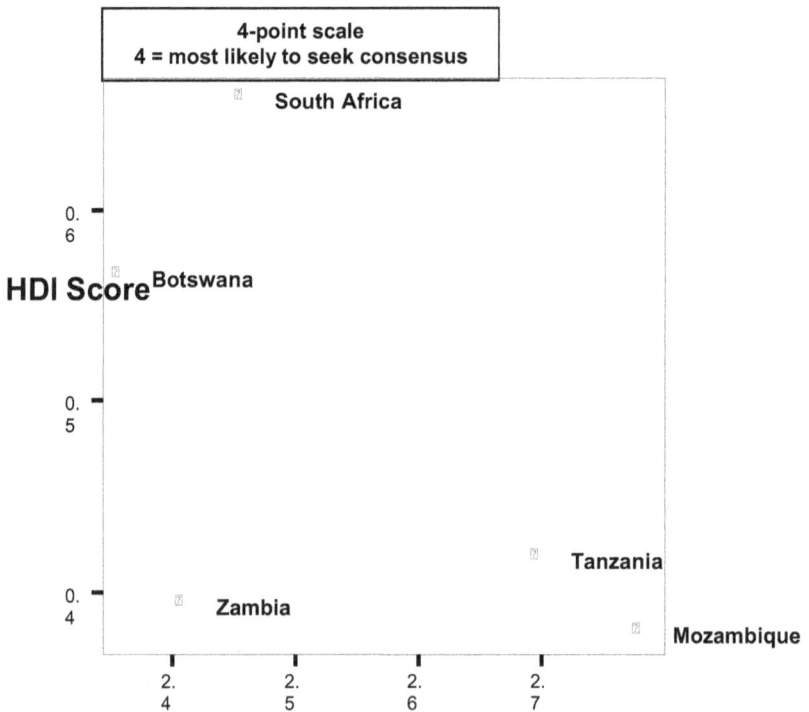

Although the above results should once again be analysed with caution due to the limited number of cases, the graph seems to indicate an inverse relationship between level of development and the need to build consensus (Pearson's $r = -.578, p > 0.05$). Mozambique represents the extreme case in this regard. As mentioned in Appendix A, Mozambique was only declared 'party free' in the 2005 Freedom House rankings. One of the major contributing factors to this low ranking was the fact that the Mozambican government has the power to restrict the freedom of the press, political parties and party members should they deem it necessary. Amongst the country's leaders, therefore, there seems to be a distinct tendency to repress opposing opinions.

The third value orientation in the realm of human qualities is support for justice vs. support for rule of law. As noted above, this value orientation can be seen to have direct consequences for development, as the emphasis on communal good prevalent in traditional African societies may lead to situations where producing "just outcomes", even if it requires the use of violence, may be valued more than procedure and "rule of law" (Mattes and Shin 2005:14).

Figure 5.3: HDI Score vs. Mean Level of Support for Justice over Rule of Law

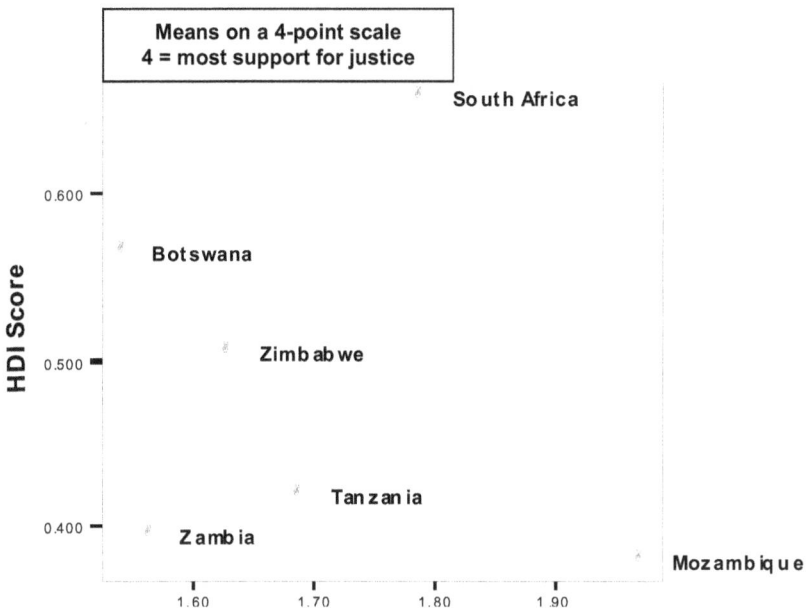

A very weak negative relationship between development and the pursuit of justice over the rule of law seems to be evident in the above graph (Pearson's $r = -.163$, $p > 0.05$). This could be explained in terms of an excessive emphasis on just outcomes clearly having the tendency to lead to vigilantism, which could have dire consequences for the peaceful resolution of conflicts. Once again Mozambique represents the extreme case, with the highest levels of support for justice over rule of law, coupled with the lowest levels of development. However, due to the weak nature of this relationship and the lack of significance, this variable does not have much explanatory power.

Nevertheless, the scores obtained by the individual countries can perhaps once again be explained by the situation on the ground. In countries such as Mozambique, structural constraints may in fact make the pursuit of rule of law untenable, with individuals forced to pursue their own form of justice. High levels of organized crime have continued to plague Mozambique after the civil war, facilitated by an understaffed and ineffective police and judicial system (Country Watch Mozambique [2007f])[29]. Similarly, South Africa has been experiencing extremely high levels of crime in recent years, possibly leading people to take justice into their own hands.

Human Relationships

Lawuyi (1998:82) emphasises the extreme importance of social relations when trying to gain an understanding of African worldviews. The mere fact of living together in society divides individuals into families, lineages and territorial units, each with its own sense of solidarity and hostility to others. In this regard, Hammond-Tooke (1974:342) highlights the fact that one of the primary functions of African religious and moral systems is to lay down norms of behaviour between individuals, with these norms and values having to be restated with a greater than human authority. Here, the role of ancestors and other supernatural or super-empirical beings comes into play. This point is reinforced by Keesing and Strathern (1998:56), who state that people's religious beliefs and their social organisation are indeed closely interrelated. Thus, in analysing human interaction during the process of development, the role played by these supernatural orders needs to be carefully considered.[30]

In more pragmatic terms, the concept of "Ubuntu" also needs to be taken into account when analysing social relations in southern Africa. This term roughly translates into 'I am because you exist' and once again emphases the extent of interconnectedness between individuals within a given society. In essence, 'the individual knows him or herself to be immersed in the community to such an extent that personality can develop only in and through it' (Maluccio 1999:67).

Taking the above dynamics into consideration, the link between development and community versus individual interest was analysed under the Human Relationships dimension. Indeed, the emphasis in traditional societies on communal relationships seems to inextricably link individuals to their social environments. The Afrobarometer questionnaire provided two items which tapped into levels of individualism. Unfortunately, these two items did not correlate very well (Chronbach's Alpha = .382) and were, therefore, analysed independently in relation to development.

Figure 5.4: HDI Score vs. Mean Level of Individualism

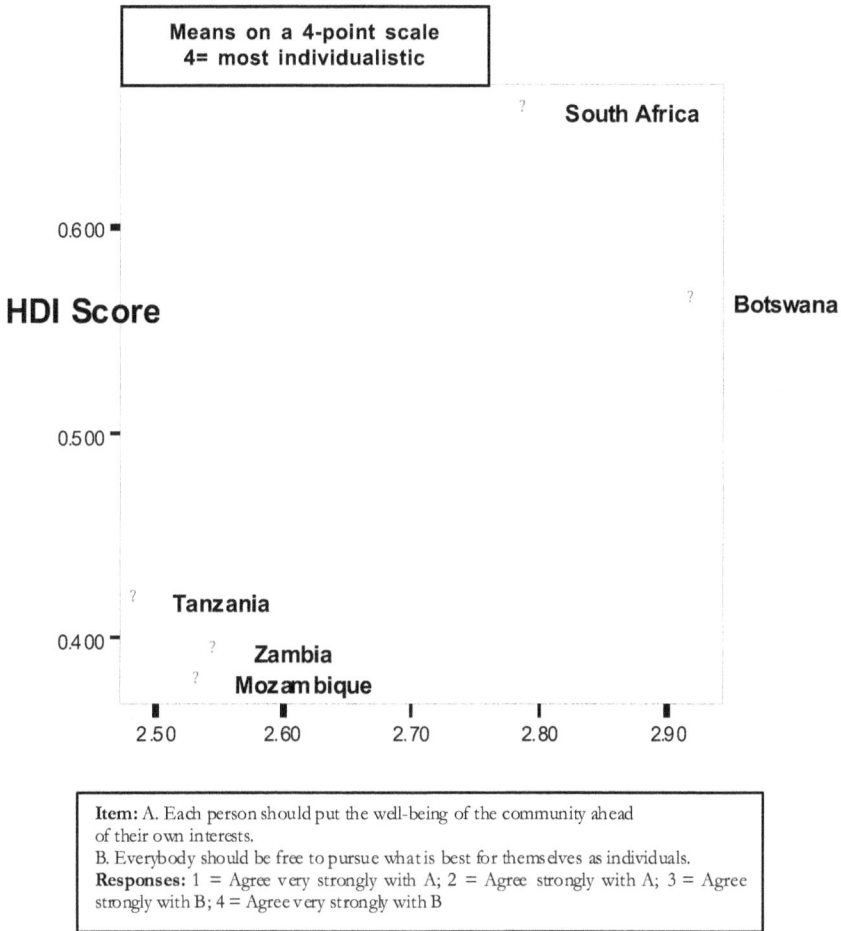

Means on a 4-point scale
4= most individualistic

? **South Africa**

HDI Score   ? **Botswana**

0.600 ■

0.500 ▬

? **Tanzania**

0.400 ▬   ? **Zambia**
                    ? **Mozambique**

2.50   2.60   2.70   2.80   2.90

Item: A. Each person should put the well-being of the community ahead
of their own interests.
B. Everybody should be free to pursue what is best for themselves as individuals.
Responses: 1 = Agree very strongly with A; 2 = Agree strongly with A; 3 = Agree
strongly with B; 4 = Agree very strongly with B

With regard to the first item, a strong Pearson's correlation ($r = .884$) was found, coming close to significance at $p = .074$. South Africa and Botswana are particularly striking in that they both show high levels of development coupled with an emphasis on individualism. This strong relationship seems to highlight the need for individual entrepreneurial spirit in terms of bringing about development within the respective countries. In line with these findings, Samli et al (2007) highlight the need for struggling economies in Sub-Saharan Africa to generate or nurture an entrepreneurial culture.

Figure 5.5: HDI Score vs. Mean Level of Individualism 2

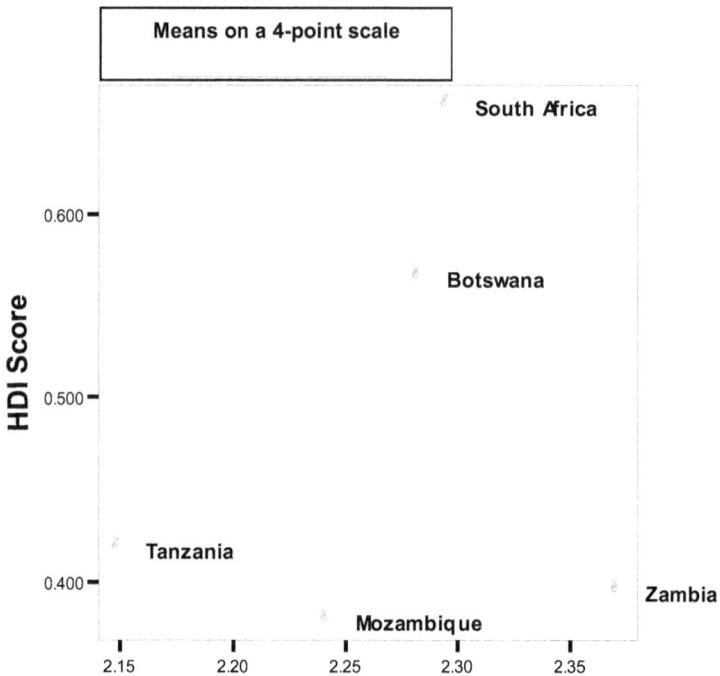

Figure showing HDI Score (y-axis, 0.400 to 0.600) vs Means on a 4-point scale (x-axis, 2.15 to 2.35) with data points labeled: South Africa, Botswana, Tanzania, Mozambique, Zambia.

Item: A: It is alright to have large differences of wealth because those that work hard deserve to be rewarded.
B: We should avoid large gaps between the rich and the poor because they create jealousy and conflict.
Responses: 1 = Agree very strongly with A; 2 = Agree strongly with A; 3 = Agree strongly with B; 4 = Agree very strongly with B
Item was recoded – higher value = greater emphasis on individualism

Surprisingly, a much weaker correlation (Pearson's $r = .182$; $p>0.05$) between individualism and development was found for the second item. This would seem to indicate that the notion of 'individual interest' may be multi-faceted and may operate differently where actual wealth differentials are involved.

The level of social capital within the societies forms another component of the Human Relationships value dimension. A wide body of literature has shown that social capital (networks between individuals and the norms of reciprocity and trust that arise from them) can be seen to have a direct influence on the attainment of developmental objectives.[31] Unfortunately, however, the Afrobarometer questionnaire only allowed us to tap into the 'network' dimension of social capital, and not its corollary, namely 'trust between individuals'.

Figure 5.6: HDI score vs. Mean Level of Social Capital

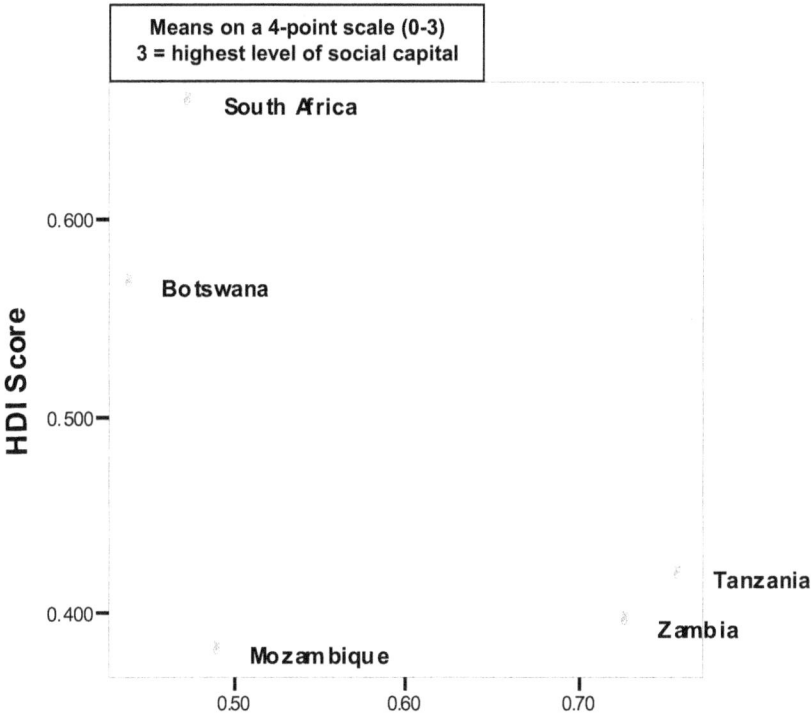

Surprisingly, there seems to be a relatively strong negative relationship between development and social capital amongst the five countries ($r=-.609$, $p>0.05$). Although the correlation is not significant, it nevertheless seems to contradict the social capital hypothesis. South Africa, which has the highest level of development, obtains a low score on the social capital index, while Tanzania, which has a much lower level of development, obtains the highest score (all countries however score lower than 1 on the index, range $= 0-3$). Further investigation into the trust dimension of social capital is however necessary, as the measure of social capital used in the survey (i.e. excluding the trust dimension) may have lead to distorted findings.

Identity politics is another major factor which needs to be taken into consideration when analysing the progress which Africa has made in terms of reaching developmental goals. The Berlin Conference of 1884-1885[32] essentially created heterogeneous national societies in Africa, which was exacerbated by the fact that kinship identities were often so strong that they resisted attempts at forming overarching identities. This can naturally be seen to have severe consequences for development, as people with strong group-based identities may be more likely to develop antipathies to others and less likely to accept competing groups in working towards a common goal. In line with an analysis of Afrobarometer data by Mattes and Shin (2005), self-reported identities of individuals were divided into traditional (including racial, ethnic, religious, regional or age identities) and modern (including occupation, class, country, political party, individual identities) categories. The subdivision of identities into these two categories can be motivated by the fact that the often still limited influences of industrialisation may have led Africans to continue to identify themselves 'according to where they live or the kinship group to which they belong, rather than by what they do or the broader polity in which they have been included by colonial mapmakers' (Mattes and Shin 2005:25).

Figure 5.7: Mean Level of Development vs. Type of Identity

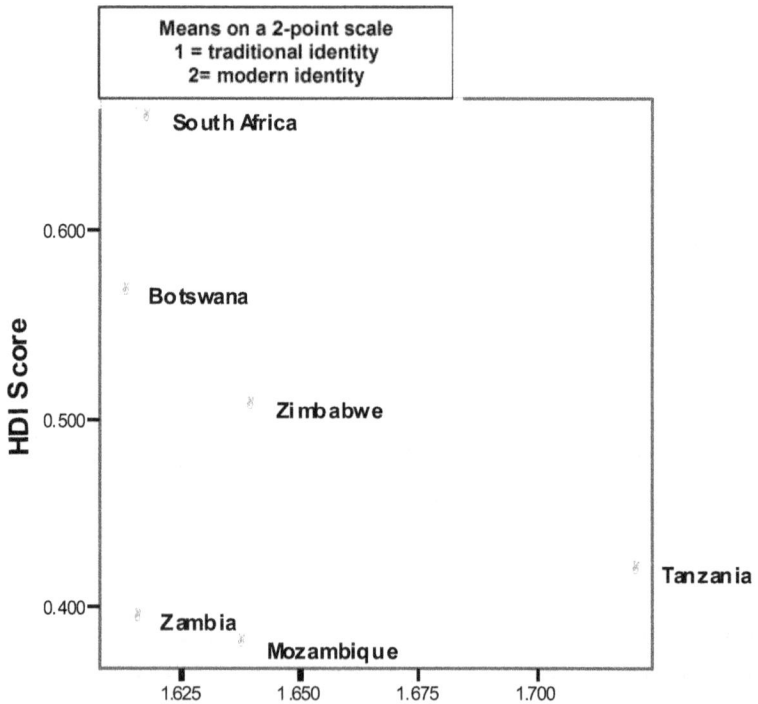

Interestingly, Tanzania seems to show the highest mean level of modern identity markers.[33] However, all the countries score higher than 1.6 (range of 1 to 2; traditional to modern), seemingly indicating that individuals in these countries generally tend towards so-called 'modern' forms of self-identification. However, no distinct conclusions in terms of the link between development and identity can be drawn, with only a weak correlation emerging (Pearson's $r = -.396, p>0.05$). Further analysis and the development of more comprehensive indicators is therefore necessary.

Power

Under the value dimension of power, support for gender equality in the respective countries was analysed. The patriarchal nature of many African polities in many cases continues to place women in inferior and unequal positions. This naturally also places severe limitations on the agency of women in the developmental context.

Figure 5.8: HDI Score vs. Mean Level of Support for Gender Equality

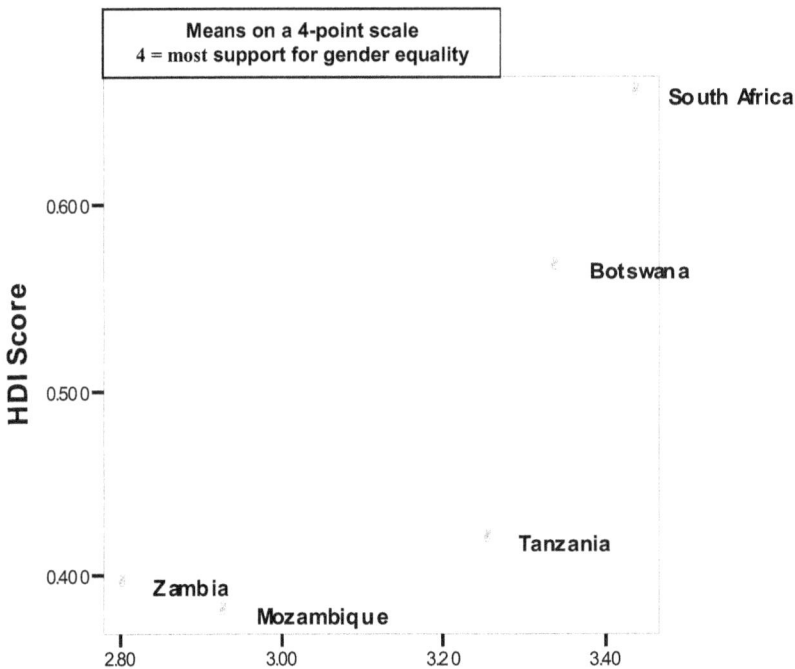

There seems to be a clear linear relationship between level of development and level of support for gender equality in these countries. The Pearson's correlation ($r = .843$) comes close to significance at $p = .073$. This finding highlights the extreme importance of developing policies that respect the rights of women in the Southern African region, allowing them to play an active role in developmental outcomes. In this regard, Appendix A provides some cursory insights into how the above countries are currently performing in terms of achieving gender equality. South Africa has made particular progress in terms of achieving gender equality in government, moving from 141 in the world before the 1994 elections to number seven in terms of women occupying seats in the national government, when the African National Congress adopted a 30 per cent quota on its party list (Garson, 2007).

The final value orientation analysed under the dimension of power was the level of support for elite rule within the respective countries. This value orientation poses a crucial question: Where should the power reside? In other words, should it reside with the masses or with economic experts and elites within the respective countries? This question has particular relevance, as traditional Southern African societies have historically been highly stratified into both kinship and political hierarchies.

Figure 5.9: HDI Score vs. Mean Level of Support for Elite Rule

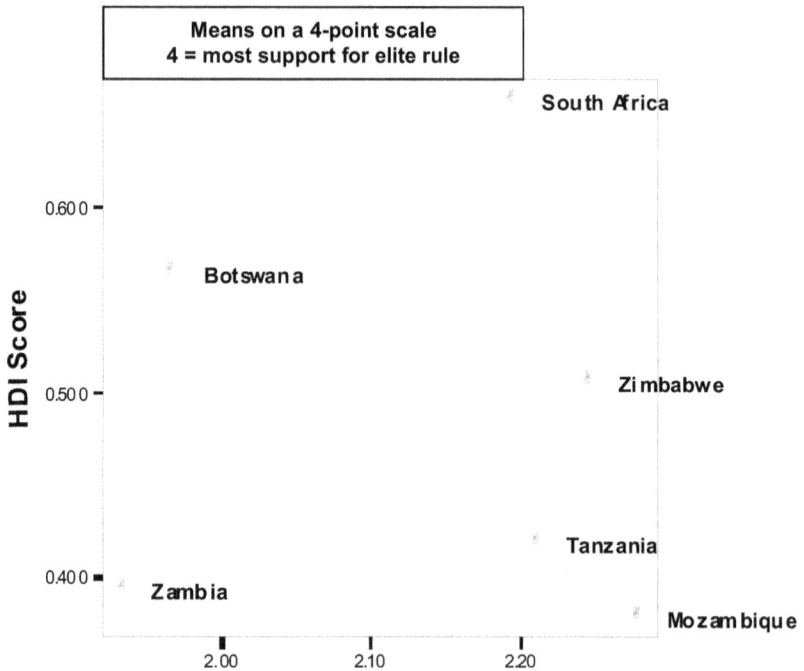

A very weak inverse relationship between development and support for elite rule emerges (Pearson's $r = -.034$; $p>0.05$). The extreme case is once again Mozambique, showing very low levels of development in conjunction with high support for rule by elites. A more comprehensive index is, however, necessary to provide more conclusive insights.

Although the dimension of cosmology could not be comprehensively analysed due to the lack of suitable items in the Afrobarometer questionnaire, it should be seen, however as a crucial component in terms of explaining developmental outcomes in Africa.

Cosmology

It is clear that in order to fully understand belief systems one cannot simply identify isolated value orientations. What needs to be developed is a deeper understanding of cosmology - how people conceptualise their universe, see the place of humans in it, and relate to unseen beings and powers. As noted by Keesing and Strathern (1998:64), 'striving to understand the religious philosophy of non-Western people, demands every ounce of one's analytical and intuitive powers, and often more'.

Hammond-Tooke (1974:320) notes that traditional systems (focusing specifically on the 'Bantu'-speaking peoples of Southern Africa) differ remarkably from the so-called 'World Religions' – they are all firmly rooted in the social structure, the objects of worship are structurally determined, and they are mostly this-worldly in orientation:

Unlike Christianity, for example, which accepts suffering as inevitable and indeed necessary, merely promising grace in the face of it, all Bantu religions are concerned with attaining the good life here on earth, and their rituals tend to be essentially pragmatic. A dualism is recognized, as in Christianity, between good and evil, but the war waged between them, with its resulting rewards and penalties, is essentially here and now, and not in an apocalyptic future existence. The witch and the sorcerer, the very embodiment of evil, is a constant threat to the well-being of man and beast, and the whole complex of witch beliefs, with its related institution of divination must, therefore, be seen as an integral part of the religious system (Hammond-Tooke 1974:318).

Keesing and Strathern (1998:67) also highlight the fact that 'magical thinking', prevalent in many African cultures, reflects a kind of model of a universe far more deterministic than the Western one, a universe where things do not just happen by chance or accident (see also Horton 1993; Lawuyi 1998). In such a universe, death, illness and crop failure call for explanation. As noted by Hammond-Tooke (1974:328), these misfortunes are almost inevitably believed to be caused by some external agent. This agent may be a supernatural being in its own right, or a human being using supernatural means. Magic, then, represents human attempts to manipulate chains of cause and effect between events which to Western eyes may seem unrelated. Yamba (1997) emphasizes that these cosmologies have daily relevance in all spheres of life, noting the impact of cosmology, and more specifically witchcraft, on the discourse surrounding AIDS in Zambia.

Despite the unavailability of suitably operationalised survey items tapping into cosmologies within the Southern African context, it is nevertheless crucial that these dynamics are further investigated. This will allow us to gain a fuller understanding, not only of their impact on everyday interactions between individuals, but also on attitudes towards achieving developmental goals. Indeed, the very notion of 'development' may take on distinct variations based on the differing cosmologies of given societies.

Conclusion

The above analysis has provided an exploratory empirical analysis investigating whether there may indeed be a link between value orientations and development within the Southern African context. Although the use of such a small sample (6 countries), the limited type of data available (quantitative and opinion survey), has precluded significant results from being found, interesting trends have nevertheless emerged. However, the development of a survey instrument which takes particular cognisance of the intricacies of value orientations in the Southern African region, particularly in the complex field of cosmology, would allow us to gain a much-needed understanding of how particular values manifest themselves in people's lived realities.

As noted above, it is particularly within the fields of gender, consensus-seeking and individualism where links with development seem apparent. Yet, these cursory findings need to be verified through adequately controlling for the effect of various environmental factors and taking a closer look at questions of causality. It is also important to note that the above findings merely provide a macro view of the link between values and development, without taking into account the vast socio-economic and cultural variation that often characterises the African landscape. Within-country analyses and the thick descriptions and confounding nature of qualitative studies of the spread of value orientations therefore also have a valuable contribution to make.

Augmenting the use of empirical analysis of survey data with qualitative analyses (such as focus groups) will go a long way in contextualising findings within diverse environments. This will ultimately allow us to gain a much-needed deeper understanding of specific values driving individual actions, thereby making crucial inroads in addressing developmental shortfalls in a sustainable manner.

Notes

1. These countries were chosen due to the fact that they form part of the Southern African region. All six of these countries were also included in Round 2 of the Afrobarometer survey, providing an ideal opportunity for comparative empirical analysis. More information on the Afrobarometer survey will be provided below.
2. Rist (Berry 2002) has questioned the very notion of national development, particularly its universality. He argues that development is one of the Western world's favourite myths and that one needs to attack the accepted truths about development held by Western 'developers'. Indeed, not every culture has a concept for development and that if there is, it may not be at all like the one in the developer's programme. It is, therefore, necessary to discern the very existence and important variations in the meaning of

development across cultures. According to Sindima (1995:xiii), liberalism is a thoroughly materialistic philosophy which understands development in 'purely economic terms'. This notion of progress and orientation towards social change 'corrupted the African way of life' and 'destroyed the African holistic concept of the world, [pushing] religion into the realm of the private'.

3. See chapter 2 on the 'comparative method' for more on these limitations.

4. See also Graeber (2001) in this regard.

5. Modernisation theory (often contrasted with dependency theory) is a socio-economic theory which highlights the role played by the developed world in modernising and facilitating sustainable development in underdeveloped nations (mostly through the acculturation of the modern policies and values of the Western world). The theory has, however, been subject to major criticisms, especially for its western, ethnocentric approach. See Rostow (1960), McCelland (1967) and Inkeles (1974).

6. Mazrui (1990:4) observed that: 'A central aspect of the gap in technique is the relationship between culture and technical modernization. In order to modernize industrially, is it necessary to Westernize culturally? Japan from 1868 decided that a country could modernise industrially without Westernizing culturally. "Western technique, Japanese spirit" was Japan's slogan. Japan proceeded on that basic assumption. Turkey under Mustafa Kemal Ataturk in the 1920s and 1930s decided that in order to modernize industrially a country had to Westernize culturally.' He goes on to state that Africa has not followed the Japanese fate of technical modernisation without cultural Westernisation, nor the Ataturk fate of technical modernisation through cultural Westernisation. Instead, Africa has followed the painful process of 'cultural Westernisation without technical modernization'.

7. In some cases Zimbabwe was excluded from the analysis, due to certain items not having been included in the Zimbabwean questionnaire.

8. For more on the pitfalls inherent in cross-cultural analysis, see Landman (2000).

9. For more on the complexity of value systems in relation to a changing environment, see Graeber (2001).

10. Data limitations did not allow us to put this into practice in this analysis. As mentioned above, Round 2 of the Afrobarometer survey was the first time the six countries under investigation in this study were simultaneously included in a survey. The release of Round 3 data will allow the evolution of values in these countries to be investigated over time, albeit over a relatively short period.

11. Hammond-Tooke is regarded as one of South Africa's most prolific authors of anthropological texts. His best-known works are those on the peoples of southern Africa and the history of Southern African anthropology. Hammond-Tooke was primarily interested in the type of topics investigated by the founders of South African anthropology, which led the more progressive of his generation of anthropologists in the 1970s and 1980s to perceive his approach as conservative and outdated. As noted by Niehaus (2005:6), from an activist vantage point, Hammond-Tooke's more scholarly concerns – such as demonstrating how old Zulu folk tales display the fundamental logic of the human mind – seemed rather pedestrian. Yet Niehaus acknowledges that the classical theories and concerns represented in his work are now seen as indispensable for understanding the complex and dynamic society we live in. His work is a reminder

that 'any vision of human nature that excludes myths, morality, symbols and religion will always be partial and incomplete' (2005:6).

12. See Afrobarometer Round 2 compendium for a summary of major findings from the surveys (Afrobarometer, 2007a). These findings however focus particularly on political attitudes rather than individual value orientations as such.

13. The values which characterize African cultures are widely seen to be the product of four formative and dominant influences. First, until relatively recently, Africans have traditionally lived in small-scale villages. Second, Africans traditionally governed themselves through a mostly patriarchal system of largely hereditary, unelected traditional leaders. Third, political rule was rarely exercised on the scale of the modern state, often extending only to the boundaries of the village, and beyond that only indirectly in loose confederation with other villages sharing tribal, clan or linguistic similarities. Fourth, Africa's modern political topography often bears little resemblance to the continent's ethnic or tribal makeup. Colonial mapmakers essentially divided and recombined Africa's agrarian and herding societies into heterogeneous national societies (Mattes and Shin 2005:8-9).

14. Similarly, Hyden (2001) argues that African values are impediments to development and the reduction of fertility in Africa. Thus, demographic change will only occur in Africa if political systems are willing to move beyond the structural limitations of populism. However, Chowdhry (1992:33), in her review of this work, argues that this focus on the negative impact of African values is disturbingly reminiscent of modernisation theory.

15. This degree of control over individual destiny naturally also relates to the degree of internal versus external locus of control which the individual experiences.

16. The identification of these four broad value dimensions resulted from a series of workshops during which African academics participating in the Southern African values project deliberated extensively regarding the most appropriate conceptual framework to guide this study.

17. The level of paternalism / dependency within the 6 countries was measured with an index consisting of the following items (across the five countries where all six questions were asked, Chronbach's Alpha = .762); Only the first and the fifth questions listed below were included in the Zimbabwean questionnaire.

Which of the following statements is closest to your view? Choose Statement A or Statement B

Response categories: Agree Strongly with A; Agree with A; Agree with B; Agree Strongly with B.

*Items were re-coded into the same direction – higher value = greater dependency

A: People should look after themselves and be responsible for their own success in life

B: The government should bear the main responsibility for the well-being of people.

A: As citizens, we should be more active in questioning the actions of our leaders.

B: In our country these days, we should show more respect for authority.

A: It is better to have wealthy people as leaders because they can help provide for the community.

B: It is better to have ordinary people as leaders because they understand our needs.

A: Since everyone is equal under the law, leaders should not favour their own family or group.

B: Once in office, leaders are obliged to help their own family or group.

A: People are like children; the government should take care of them like a parent.

B: Government is an employee; the people should be the bosses who control the government.

Across five countries, these items produce a Chronbach's Alpha of .762 (Zimbabwe was not included as not all of the items where asked in this country).

18. Consensus-seeking was measured using the following variable:

Which of the following statements is closest to your view? Choose Statement A or Statement B.

Response categories: Agree Strongly with A; Agree with A; Agree with B; Agree Very Strongly with B.

A: In order to make decisions in our community, we should talk until everyone agrees.

B: Since we will never agree on everything, we must learn to accept differences of opinion within our community.

*Response categories were reversed – higher value = increased consensus-seeking

Unfortunately other variables testing the same concept were not available, preventing an index from being constructed.

19. The following items were included in an index, testing whether the pursuit of justice takes precedence over respect for the rule of law (Chronbach's Alpha = .645). In Zimbabwe only the 'violent crime' item was included in the questionnaire.

Which of the following statements is closest to your view? Choose Statement A or Statement B.

Response categories: Agree Strongly with A; Agree with A; Agree with B; Agree Very Strongly with B.

A: If you were a victim of violent crime, you would turn to the police for help

B: If you were a victim of a violent crime you would find a way to take revenge yourself

A: The use of violence is never justified in [this country's] politics.

B: In this country, it is sometimes necessary to use violence in support of a just cause.

20. The following two items were assessed individually in relation to individualism. These items were not asked in Zimbabwe.

Which of the following statements is closest to your view? Choose Statement A or Statement B.

Response categories: 1 = Agree Strongly with A; 2 = Agree with A; 3 = Agree with B; 4 = Agree Very Strongly with B.

Item 1:

A: Each person should put the well-being of the community ahead of their own interests.

B: Everybody should be free to pursue what is best for themselves as individuals.

Item 2:*

A: It is alright to have large differences of wealth because those that work hard deserve to be rewarded.

B: We should avoid large gaps between the rich and the poor because they create jealousy and conflict.

---

*Item 2 was recoded – higher value = greater emphasis on individualism.

21. The following items were combined into a social capital index (Chronbach's Alpha = .803); Items not asked in Zimbabwe.

Now I am going to read out a list of groups that people join or attend. For each one, could you tell me whether you are an official leader, an active member, an inactive member, or not a member.
- A religious group
- A trade union or farmers association
- A professional or business association
- A community or development organisation

22. The following question testing identity was asked of respondents:

We have spoken to many [South Africans] and they have all described themselves in different ways. Some people describe themselves in terms of their language, ethnic group, race, religion, or gender and others describe themselves in economic terms, such as working class, middle class, or a farmer. Besides being [South African] which specific group do you feel you belong to first and foremost?

Responses were recoded into the following categories:

Traditional: racial, ethnic, religious, regional or age identities.

Modern: occupation, class, country, political party, individual identities.

23. The following items were combined into a 'support for gender equality' index (Chronbach's Alpha = .896):

Which of the following statements is closest to your view? Choose Statement A or Statement B.

Response categories: Agree Strongly with A; Agree with A; Agree with B; Agree Very Strongly with B.

A: Women have always been subject to traditional laws and customs, and should remain so.

B: In our country, women should have equal rights and receive the same treatment as men do.

A: A married man has the right to beat his wife and children if they misbehave.

B: No-one has the right to use physical violence against anyone else.

24. The following items were used to measure support for elite rule (Chronbach's Alpha = .468):

Item 1: Which of the following statements is closest to your view? Choose Statement A or Statement B.

Response categories: Agree Strongly with A; Agree with A; Agree with B; Agree Very Strongly with B.

A: All people should be permitted to vote, even if they do not fully understand all the issues at hand.

B: Only those who are sufficiently well educated should be allowed to choose our leaders.

Item 2: There are many ways to manage an economy. Would you disapprove or approve of the following alternatives:

Economic experts (including foreign donors and investors) make the most important decisions about our economy.

Response categories: Agree strongly, agree, disagree, disagree strongly.

25. Various criticisms have, however, been levelled against the HDI in recent years. Although it has many strengths, the HDI remains a very blunt instrument since it relies on incomplete sets of cross-national aggregate data that (particularly in developing countries) are not necessarily collected systematically on an annual basis (Lindenberg 2002:307). In addition, the HDI seems to fall short of providing a context-sensitive measure of development, which can be seen to be particularly important in Africa. What is, therefore, needed is the development of indices constructed from culturally rich data, which take into account the local way of life. Global developmental measures are inherently problematic in this regard, as they are designed to be applicable in diverse contexts, yet often miss out on valuable context-specific information. For more on this, see Alkire (2002); Anand & Sen (2000) and Atkinson (1973). See also chapter on the 'Comparative Method' for more on aggregate data collection in developing countries.

26. Paternalism, as it is used in this context, can be defined as the policy of governing or controlling people through providing for their needs, but giving them no responsibility during this process. More specifically, the survey items used to measure this concept tap into whether or not individuals consider it to be acceptable to be governed in a paternalistic manner.

27. See also Mamdani (1996); Etounga-Manguelle (2000).

28. By contrast, Wiredu (2001) argues that the value of consensus was pivotal in the organisation of non-centralised African states. He claims it constituted African democratic culture and that it is still important for post-colonial Africa to promote it.

29. See Appendix A.

30. This will be more closely analysed in the section on cosmology.

31. The central premise of social capital is that social ties have value. Of course this value is conceptualised in capitalist terms (Fine 2001). Social capital refers to the collective value of all social networks (who people know) and the inclinations that arise from these networks to do things for each other (norms of reciprocity and trust). The term, therefore, emphasises a wide variety of specific benefits that flow from the information, and cooperation associated with social networks (Cohen and Prusak 2001:65). In this way, value is created for people that are connected and - at least sometimes - for bystanders as well. Indeed, there is considerable evidence that communities with a good stock of social capital are more likely to benefit from lower crime figures, better health, higher educational achievement, and better economic growth (Putnam 2000:296-306; 307-318).

32. For more on the impact of the 'Scramble for Africa' on African consciousness, see Petringa (2006).

33. This seems to stand in sharp contrast to the agricultural policy of collectivisation - *ujamaa* or 'familyhood' - instituted by Nyerere in Tanzania. This policy was based on the belief that life should be structured around the *ujamaa*, or extended family found in traditional Africa (Yakan 999).

6

Values, Development and Demography

Marvellous Mhloyi, Noah Taruberekera and Musonda Lemba

Introduction

There is an intricate reciprocal relationship between values, development and demography (and the components of population growth). In effect, values impact on development that in turn affects trends in fertility, mortality and migration. On the other hand, development also impacts on values. It should be noted that Africa, which is the least developed continent, experiences the highest fertility and mortality rates, while its migration patterns and trends are determined by the respective countries' and global development trends. Within the respective countries, there are pockets of development such as the urban settings, educated and high income groups of people; these differentially distributed development factors are in turn highly causal for the differentials in fertility, mortality and migration of people within and between countries.

This chapter will briefly trace the changes in development and the demography of the world, paying special attention to the African continent and the Sub-Saharan region in particular. Data from Zimbabwe and Zambia are used as specific examples of the relationship between demographic phenomena and development. An effort is made to show data on the changes in fertility and mortality over the past two and half decades. Subsequently, a discussion of factors underlying the observed trends is provided. Given the limited space, factors underlying fertility are covered in greater detail compared to the brief discussion on factors underlying mortality and migration respectively. The discussion on underlying factors to demography will highlight the interaction between values, development and demography.

Global Levels of Development and Demographic Characteristics

As noted earlier, the world is characterised by differential developmental levels that qualify respective countries to be classified as either developed or less developed. Two indices of development, the proportion of the population that resides in urban areas and gross national product (GNP) per capita are used as proxies for development. Two mortality indices, infant mortality rate and life expectancy, and total fertility rate are the demographic aspects that are compared between and within regions. The composite rate of population growth is also used. These indices, covering the period 1981- 2005 are shown in Table 6.1. World indices and those for developed and less developed regions are covered. Indices for respective aspects within Africa, for Zimbabwe and to a lesser extent, Zambia, are also shown.

There is, of course, a marked difference in GNP per capita between the developed and less developed nations; with per capita GNP in the developed nations being about ten times higher than in the less developed nations. The rate of increase of the GNP is also higher in the developed nations compared to the less developed nations. For instance, while GNP per capita for the developed nations ranged from US$8,657 in 1981 to US$19,480 in 2000, it ranged from a meagre US$728 to US$1,260 for less developed nations. The gross national product (GNP) per capita for the developed nations was US$26,320 in 2005 compared to only US$4450 for less developed regions. On the other hand, GNP per capita for the African region falls below the average of less developed nations; and the GNP per capita declined over the two decades as it ranged between US$783-670. Within Africa, the Southern African region fares better than other regions. GNP per capita for Southern Africa ranged between US$2,349 in 1981 to US$3,100 in 2000; as compared to a meagre US$305 to US$260 for Eastern Africa. Consistent with the trend in the less developed countries, Zimbabwe's GNP per capita declined from US$630 in 1981 to US$620 in 2000.

The developed regions of the world are also more urbanised than the less developed regions, albeit with increasing urbanisation over time in less developed regions. For instance, while the proportion residing in urban areas ranged between 70 per cent in 1981 to 76 per cent in 2005 in the developed nations, such proportions ranged from 29 per cent to 41 per cent in the less developed nations. It should be noted that the rate of increase of urbanisation is higher in the less developed compared to the more developed nations. Urbanisation is not the most accurate indicator of development as it differs significantly between the developed and the developing nations and within these categories; and we only use it as a proxy for an admittedly complex dynamic.

As alluded to earlier, the developed nations have more positive general demographic indices than the less developed nations. The developed nations experience better health than less the developed nations. The infant mortality rate reduced from 19 to 6 deaths for 1,000 live births between 1981 and 2000 for the developed regions. Infant mortality for the less developed nations reduced from 93 to 59, while that for the Africa region reduced from 120 to 88 over the same period. It should be further noted that while the infant mortality rate ranged between 97 and 46 deaths per 1000 births in 1981 and 2000 respectively for Southern Africa, it ranged from 111 to 90 for Eastern Africa. Consistently, life expectancy is higher in the developed compared to the less developed nations. It ranged from 73 to 76 years between 1981 and 2005 respectively, for the former compared to 58 and 65 years respectively for less developed nations. This compares with only 50 and 52 years, respectively for the African continent. While life expectancy for Southern Africa ranged between 60 and 50 years for the same period, it ranged between 46 and 48 years for the Eastern African region and declined from 54 to 41 years respectively for Zimbabwe.

The less developed regions experience higher fertility than the more developed regions. While the total fertility rate ranged between 1.9 and 1.6 children between 1981 and 2005 in the developed regions of the world, it ranged between 4.5 and 3.0 children respectively, for the less developed nations; and between 6.5 and 5.1 children for Africa. Fertility rate ranged from 5.2 to 2.9 children for the Southern African region, and from 6.6 to 5.7 children respectively for Eastern Africa. Zimbabwe's fertility ranged between 6.7 and 3.8 children, respectively. In Zambia, fertility declined 7.1 in 1980 to 6.3 in 1990, and then 4.9 in 2000. Estimates based on the Zimbabwe Demographic and Health Survey has shown a similar downward trend in fertility. This showed a decline from 6.5 births in 1992 to 6.1 in 1996 and 5.9 in 2001 to 2002.

The high fertility rates in the less developed nations coupled with declining, albeit high mortality rates give rise to high rates of population growth. While the rate of natural increase ranged between .6 and .1 between 1981 and 2000 in the developed nations, this compares 2.1 and 1.5 respectively for the less developed nations. The African region experienced rates of increase of between 3.0 and 2.3 per cent, with the Southern African region experiencing a decline in the rate from 2.6 to .7 per cent compared to 3.1 to 2.5 per cent for the East African region. What is it in development, or the lack of it, that explains the differentials in the demography of the world?

Table 6.1: Development and Demographic Indices for the World

Socio-demographic Data 1980-2005

	1981	1985	1990	1995	2000	2005
World						
Population (millions)	4677	4845	5321	5702	6067	6477
Rate of Natural Increase (%)	1.8	1.7	1.8	1.5	1.4	1.2
IMR (per 1000)	84	81	73	62	57	54
TFR (per woman)	3.9	3.7	3.5	3.1	2.9	2.7
Life Expectancy	62	62	64	66	66	67
Urban Population (%)	39	41	41	43	45	47
GNP per capita (USD)	2754	2760	3470	4500	4890	8540
Developed Regions						
Population (millions)	1158	1174	1214	1169	1184	1211
Rate of Natural Increase (%)	0.6	0.6	0.5	0.2	1.7	0.1
IMR (per 1000)	19	18	16	10	8	6
TFR (per woman)	1.9	2	2	1.6	1.5	1.6
Life Expectancy	73	73	74	74	75	76
Urban Population (%)	70	72	73	74	75	76
GNP per capita (USD)	8657	9380	15830	17270	19480	26320
Less Developed Regions						
Population (millions)	3519	3671	4107	4533	4883	5266
Rate of Natural Increase (%)	2.1	2	2.4	1.9	1.7	1.5
IMR (per 1000)	93	90	81	67	63	59
TFR (per woman)	4.5	4.2	4	3.5	3.2	3
Life Expectancy	58	58	61	65	64	65
Urban Population (%)	29	31	32	35	38	41
GNP per capita (USD)	728	700	710	1030	1260	4450

Africa

Population (millions)	513	551	661	720	800	906
Rate of Natural Increase (%)	3	2.9	2.9	2.8	2.4	2.3
IMR (per 1000)	120	110	109	90	88	88
TFR (per woman)	6.5	6.3	6.2	5.8	5.3	5.1
Life Expectancy	50	50	52	56	52	52
Urban Population (%)	27	31	31	31	33	36
GNP per capita (USD)	783	750	600	660	670	2300

Northern Africa

Population (millions)	120	128	144	162	173	194
Rate of Natural Increase (%)	3.1	2.9	2.8	2.4	2	2
IMR (per 1000)	109	97	87	63	51	45
TFR (per woman)	6.4	6	5.2	4.4	3.6	3.3
Life Expectancy	55	56	59	65	64	68
Urban Population (%)	42	42	41	45	46	47
GNP per capita (USD)	1165	1190	1110	1040	1200	4050

Western Africa

Population (millions)	155	166	206	199	234	264
Rate of Natural Increase (%)	3.1	3	3	3.1	2.8	2.5
IMR (per 1000)	139	118	119	86	89	105
TFR (per woman)	6.8	6.4	6.6	6.4	5.9	5.9
Life Expectancy	47	48	48	55	51	47
Urban Population (%)	22	29	30	23	35	40
GNP per capita (USD)	681	580	340	370	340	1200

Eastern Africa

Population (millions)	146	159	199	226	246	281
Rate of Natural Increase (%)	3.1	3.1	3	3	2.4	2.5
IMR (per 1000)	111	109	116	106	102	90
TFR (per woman)	6.6	6.8	6.7	6.4	6	5.7

Life Expectancy	48	49	5	52	46	47
Urban Population (%)	14	17	18	21	20	24
GNP per capita (USD)	305	300	230	210	260	1020
Middle Africa						
Population (millions)	58	62	68	83	96	112
Rate of Natural Increase (%)	2.7	2.7	3	2.9	3	2.8
IMR (per 1000)	121	119	118	107	106	98
TFR (per woman)	6	6.1	6.1	6.3	6.6	6.3
Life Expectancy	46	48	50	51	49	48
Urban Population (%)	30	34	37	33	32	35
GNP per capita (USD)	483	420	420	-	320	1240
Southern Africa						
Population (millions)	34	37	45	50	50	54
Rate of Natural Increase (%)	2.6	2.2	2.7	2.3	1.3	0.7
IMR (per 1000)	97	92	61	49	51	46
TFR (per woman)	5.2	5.2	4.7	4.2	3.1	2.9
Life Expectancy	60	53	62	67	54	50
Urban Population (%)	46	52	53	59	42	50
GNP per capita (USD)	2349	2280	2150	2720	3100	10360
Zimbabwe						
Population (millions)	8.0	8.6	9.7	11.3	11.3	13.0
Rate of Natural Increase (%)	3.4	3.5	3.2	2.7	1.0	1.1
IMR (per 1000)	74	70	72	53	80	62
TFR (per woman)	6.7	6.6	5.8	4.4	4.0	3.8
Life Expectancy	54	56	58	54	40	41
Urban Population (%)	20	24	25	27	32.0	34
GNP per capita (USD)	630	740	660	540	620	590

(PRB, 1981, 1985, 1990, 1995, 2000c)

Demography and Development

As noted earlier, there is reciprocal relationship between development and population. The simple causalities are often argued as follows. First, for a country to develop economically, it is necessary that there be investment. Investment is only possible in a situation where the country is able to save, *ceteris paribus*. In situations where there is a high rate of population increase as was the situation in most less developed nations during the past twenty-five years, saving and investment become minimal if not impossible; and this impacts negatively on development. The minimal savings are largely a result of higher consumption patterns necessitated by large proportions of dependants. For instance, the proportion of the population less than fourteen years averaged about 35 per cent in the less developed nations during the period under discussion. This compares to an average of 20 per cent in developed nations, and about 43 per cent in Africa. On the other hand, development impacts on demographic characteristics especially because it changes values underlying the demographic determinants.

The ensuing section covers the relationship between development and components of population growth in Africa. The bulk of the discussion is on development, values and fertility in Sub-Saharan Africa (SSA). Brief discussion will be on mortality and migration for two reasons. First, human beings value mortality to the extent that all population policies are unidirectional with regard to mortality. They are aimed at reducing mortality and increasing longevity. Second, even when there is high population growth, a country cannot ask its people to emigrate in order to reduce population pressure, for country of residence is an unalienable human right. Thus, fertility remains the component of growth most amenable to intervention with minimal negative impact, if any, on people's rights. Yet policies that are insensitive to respective people's norms and values regarding fertility have had minimal impact on such fertility. Hence, a discussion of the relationship between demography, values and population can best be started within a context of fertility and its determinants.

Development, Values and Fertility in Sub-Saharan Africa

Pre-transitional Fertility Regimes
The Sub-Saharan African (SSA) region has experienced very high fertility levels for decades amidst sustained fertility declines in the developed world. However, it is clear that fertility decline is now underway in SSA (Table 6.1). What explains the sustained high fertility levels in pre-transitional (integration in the world economy and relative democratisation of political society are two important dimensions of the transition) SSA, and what has changed in the mix of such interacting variables that has ushered in fertility decline in the region? In answering these two

questions, this discussion focuses on factors underlying high fertility levels and subsequently the fertility decline, highlighting the interplay between development, values and fertility.

It must be noted that pre-transitional Africa has been characterised by a mosaic of strongly contrasting levels of fertility and a commensurate variety of socio-cultural practices whose underlying values are indeed variable (Mhloyi 1988). Pre-transitional fertility regimes are largely governed by supply variables to the extent that a shift from a natural to a controlled fertility regime is often paralleled by a shift not only in the relative importance of supply vis-à-vis demand variables, but also a change in the relative importance of the supply variables (1988). The most important supply variable in transitional societies is contraception which is intended to regulate fertility in order for couples to realise their desired number of children (demand for children).

In this chapter, fertility is perceived as a function of proximate determinants or supply variables which are, among others, duration of marriage, primary and secondary sterility, birth intervals, breastfeeding, pregnancy wastage and infant mortality in pre-transitional societies. In addition to these variables, a proximate determinant which typifies transitional societies is contraception. In turn, these variables are affected by background or development factors. The development variables include, among others, education, urbanisation, public health, employment, income, media or information. These variables have a reciprocal relationship with values. What happens as countries move from a pre-transitional to a transitional fertility regime?

In pre-transitional, SSA high value is placed on fertility to the extent that fertility supply variables are the dominant determinants underlying such fertility. In SSA, fertility has had, and continues to have, an economic and psycho-social value which is commensurate with the level of development in respective communities. In pre-transitional subsistence and agrarian societies, children are perceived as assets since they provide labour along with their mothers whose productivity in the fields is perceived only as a necessary support for their most important role: reproduction (Boserup 1970; Kamuzora 1987; Mhloyi 1987). In these communities, fertility is the essence of femininity, while infertility is generally perceived as a curse from the gods (Mhloyi 1987). As children were perceived to offer economic security to their mothers, such mothers also accrued status with increased childbirth.

Generally, women in pre-transitional Africa were not educated nor employed, hence their consequent low status. With colonisation, came pockets of development in urban areas. In Southern Africa, these pockets necessitated the splitting of African families as men were expected to migrate to urban areas for work while women remained in their rural homes. At that time, it was worthwhile to educate the boy-child who had to be prepared for urban employment. The girl-child was not expected to migrate to urban areas, for such was associated with prostitution.

Note that the education of the boy-child was also linked to the utility of children who are also perceived as old-age security especially for mothers (Robertson 1984; van de Walle 1987). As noted by the Caldwells (Caldwell and Caldwell 1987:51) '[t]he African knows from personal experience that high fertility does not carry economic penalties'. Instead, numerous children are economic assets since they provide labour from childhood through adulthood; they provide old-age security and prestige to their parents. Granted that children are so valued within high mortality contexts, high fertility is valued because it assures parents of some surviving children.

High fertility also has a cultural value attached to it. As maintained by van de Walle (1987), in the mind-set of the traditional man, in his world of hunting, sowing and reaping, fertility is the first value: fertility of the fields, of domestic and wild animals, indeed fertility of the woman. Children are valued for the extension of the family line; boys retain and sustain the father's name. Note that within this context, the family comprises the couple and the next of kin, the woman is only connected to this kin group via her fertility. As noted by Fortes (1978), a woman does not gain adult status fully until she is a mother and not just a wife. Her future depends not on old pension, but on having sons who win her the respect of her husband and mother-in-law.

Transitional Fertility Regimes

The discussion on transitional fertility regions will draw heavily from the Zimbabwean and Zambian cases assuming that the values discussed above for SSA also pertain to these two countries which are also undergoing fertility transition with a total fertility rate which declined from over 7 children prior 1980, to 6.7 in 1981 down to 3.8 in 2005 in Zimbabwe. What has changed in the proximate determinants, indeed, the values and background factors underlying fertility?

In order to understand those factors that facilitated the decline, and their relationship to values, it is important to discuss the developmental stages that Zimbabwe has gone through in broad terms. It is argued that Zimbabwe has gone through five developmental stages: hunting and gathering, sedentary pre-colonial rural, colonial rural/urban, post-colonial rural/urban and the distant modern semi-developed stages.

In the first stage, division of labour was based more on convenience and support between sexes, and not necessarily on subordination. A large number of children was an asset. At that stage, fertility is perceived to have been low since it was necessary for the population to move from place to place in search of the means of survival.

In the second stage, the sedentary stage, predominance of the patriarchy took shape as women's contribution through fertility and food production on land which belonged to the patriarchy was perceived to enhance women's major role of child bearing. Fertility was then high, albeit not recorded. The colonial stage, which is the third stage, saw men getting more educated and urbanised with the bulk of the women remaining in the rural areas as de facto heads of households. Children were an economic asset to such mothers who depended on the assistance of their children in the cultivation of the land, the herding of animals and the building of the necessary infrastructure needed for the running of homes. Children were a source of economic, social and physical security. Fertility increased in this stage up to over 7 children per woman. The role of Christian missions in changing the valuation of types of work and thus gender relationships, should not be underestimated (Comaroff and Comaroff 1992:113-114).

The fourth stage, the post-colonial era which started in 1980, saw the government of Zimbabwe making concerted efforts to reverse the sex imbalance in education and employment. Government endeavoured to provide education to all citizens regardless of sex with the hope of enhancing marketability in the common modern labour market. More women got education and training in a number of areas such as nursing and teaching. Legislation stipulating equal pay for equal jobs were stipulated while a number of women were also appointed in positions of power, a situation which not only accrued women another source of income as they were also contributing to household incomes, but served as role models for the girl-child. More and more women were now living with their husbands in the urban areas. Within the urban context, women's decision-making powers increased. On the other hand, children became more expensive as there was need to pay for housing, food and clothing. During this period, fertility declined to 6.5 in 1984. However, urban women were further ahead in the transition with lower levels of fertility than their rural counterparts. Rural fertility declined for different reasons; education increasingly became necessary for children to be marketable in the modern labour sector hence maintaining their role of providing old-age security. Although such children were still helping with their manual labour, some parents found it necessary to reduce their fertility to the educable number of children. This need increased as the economic situation in Zimbabwe deteriorated and the cost of both children's education and health was transferred from the state to parents. Thus, fertility declined because of development and the lack of it; it became a crisis-driven fertility transition.

Zimbabwe is currently experiencing all the five stages. There are still semi-sedentary, hunting and gathering groups such as the Tembomvura of the Zambezi valley (Marindo-Ranganai 1995). These women are experiencing high fertility, approximately seven children. The bulk of Zimbabwean women still live in rural agrarian communities where children remain economic assets for a number of reasons: they provide labour to their mothers, but most importantly, they provide old-age security to their parents. Education and training for children is essential if such children will manage to provide the needed security; yet such education and training are increasingly becoming expensive. Such couples reduce their fertility to the educable number of children. In this situation, it is the lack of development that is driving fertility downwards. Note that the high cost of children is worse in urban compared to rural areas; hence, urban women have declining but lower fertility than their rural counterparts. Both groups are, however, reducing their fertility to lower levels than could have been achieved if the economic situation or development was sustaining. But the urban, thus more developed, couples are further ahead in the fertility transition. Both groups are managing to effectively achieve their desired number of children because of yet another developmental factor, availability of contraception.

A small proportion of women can be described as living in the fifth stage, the modern developed stage in which they are educated, employed and holding positions of power in work places. Such women have status not only in society, but also in the extended families within which they are daughters-in-law. Such status affords them the opportunity of having small families with minimal or any reprisals from in-laws – a reversal of a cultural value because of development. It is important to highlight at this juncture that these women are a "squeezed generation"; they feel obligated to help their parents while at the same time do not like to depend on their children for their old-age security. Such women are investing for themselves for the future through life insurances and other investments. At the same time, they are also investing heavily in their children, not for parent's old age security per se, but in order to make sure their children will be able to support them in the future. Fertility for this group of women is declining because the cost of children is high as they send their children to expensive schools. These parents also have competing needs and tastes that are incompatible with high fertility. Such tastes are ushered in by development that is thus eroding pro-natalistic values.

One can summarize this brief exposition by noting that the interplay of development and values has culminated in the observed fertility levels, hence demographic transition in Zimbabwe. First, the lack of development in pre-transitional Zimbabwe supported high levels of fertility since children were an economic asset with minimal economic costs. In addition, couples had not been exposed to the whole notion of family planning and family limitation of the nature necessitating substantial fertility decline. Family planning during the colonial era was only perceived as a colonial gimmick to reduce the African population. Second, the ushering in of development in the form of increased urbanisation and education altered values regarding production and reproduction. Yet the high value placed on sons as the inheritors of their fathers negatively impacted on the education and employment of women. "High producers" were those people who were educated and working in the modern labour market. They were valued in society for their ability to produce incomes that could purchase goods and services unavailable to the agrarian communities. Within the urban settings, the cost of children also increased, people were also exposed to new goods and services commensurate with modernisation. Such modernisation not only eroded the value of children, but it also redefined the status of women. Fertility and income-generation complemented to define high status for women. Such development shifted the tastes away from children towards consumer goods. At the same time it ushered in family planning services while legitimising the whole notion of family planning. Today, even the least developed couples are exposed to their successful low fertility urban counterparts and desire to achieve such success, albeit at modest levels. The role model family has commensurately shifted from a high fertility to a low fertility one. High fertility increasingly gets associated with backwardness; it is development that changes values which in turn determines population.

A cursory assessment of the Zambian situation also shows that fertility levels and trends are influenced by developmental variables. For instance, education has persistently shown a depressant impact on fertility since 1980. In all census years, women with no education had half a statistical child more than those with tertiary education. Furthermore, between 1980 and 2000, women with no education, primary, and secondary education experienced increases in the TFR (Total Fertility Rate). In contrast, those with tertiary education experienced a slight decline in fertility. Similar findings were observed on the basis of Zambia Demographic and Health Survey findings. These, for example, show that women who have some secondary education experienced a steady decline in fertility, with the fertility rate for such women dropping buy one birth over the period from 1992 to 2001/2002.

Table 6.2: Total Fertility Rate by Educational Background: Zambia Census Year

Education	1980	1990	2000
No education	6.1	7.6	7.4
Primary	6.9	7.4	7.4
Secondary	4.7	5.9	6.4
Tertiary	3.9	3.2	3.5

(CSO, 2003a: 105)

Development, Values and Mortality

As noted earlier, people, regardless of level of development, value life to the extent that policies and programmes on mortality are often aimed at reducing morbidity and mortality. However, development has a significant impact on the achievement of health. It impacts on factors underlying morbidity and mortality; hence the differential mortality levels between developed and less developed nations. A discussion on factors underlying the modern rise in world population will assist in showing the relationship between development, values and mortality.

Factors Underlying Massive Mortality Decline

Although there are at least three schools of thought on factors underlying the decline in mortality, hence modern rise in population since 1650 – which include the medical (Razzell 1974), public health (Griffith 1967) and nutrition (McKeown 1976) – it is clear that all these factors are developmental. It is often argued that mortality decline was underlined by a host of factors that include: improved agriculture that necessitated the production of food and the consequent reduction in malnutrition. It is argued that industrialisation reduced mortality through the production of useful goods and services such as iron ploughs, steam engine, soap and other things. In turn, the production of soap facilitated the improvement of personal hygiene. Public health in the form of improved water supply and sewage disposal, and the reduction of water and airborne diseases all conspired to reduce mortality. The discovery of asepsis and anti-sepsis by John Lister facilitated the killing of disease-causing agents. This was complimented by the discovery of immunology that necessitated immunisation against killer diseases such as smallpox by Jenner, chicken pox by Koch and diphtheria by Behring and Roux. The discovery of drugs against syphilis by Ellick also enhanced health. Transport facilitated the transportation of all these discoveries, including that of food to the rest of the developed regions. As people's nutrition improved, as they got used to certain disease causing agents, people became more resistant to diseases, while the virulence of certain diseases also reduced. In addition to these discoveries was a change in attitude towards workers that led to social reforms that improved working conditions while prohibiting child labour.

Note that all these factors are a consequence of the overall development within contexts where life was, and continues to be valued. Mortality in the developing nations started to decline fairly substantially in the 1950s. In SSA the decline was necessitated largely by the importation of medical technology such as the wonder drugs. As colonialists built cities, they imported the public health knowledge and measures that they had enjoyed in their homes into the urban areas which became islands of development. Tertiary care was facilitated at central hospitals. However, substantial public health measures such as public sanitation, safe water and personal hygiene could not be implemented especially in the rural areas where the bulk of people reside. Agriculture has also not improved to the levels of the developed nations; to the extent that malnutrition remains the most important underlying cause of infant and child deaths especially in SSA. As one can note, mortality declined to the extent that life expectancy increased to as high as 60 years in some countries in SSA; mortality levels of the developed nations will be achieved in Africa once there is significant developmental gains. What underlies the increase in mortality in SSA in a context of declining mortality in the developed world?

The increase in mortality in SSA since the mid-1980s is a consequence of high levels of HIV and AIDS. Lack of development enhances the spread and impact of HIV in SSA. First, little knowledge regarding the aetiology of disease makes it difficult for people of SSA to even appreciate HIV as the cause of the increasing mortality so far observed. Within SSA there are many social practices that enhance the spread of HIV. Such practices include, among others, polygamy, levirate, widow cleansing ceremonies, virginity testing by fathers-in-law, betrothal of young girls to older males and ceremonial and social sharing of sexual partners. Perennial poverty not only exposes a population to more disease, but also necessitates commercial sex work, and the moral/spiritual poverty that enhances the demand for such commercial sex work characterises the SSA region. For all these reasons, the entire sexually active population in SSA is at risk of HIV infection, unlike in the developed nations where high-risk groups could be clearly identified. This poverty, or lack of development, makes HIV a death sentence for most of the people who get infected by the virus, especially because most people cannot afford the anti-retroviral drugs now commonly used in the developed world to delay the progression of HIV to AIDS. One can simply argue that people die in their thousands from AIDS in Africa not because they do not value life. To the contrary, SS Africans value life; however, the lack of development does not enable the African man and woman to preserve their lives!

Development, Values and Migration

Introduction

Most theories of migration maintain that people migrate from areas of less development, and therefore less opportunities, to areas of development and opportunities (Lee 1968). In SAA such migration is dominated by the rural-urban type. Consistent with this argument is the argument that people are attracted by education and employment opportunities and a more comfortable life-style, the so-called pull factors, while they are pushed away from the rural areas by lack of such amenities, the push factors. This argument holds for migration within and between countries. The ensuing discussion intends to support these assertions drawing heavily from the Zimbabwean and Zambian experiences.

The Zimbabwean Experience

Data from Zimbabwe (Table 6.3) shows that Zimbabwe's net migration was negative since 1980. During the 1980-1984 period, there was a mass exodus of the white population from Zimbabwe. Indeed, this was largely politically precipitated. In fact, the white emigration was somewhat counterbalanced by the immigration of black Zimbabweans who had been in the Diaspora, having run away from the war. The massive emigration fairly stabilised from the late 1980s to the end of the 1990s. From 1998, emigration started to increase from about 1,375 emigrants and peaked in 2005 that recorded about 10,986 emigrates. We should note that the current emigration is paralleled by the deterioration of the economic situation and hence the lack of development. Zimbabwe has lost large numbers of both professionals and non-professionals alike to other countries where they go in search for better employment opportunities. These opportunities are being sought in the developed nations such as Britain, Australia, New Zealand and the United States of America.

During the 1992-2002 period, a significant proportion of the internal migration was between rural and urban areas within Zimbabwe. For instance, while net migration for the two largest cities, Harare and Bulawayo, respectively, was about 25 per cent and 50 per cent respectively, these rates had declined to 23 per cent and 28 per cent respectively (CSO 1994; CSO, 2004). During this same period, the bulk of the rural areas had a negative net migration. Thus, both short and long-distance migration are dependent on developmental situations, while the actual migration process is also facilitated by development which is facilitating travelling for long distances.

Table 6.3: Migration in Zimbabwe 1980-2005

Year	Immigrants	Emigrants	Net Migration
1980	6407	17240	-10833
1981	7794	20534	-12740
1982	7715	17942	-10227
1983	6944	19067	-12123
1984	5567	16979	-11412
1985	5471	6918	-1447
1986	4897	3787	1110
1987	3925	5330	-1405
1988	2915	4305	-1390
1989	3342	4565	-1223
1990	2964	4224	-1260
1991	3583	4031	-448
1992	3171	2620	551
1993	3461	3056	405
1994	2921	3474	-553
1995	2901	3282	-381
1996	3286	1629	1657
1997	2483	1821	662
1998	1286	2661	-1375
1999	3152	3860	-708
2000	1747	5531	-3784
2001	752	6739	-5987
2002	966	8524	-7558
2003	643	8950	-8307
2004	987	12110	-11123
2005	643	11629	-10986

The Zambian Experience

Historical Oatterns of Migration

Early migratory trends were spurred on by policies pursued by the British Colonial Office and its agent, the British South Africa Company. These policies were all designed to encourage labour migration, first to the mines of South Africa and later to Northern Rhodesia's own Copperbelt. Among these policies were those that prevented alternatives to wage labour, which included outlawing traditional subsistence systems and cash cropping, and enforcing hut and poll taxes (Chipungu 1992; Seleti 1992; Vail 1983).

Colonialism established a system by which migrant labourers were temporary town dwellers, in town solely for employment, while maintaining their real home in the village. Residence and housing were restricted to specific areas of town, and for men only. Women's employment in town was banned until the late 1950s and licences for business were given to Africans only in the Native Territories (Seleti 1992). In the late 1950s, however, restrictions on travel, work and housing were eased and employment opportunities for women became more readily available (Schuster and Van Pelt 1993; Schuster 1979). By the time of independence in 1964, all such restrictions were lifted, and people could flow to and from town, and more importantly, find better and more permanent employment, as well as establish long-term households there.

Yet, despite the potential for decreasing links with the rural family that more freedom of movement and longer residence in town might encourage, the pattern of circulatory migration persisted into the 1970s (Chilivumbo 1985; Ohadike 1981). Using data from the 1980s, Ogura (1991) suggests that while circular migration might have decreased during recent years in Zambia, town migrants still ultimately return to their home villages upon retirement, and thus maintain some kind of link with home communities. Rural-to-urban migration is necessitated by the search for education and jobs, from areas of little development to areas of greater development.

Contemporary Patterns of Migration

Post-independence migratory flows between 1963 and 1980 followed the normal "gravity" pattern whereby the nearest attractions were preferred. It was from the less developed rural areas to the more developed urban areas.

An analysis of migratory patterns between 1980 and 2000 shows the pattern decreasing the importance of rural-urban migration and the emergence of urban-rural and urban-urban migration. Overall, the picture that emerges shows that urban-rural migration is taking dominance over rural-urban migration. The economic recession has made migration to the Copperbelt, Central, and Lusaka less attractive than it was before independence. The economic recession has been more pronounced in the mining industry whilst the more diversified economy of Lusaka still exerts an influence in attracting migrants.

It is clear that migration is influenced by development patterns as shown in Table 6.4 below that compares net migration, poverty, levels and income. This shows that between 1980 and 2000, the more impoverished provinces like Northern, North-Western, Eastern, Luapula and Western provinces experienced significant losses, whilst richer and more developed provinces like Lusaka and the Copperbelt had net gains in population.

Table 6.4: Relationship between Migration and Development Indicators in Zambia

	Per capita Income (US$)	Overall	1980 Poverty	1990	2000
Zambia	347.4	73			
Residence					
Rural		83			
Urban		56			
Province					
Central	271.6	77.0	12.4	13.6	12.8
Copperbelt	414.5	65.0	22.2	7.0	-6.1
Eastern	311.8	80.0	-26.9	-14.0	-5.7
Luapula	243.1	81.0	-15.1	-10.2	-3.4
Lusaka	588.6	52.0	33.1	27.8	21.2
Northern	265.7	81.0	-23.8	-14.2	-6.9
North –Western	263.7	76.0	-21.1	-13.6	-5.2
Southern	362.8	76.0	-3.3	-4.2	-5.8
Western	210.2	89.0	-13.8	-11.3	-6.3

p103 p. 4 (ZDHR, 2004 estimates)

(CSO, 2003a:4, ZDHS, 2007i:103)

The patterns of migration in Zambia and Zimbabwe, therefore, are broadly similar as economic and political change and legal and social restrictions determine most of the dynamics. However, it is interesting that the connection to a cultural and social setting in a rural context retains some purchase as can be seen in the circulatory migration patterns – even if the circulation is co-determined by economic factors.

Conclusion

The demography of any nation is affected by three components of population growth: fertility, mortality and migration. In turn, these components of growth take place within socio-economic and cultural nexi with variable values, hence differential demographic characteristics between and within countries. The values regarding reproduction, mortality and migration are affected by development, yet values also affect development. And demography impacts upon development: it is an interplay of reciprocal relationships as shown in Figure 6.1 below.

Yet, this simple causality that underlies most of the argumentation above only works on an aggregate level and the explanation is a rational choice-based model of a complex reality in which new meaning develops over time and with many variations. The fact that it does seem to play out in the terms that were suggested at the beginning does not mean that a closer reading of the material and the data from other methodologies will not enhance our understanding of the dynamics and the mechanisms of change. We still cannot conclude decisively what the direction of causalities is. To answer that question, a qualitative analysis is needed and, even then, such an analysis will be dependent on theoretical points of departure.

Figure 6.1: Interplay of Reciprocal Relationships between Demography and Development

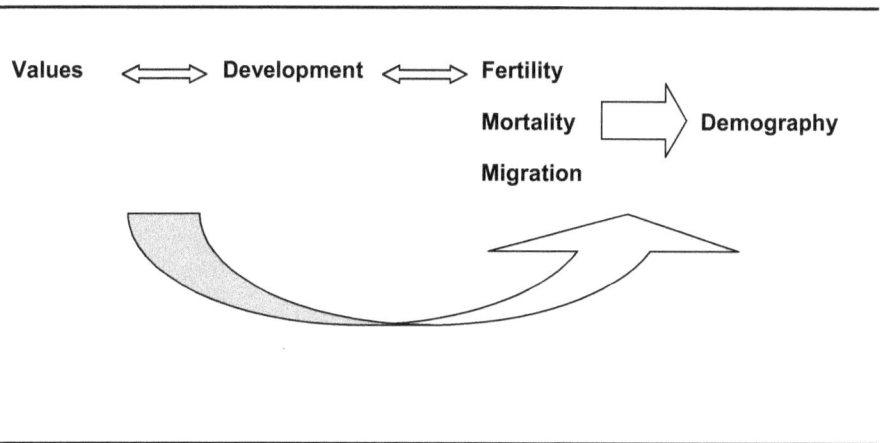

The intricate relationship between values, development and demography also emphasizes the need for holistic intervention programmes if changes, especially, in values, development and demography are to be effected. For instance, efforts to reduce the rates of population growth, especially in Africa where children were highly valued, through the provision of family planning did not yield results. However, as developmental factors changed, such undermined the value of children, thereby rendering contraception logical. And if mortality is to be significantly reduced in Africa, it is necessary to tackle poverty thereby enhancing development, the driver to good health. It is imperative to repeat the cry by developing nations in the 1970s when family planning was being pushed into the region: "Development is the best pill". With development, the exodus of professionals from the poor countries of Africa to the developed nations will abate; the high levels of fertility will reduce, while the high levels of morbidity and mortality will be the story of the past. Such changes will be the bedrock of increased development and human welfare in Africa. The value system will change commensurately.

7

Human Values, African Values, Southern African Values? On Work[1]

Hans Müller (with Tania van Heerden)

Introduction

In this chapter, we explore and compare work value orientations of people in Europe and Africa and then focus on work ethic and religion in three African countries in the Southern African region. The two themes deal with a key aspect of perceptions about Africa in that work orientation and work ethic would somehow explain something of the lack of development in Africa. The analysis follows previous analyses of work orientation and work ethic closely in order to attempt a duplication of the methodology that is used in other contexts and learn from the result of such a study when including Africa or focusing on Africa.

Of course, comparative research that attempts to come to some conclusion about African culture and values would do well to compare Africa to other parts of the world. We have mostly compared African countries among themselves in the previous sections as the main aim of the project has been to compare African countries in Southern Africa. In this chapter, some effort is made to also compare work orientation in Africa to work orientations in a part of the world that is often transposed as 'the other' of Africa, namely Europe.

The second comparison between South Africa, Zimbabwe and Tanzania (sample determined by data available, but useful in spite of that) echoes the European-African comparison in that it compares the most industrialised and modern country in Africa with close neighbours that are significantly different economically, but could be seen as relatively similar in terms of culture and cultural exposure to Europe – especially on the level of exposure to Christian missionary activity.

Work Values Analysed in Europe and Southern Africa

The African and European continents differ not only in terms of economic wealth and development or the existence of welfare states, but also in political development, religion, labour markets and working conditions. Not only have African workers increasingly been exposed to the quick changes of a globalised labour market (Castells 1996a; Kothari et al. 2002:32) and have adapted to a certain extent through migration (Crush and Fraynes 2010; Bush 2007:49-80), but the even more massively momentous changes of global markets in terms of commodity prices, primary resource supply and demand and capital and currency fluctuations require even more extreme adaptation (Kothari et al. 2002:17-21). Large majorities of the African people still live under conditions of (extreme) poverty and physical insecurity and most African economies are currently still predominantly agrarian. Work, therefore, means something different for most Africans than for most Europeans in that African work is mostly agrarian, often subsistence farming, and if urban and industrial, mostly significantly more uncertain than in Europe. One has to be careful not to fall into the trap of thinking that African communities and people are fixed in the agrarian mode. The reality is that Africa will be a majority urban continent by 2030 (Cohen 2006) while Southern Africa as a region already has more than 50 per cent of the population living in cities. At the same time, globalisation and Africa's exclusion and marginalisation through many different dynamics has meant the concept 'work' has a significantly different meaning in the 'Fourth World' (Castells 1998).

One of the most damning indictments of colonial, neo-colonial and neo-liberal global arrangements in Southern Africa has been the way in which labour was first of all created (Bundy 1988; Comaroff 2001), then moved around almost at will (Burawoy 1976) and now mostly discarded as insignificant or 'irrelevant' (Castells 1998:341)

On the other hand, industrial production has occurred in Africa for at least a century in mining and agriculture and currently, globalisation and the internationalisation of labour and business play a role – significantly so in Southern Africa. Wage-labour itself and processes of specialisation, changing work-place authority, and cost-benefit calculation have been part of African work experience for quite some time (Sharp and West 1982). The dynamics that cause uncertainty in labour conditions in Europe have also reached Southern Africa or at least South Africa. South African firms are now also moving toward a greater use of 'flexible workers, through casual labour, contract labour, subcontracting to smaller firms, homeworkers and other "outworkers", and agency workers' (Webster 2002:186). However, the legal and organisational protection in South Africa is considerably lower than in Europe and this may be even more so in the rest of Africa. Thus, it seems likely that the African's work orientations will differ from the European's orientations to work.

But within Europe, differences do exist. The trajectories of modernisation, individualisation, emancipation, globalisation, internationalisation, etc., are far from uniform (Ester et al. 1994; Hagenaars et al. 2003), and there are obvious differences in working conditions, work activities and organisations, (use of) production technologies, and employment opportunities also within European borders. Hence, in Europe also differences in work orientations are likely to be found.

The main purpose of this section is to explore people's orientations to work and to investigate if and how these orientations are shaped by characteristics of each individual as well as by distinctive features of the societies they are living in. Kalleberg and Stark (1993:182) argued that 'structures operating at macroscopic levels (such as states)' affect people's interests, motivations and their '"conceptions of the desirable" regarding work'. Since these 'structures' differ so much, it seems likely to assume that they are important attributes of people's work orientations.

A large body of research has developed suggesting that work orientations can be classified along a small number of categories. Such orientations are usually based on motives of why people work (Yankelovich et al. 1985:39) or on answers to questions about what one wants from a job (Herzberg et al. 1959:6). Although several dimensions can be distinguished, broadly speaking the motives to work and job attributes mentioned are organised around two kinds of work orientations that strongly correspond with Arendt's (1958) distinction between work attributes that stimulate personal development ('work'), and the less pleasant attributes of a paid job ('labor'). A distinction is, therefore, made between intrinsic and extrinsic work qualities.

An intrinsic work orientation refers to the idea that the main goal of labour is in the work itself: work provides the 'opportunities for further development of personal skills and an interest in the work promoted by the activity' (Tarnai et al. 1995:140). In other words, work is regarded as a means to utilise one's capacities and providing opportunities for personal development and unfolding. Another commonly used term for this orientation is expressiveness because it emphasises 'inner growth rather than external signs of wealth' (Yankelovich et al. 1985:34).

A work orientation is called extrinsic when work is regarded a means of achieving goals that are outside work. 'Expectations of work are in direct relation to the effects of employment (high income, advancement)' (Tarnai et al. 1995:140). Work is mainly seen as 'serving the immediate needs for the maintenance of life' (MOW 1987:3), a means to get an income and other life securities. In other words, the 'key words are "standard of living" and "productivity," and the values center on being part of the productive process and on the creation of capital' (Yankelovich et al. 1985:34). Favourable circumstances and working conditions, good pay, job security, good physical working environment, not too much stress and pressure, good working hours, and generous holidays are stressed because they reduce unpleasant job characteristics.

These orientations have been validated in scores of studies. However, these studies were mainly confined to highly developed, industrial and post-industrial, mostly Western societies (Zanders 1994; Harding and Hikspoors 1995; Zanders and Harding 1995; Tarnai et al. 1995); and the question is whether similar dimensions can be found in non-Western, e.g., African and Eastern European countries, as well.

Another question deals with how to understand and explain why people adhere to these orientations. Although work orientations have been studied at individual level, investigations on the effects of individual features and societal characteristics are rare. Part of the explanation will be found in individual characteristics, but as we argued above, it seems also likely that the context will have an impact too. Both will be further explored, and in section 2, we start with formulating some hypotheses on the impact of country or macro characteristics on people's work orientations.

In section 3, we turn to the individual level. We focus on some basic socio-demographic features of individuals that are often seen as determinants of values in general and thus likely also of work values. As said, work orientations have been investigated mainly in the West and the distinction between expressive or intrinsic and extrinsic or extrinsic work values was invented to understand the transformation in such orientations in societies that gradually were transforming from agrarian into industrial and modern, highly developed welfare states (Yankelovich et al. 1985). It remains to be seen if similar work orientations can also be found in non-western contexts, and if the determinants of (Western) work orientations are also the determining attributes of people's work orientations in non-Western contexts.

In section 4, we present the data, measurements and analytical strategy, and the results of our analyses are presented in section 5. In section 6, the main conclusions from our analyses are drawn and we discuss the implications for our theoretical views.

Work Values and their Antecedents

The literature suggests links between orientations towards work and the stages of societal development. In *The World at Work* (Yankelovich et al. 1985:33-34), it is argued that in traditional, agrarian societies, sustenance predominated people's reasons to work. Work was regarded a 'necessary evil' to survive. In industrialised society, the main focus was on economic growth and the accumulation of money and possessions. In work, material success was strongly emphasised or in other words, an instrumental or extrinsic work orientation had developed. In contemporary advanced welfare states, work is not any longer a necessity to provide security and the satisfaction of fundamental or 'lower' needs. Instead of focusing on economic growth and material expansion, quality of life issues, care for the environment, individual autonomy and well-being became key issues. These were increasingly seen as dependent upon self-development and self-realisation. This development could not have happened if in society certain conditions were not met, such as securing people's basic needs. In modern advanced, rich, welfare states, such conditions are satisfied and 'work no longer means "Adam's curse" – a disagreeable necessity undertaken solely for survival purposes' (Yankelovich et al. 1985:13).

We are, of course, interested in whether this conceptualisation of work makes sense in an African context. The comparison between Africa and Europe is interesting in its own right, but the focus here is the relevance and staying power of the conceptualisation of work in terms of the distinction between expressive and instrumental orientations to work.

Due to an unprecedented economic growth and the emergence of the modern welfare state, people's priorities shifted from an emphasis on survival and economic security to achieving psychological benefits and concerns of personal well being and the fulfilment of higher needs such as personal development, creative self-expression, recognition (Yankelovich et al. 1985:13). With regard to work values, these developments are assumed to have triggered the emphasis on intrinsic work qualities.

Economic development and the resulting increase in wealth and welfare are considered 'determining forces' for the expansion of individual choice in some (mostly European) countries. The economic expansion, especially after World War II, produced unprecedented high levels of affluence for an expanding middle class in Europe, but also significant growth in African countries. This affluence enabled, in some countries in Europe, but not really in Sub-Saharan Africa, the creation of a system of welfare arrangements guaranteed by the state, which eventuated in a comprehensive de-commodification of labour. The welfare state has made its citizens much more independent of the labour market, because people's incomes are guaranteed by the state and no longer solely dependent upon a job. Therefore, it can be assumed that work orientations are linked with a country's level of prosperity. Our hypothesis is that the inhabitants of more prosperous and secure societies (in terms of quality of life as well as in economic securities) would have a greater tendency towards an intrinsic work orientation than people in less affluent and less secure societies. We, therefore, also suppose that the opposite will mostly be true in African countries.

In post-modern, post-industrial society, the applications of 'mechanical labour' have increased tremendously due to rapid technological innovations in general and the introduction and advancement of the computer in particular. Labour tasks in information society shifted gradually into services using the latest information and communication technologies which implied a loss of lower or semi-skilled manufacturing jobs and the gain in high-technology, high-skilled service positions (Turner 1997:38). Such jobs require knowledge, high-tech skills, the application and use of modern communication means, innovation as well as creativity and flexibility of employees in post-industrial societies. These are all elements that seem to go with an intrinsic orientation to work that emphasise inner growth and individual autonomy. Thus, people will be more inclined to emphasise intrinsic work qualities in societies which have high levels of education, high tech communication means, and where a large proportion of or most working people are occupied in the service sector.

Because as argued above, in industrial society the main focus was on pay, fringe benefits and work security or in other words on instrumental, extrinsically rewarding work attributes, it is to be expected that, the larger the secondary or industry sector in a society is, the more its people will stress extrinsic work values.

Large income inequalities may motivate people to find ways to decrease the differences in incomes. One way to achieve that is to get higher payments for work. Thus, it can be suggested that large income inequalities in society are conducive to stressing material work qualities because work is regarded a means to improve one's financial position and as such lowers the inequality in society. In case the income gap is not so big, people will be less inclined to work for money, because it will not improve their position on the social ladder. In case of small income inequalities, work is likely to be seen as a means to satisfy personal needs of self-fulfilment. Hence, people in societies with large income inequalities will emphasise material aspects in work, while people in more equal societies will emphasise intrinsic work values.

Apart from such structural factors, characteristics of a cultural nature may also play a role in explaining the differences and similarities in work orientations between the countries. For example, Lipset (1996:72) noted that individual freedom and personal responsibilities are much more valued by Americans than by Europeans. Browne (1997) argued that because American society is pragmatic, stressing efficiency, productivity and competence, while Australian society is less oriented towards success, personal achievement and organisational growth, it seems likely that 'extrinsic factors, such as salary and promotion, would be more important to Americans than Australians' and that 'intrinsic motivators, such as self-expression and affiliation, would be relatively more important to Australians than Americans' (Browne 1997:63). Following such arguments, it can be expected that the more individualistic a society is, the stronger the emphasis will be on material work qualities.

Finally, Hofstede (2001:15) qualifies cultures in terms of masculine and feminine – as one of five critical dimensions of cultural difference. The key characteristics of masculine society are material success, money and things, being ambitious, living for work, stressing competition and performance. Feminine societies are the opposite. Typical of feminine societies is that work is seen as a means to live, and cooperation, solidarity and quality of work life are emphasised (Hofstede 2001:318). Thus, the more a national's culture stresses competition, material success, being ambitious, etc., the more likely its people will prefer extrinsic work values and the less emphasis will be found on intrinsic work qualities.

Individual Determinants of Work Orientations

The literature on work orientations reveals a number of interesting determining factors for differences in work values at the individual level.

It is often argued that, at least in Europe, young people will display a more intrinsic work orientation, because they were raised and socialised in a prosperous society where all their basic human needs are satisfied. For young people, work is not so much a necessity to survive, but merely 'a means to acquiring the good things in life and for achieving [....] the intangibles of social identity, independence, self-esteem, creative self-expression, recognition, fulfilment of potentials, and social stimulation' (Yankelovich et al. 1985:13). Older people, who were raised and socialised during a period when scarcity and insecurities played an important role, are likely to display higher levels of extrinsic work values and lower levels of intrinsic work values.

It remains to be seen if such arguments also apply to the African context. In general, Africans have become poorer in the last three decades and there have been more violent wars than before. Further, only South Africa seems on track to reach some of the Millennium Goals. The other African countries that we analyse here were slipping back on many of these Goals (Human Development Report 2002:47-49). Because contemporary youth in African societies are worse off than their parents, they may be more inclined to stress extrinsic work qualities than older people.

One can also expect a correlation between work orientations and level of education, because education increases people's 'breadth of perspective' (Gabannesch 1972:183), and their abilities and cognitive skills, which make them more critical towards authority, and enhances their levels of personal autonomy and ability of individual judgements. Earlier studies revealed, indeed, that the more educated people are more in favour of personal development qualities in work than less educated people (Zanders 1994:140).

Differences between men and women in their work orientations have been investigated in numerous studies, but the results are puzzling and often contradictory. It is argued that typical gender roles are rooted in socialisation and education where men and women learn and internalise to behave in accordance to 'what is required and expected on the basis of gender' (Marini et al. 1996:51).

Nevertheless, empirical research does not find substantial evidence for dramatic gender differences in work values (Rowe and Snizek 1995). Some argue that, as a result of increased gender equality, differences in work orientations have gradually disappeared (Marini et al. 1996:52). According to Hakim (1991), the reason why gender differences do not appear is because the distinction in men and women is too crude. She suggests a differentiation of women according to their commitment to work. Women who are committed to work resemble men in sharing 'long-term work plans and almost continuous full-time work, often in jobs with higher status and earnings than are typical for women' (Hakim 1991:113). Women who are not so much or not all committed to paid work prefer the homemaker role, and thus do not regard work as a means to provide opportunities for personal development and unfolding. These housewives will be less inclined to value intrinsic work qualities than work-committed women for who work provides satisfaction and self-development. Housewives may regard paid employment a necessity to earn a supplementary wage to the breadwinner. Such employment is more often 'in low-skilled, low paid, part-time, casual and temporary jobs... than in skilled, permanent jobs' (Hakim 1991:113). Hence, housewives will emphasise extrinsic or material work qualities more than work-committed women. On the other hand, it is said that because men see themselves playing the bread-winners role, they value high pay and job security. If that conventional view of men is true, it can be expected that they also will stress extrinsic work qualities more than work-committed women. If work-committed women see work indeed as an opportunity for personal development and unfolding they will emphasise extrinsic work qualities more than men and housewives. If such claims are justified, we could expect that men and housewives resemble each other in a stronger emphasis on intrinsic or material work qualities than work-committed women who in turn emphasise extrinsic work qualities. We should note that the notion of a 'housewife' would have different connotations in France than in Moldova or in Tanzania. Some of the data that we will be looking at could just be a reflection of these differences.

Finally, we not only include income as a control variable, e.g., for women who work in order to raise additional money for the household; we also have some clear expectations as to how it will affect both work orientations. The higher the income, the more the material needs will be satisfied and thus such work qualities do not have high priority. Higher incomes are usually in better jobs with better labour conditions and thus it may be expected that higher income groups will emphasise intrinsic work values.

Data, Measurements and Analytical Srategy

The individual level data come from the 1999/2000 European Values Study (www.europeanvalues.nl), and the 2000/2001 World Values Surveys (www.worldvaluessurvey.org). For information on these projects we refer to

Halman (2001), and Inglehart, Basáñez, Díez Medrano, Halman & Luijkx (2004). The selected countries (their abbreviation and number of respondents) are: Albania (al) 1,000; Austria (at) 1,522; Belgium (be) 1,912; Bulgaria (bg) 1,000; Belarus (by) 1,000; Croatia (hr) 1,003; Czech Republic (cz) 1,908; Denmark (dk) 1,023; Estonia (ee) 1,005; Finland (fi) 1,038; France (fr) 1,615; Germany (de) 2,036; Greece (gr) 1,142; Hungary (hu) 1,000; Iceland (is) 968; Ireland (ie) 1,012; Italy (it) 2,000; Latvia (lv) 1,013; Lithuania (lt) 1,018; Luxembourg (lx) 1,211; Malta (mt) 1,002; Moldova (mo) 1,008; Netherlands (nl) 1,003; Poland (pl) 1,095; Portugal (pt) 1,000; Romania (ro) 1,146; Russian Federation (ru) 2,500; Slovakia (sk) 1,331; Slovenia (sl) 1,006; South Africa (za) 3,000; Spain (es) 2,409; Sweden (se) 1,015; Turkey (tr) 4,607; Uganda (ug) 1,002; Ukraine (ua) 1,195; Macedonia (mk) 1,055; Great Britain (uk) 1,000; Tanzania (tz) 1,171; Zimbabwe (zb) 1,002.[2] Although the merged WVS/EVS data set al.so includes data from Nigeria, this country was excluded from our analyses because the Nigerian sample is skewed towards the higher educated and thus not representative for the population. Unfortunately, data of other African countries (south of the Sahara) is not available, because surveys have not been conducted in these countries. Of course, it is not very likely that the four African countries now included in our analyses, represent the whole of Africa. But in this regard, we are limited to the availability of survey data.

The Dependent Variables

The questionnaires included a number of work qualities and the respondents were asked to indicate the importance of each of them.[3] In Figure 7.1, we have displayed the overall responses in Western Europe, Central/Eastern Europe and Africa.

Work qualities such as 'good pay' and 'job security' are (still) highly valued in all countries, even in modern welfare states with low levels of insecurity. Perhaps because in 1999, jobs were not so secure (anymore) in many countries in Western Europe, while in Eastern Europe socialist ideology had assured people jobs and officially, there was not unemployment until the Iron Curtain dropped, at the time of the interviews, many people in Eastern Europe were very concerned about their job security. People in Africa, where about 80 per cent of the respondents indicated that good security is important, appeared most concerned.

Least important work qualities appear generous holidays and not much pressure. In Eastern Europe, a responsible job is less important than in Western Europe and Africa. Perhaps, this is still a heritage of Communist ideology where individual responsibility was not valued highly. There are hardly any differences with regard to the importance of a respected job, and meeting one's abilities. Western Europeans find most of these qualities less important than Eastern Europeans and Africans. Africa scores highest on 8 of the 11 work qualities, but most of all on job security and generous holidays.

Figure 7.1: Percentages of Respondents in Western and Eastern Europe and Africa Saying that these Work Qualities are Important

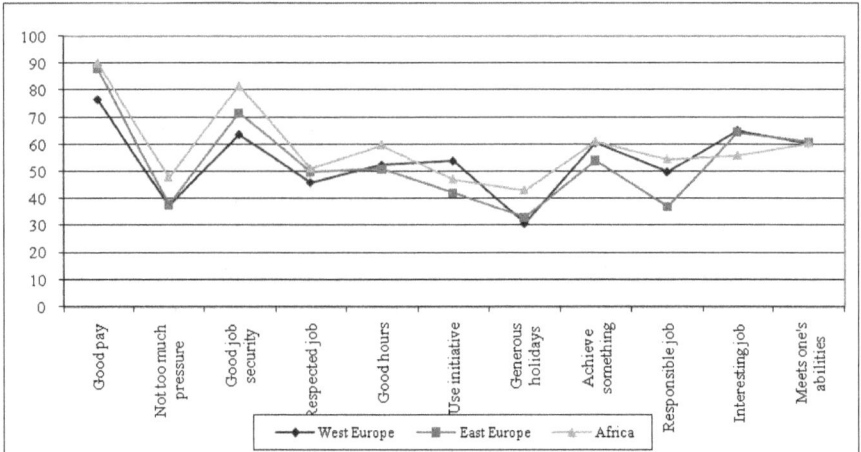

Factor analysis was applied to examine the dimensionality. Previous analyses of a more limited number of countries in Europe (Zanders 1994; Halman and Vloet 1994), yielded three factors that resemble the dimensions Yankelovich et al. (1985) had discovered. The dimension of personal development included items referring to intrinsic qualities of a job, the comfort dimension contained qualities relating to secondary work conditions and material conditions concerned financial reward and job security (Zanders 1994:136).

Our analysis using the data of all countries and weighting each country equally[4] yielded only two dimensions. The items of the comfort and material dimensions appeared to refer to one common dimension that expresses material qualities in work. The other dimension is clearly intrinsic in the sense that it includes all expressive work qualities. Respected job does not turn out to be strongly associated with the other intrinsic work qualities. It has a low loading and also appears to belong to the material conditions dimension. This may be because respect can be regarded as the consequence of being paid very well, but can also be seen as a means of self-employment and fulfilment. A respected job does not refer clearly to either intrinsic or extrinsic work values in West Europe and Africa, but appears to have an intrinsic meaning in Eastern Europe. Perhaps, this is still a manifestation of Communist era values when jobs were equal and equally respected officially.

Either way, we decided to exclude this item from our analyses and the result of a second factor analysis was much clearer in line with the two dimensions that were expected. Although good job security has a clear extrinsic connotation in Western Europe, in Africa it appears to have an intrinsic meaning while in Eastern

Europe it has neither. Again, the Eastern European finding may reflect what pertained during the Communist times when job security was not an issue. Perhaps, the importance of job security has increased in the last decade because jobs are less secure these days than before the fall of the Wall. If these 1999/2000 figures on this item are compared with the results of the 1990 survey, this indeed seems to be true. On the whole, job security is becoming of increasing importance to many people in Eastern Europe (Inglehart et al. 1998:102).

Analysing the African countries, there is some evidence that as in Europe in the past (Zanders 1994), the extrinsic orientation has two dimensions: the one referring to real material aspects like job security and good pay, the other including the comfort issues. Such results seem evidence that indeed the African context differs from the European. Elsewhere, it has been demonstrated that in the debate on materialism and post-materialism, an additional concept was needed in order to address the stage of 'pre-materialism' or underdevelopment (Lategan 2000; Kotze and Lombard 2002; Müller 2004). Our finding that in the African context a sustenance dimension can be distinguished seems to confirm that point of view. Many Africans are (still) in a struggle for survival and thus much concerned about securing their basic needs. Consequently, work values centre on sustenance and physiological security.

Because good pay and job security appeared to be problematic in the African context, we also decided to exclude these two items from our analyses. The common theme in the remaining items of the extrinsic work dimension is 'a relaxed job': not too much pressure, good hours and generous holidays.

In Table 1, the two-dimensional factor structure is displayed for the three regions separately, and from this table it is clear that the factor structures are highly similar in Western Europe, Eastern Europe and Africa. We concluded that the two work orientations are sufficiently similar in the three different contexts and thus can be used in our further analyses. We ran factor analyses on the pooled data set on the items of the two dimensions separately and factor scores have been calculated to tap the extrinsic and intrinsic work orientations.

Table 7.1: Results of Factor Analysis for each Dimension Separately in Western Europe, Eastern Europe and Africa

Instrumental qualities	Western Europe	Eastern Europe	Africa
Good pay	0.562	0.491	0.408
No pressure	0.707	0.668	0.645
Job security	0.600	0.614	0.501
Good hours	0.784	0.721	0.746
Generous holidays	0.706	0.713	0.747
% variance	45	42	39
Cronbach's alpha	0.60	0.65	0.61
Expressive qualities			
Use initiative	0.753	0.770	0.764
Achieve something	0.704	0.750	0.655
Responsible job	0.691	0.734	0.722
Interesting job	0.600	0.656	0.656
Use abilities	0.674	0.700	0.685
% variance	47	52	48
Cronbach's alpha	**0.72**	**0.77**	**0.74**

Structural and Cultural Macro Characteristics

As far as the structural macro determinants are concerned we rely on various international sources. Unfortunately, it proved impossible to find comparable measures on working conditions and labour markets. For example, unemployment statistics or welfare spending statistics for all the countries and in the same time-period appear not available particularly not for African countries. However, we were able to find some indicators on economic development, material well-being, quality of life issues, education, use of modern communication means, income inequality and characteristics of the labour market in terms of employed people occupied in the three economic sectors: agriculture, industry and services.

The data sources providing information for all countries on levels of security, welfare, quality of life, wellbeing, education and prosperity are rather limited and we had to confine ourselves to some data on economic development (GDP), and quality of life issues, such as life expectancy and adult literacy rate and the availability and use of modern communication means such as numbers of telephone mainlines, cellular mobile subscribers and Internet hosts (all per 1,000 and in the year 2000). Factor analyses on these latter three indices yielded a combined score for what we call 'communication'.

An obvious problem in analyses in which such measures as explanatory variables are included is, of course, that these characteristics are strongly correlated. Indeed, life expectancy and adult literacy rates as well as adjusted per capita income are the components of the Human Development index (HDR 2000a:147). Also our measure of communication is strongly associated with economic development measured in terms of GDP per capita (ppp) (r = .889; p < .0001 (2-tailed)). One measure of (economic and human) development seems sufficient and is calculated by means of a factor analysis on life expectancy, adult literacy, GDP per capita and communication. A high score on this dimension refers to high level of development

Income inequality is measured by the often used and well-known GINI coefficient (HDR 2000a).[5] The higher the coefficient, the more unequal the society is.

As for cultural traits, we have relied on aggregate measures on the basis of our individual level data set. The degree to which a cultural trait is favouring individual freedom appears from the percentages of people in each country that is of the opinion that people should take more responsibility for themselves. The more individualistic feature appears from agreement with individual responsibility.[6]

We relied on aggregate measures from our individual data set to establish whether cultures are more masculine or feminine, because scores calculated by Hofstede (2001) are available only for a limited number of countries. People in masculine societies stress material success, money and things, being ambitious, live in order to work, competition and performance. EVS includes few items that partially tap this concept. Material success appears from emphasising the importance of money and work.[7] Competition appears from the responses to the question whether competition is good or harmful,[8] while being ambitious appears from the opinion that hard work and determination are important qualities to encourage children to learn at home.[9] A factor analysis on these (macro) items yielded that determination as quality to teach children at home refers to another dimension. The other attributes at aggregate level appear to have something in common that resembles the dimension of masculinity-femininity. A high score indicates a masculine society.

The Independent Variables at Individual Level

Age can be simply re-coded from the question in which the respondent was asked to indicate his/her year of birth. However, our hypothesis with regard to the age effect is not so much on age in terms of 'life phase', but more in terms of generations and the different experiences of older and younger age groups in their formative years. For our purpose we distinguish six age groups: 18-24; 25-34; 35-44; 45-54; 55-64 and 65-75.

Gender is a dummy variable: 0 = male; 1 = female, but following Hakim, the category of women is further differentiated in order to tap women's commitment to work. She agreed that commitment is hard to measure, but the best available proxy for work commitment at macro level 'seems to be the percentage of women working age who are working full-time' (Hakim 1991:116). At individual level we differentiated between women who were employed and those who were housewives. It remains to be seen if 'housewife' has similar meanings in Europe and Africa even though this category is the result of self-identification of African women.

Level of education is a three-fold division in terms of qualifications attained. For each of these three levels we made a dummy variable. The top category includes all those with post-secondary school qualifications attained, the middle category includes all levels of secondary school qualifications attained and the last category includes all levels of primary school attained as well as those with no formal schooling (see also Inglehart et al. 2004:204).

Income is measured by national income variables which were re-coded into three categories (three dummy variables) in such a way that each category comprises a third of the sample as closely as possible: 1 = lower; 2 = middle; 3 = upper (see also Inglehart et al. 2004:204-210). We also added a category (dummy) for the missing responses on this variable. Income is one of these variables many people do not want to give information on. In order to avoid the number of cases dropping too much in our analyses, we have included this category. It often appears that especially higher income groups are less willing to provide information on their incomes.

Analytical Strategy

We start with some descriptive analyses comparing the countries' mean scores on both dimensions in order to find patterns in the country positions on the two work orientations. Next, a number of bi-variate analyses at macro- and individual level have been performed to test our hypotheses. Since these analyses reveal that the associations are not similar in Africa, Eastern Europe and Western Europe, we decided to run for each region separately multi-variate regression analysis to test the individual level hypotheses. It turns out that apparently, the context not only affects people's orientations, but also the determinants and the relationships between dependent and independent (determining) variables.

Results

We start our analyses with a comparison of the countries with regard to the two work orientations. The countries' mean scores are displayed in Figure 7.2.

Figure 7.2: Countries' mean Scores on the two Work Dimensions

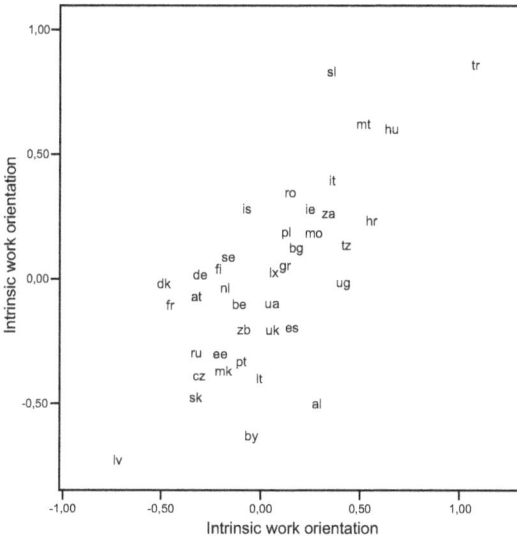

$(r = .388, p = .015;$ Spearman's rho $= .395, p = .013).$

Turkey and Latvia appear each other's opposites. In Latvia, the work qualities are far less important than in other countries, whereas in Turkey all work qualities appear important. The patterns in Denmark, France, Germany and Austria are characterised by a stronger emphasis on intrinsic work qualities and less emphasis on extrinsic qualities. Albania seems to represent the more traditional pattern of emphasis on extrinsic work qualities and low emphasis on intrinsic work values. Slovenians appear much in favour of the intrinsic work attributes, but have no strong preferences with regard to extrinsic qualities. People in Belarus share the latter indifference with regard to extrinsic qualities, but they reject intrinsic qualities most of all people. Three of the African countries are not far from each other in their work values. In particular, Uganda and Tanzania are very similar. So, the people in these two African countries are not only geographically close to each other, they are also very similar in their preferences of work attributes. In particular, Zimbabwe appears an exceptional case in the African context. The work value preference in Zimbabwe resembles the preferences in Belgium, while the work value preferences of South Africans is very similar to that of Irish people. At first sight, there are no obvious patterns in the country positions on the two work orientations. No clear distinctions appear between East and West, or Europe versus African countries.

We hypothesised that such differences may be attributed to a number of country characteristics or macro features. In Tables 7.2 and 7.3 we have displayed the simple correlations between the country characteristics and the two work dimensions for the pooled data set and for each region separately.

Table 7.2: Pearson Correlation Coefficients between Country Features and Extrinsic Work Qualities

Correlations	Pooled	W. Europe	E. Europe	Africa
Individualism	0.333*	0.766***	-0.140	-0.244
GINI	0.210	0.522*	-0.134	-0.448
Agriculture	0.356*	0.562**	0.267	0.336
Industry	-0.250	-0.060	-0.339	-0.649
Service	-0.149	-0.348	0.092	-0.037
Development	-0.370*	-0.679**	-0.013	-0.344
Masculinity	0.069	0.405*	-0.599**	-0.295
N	39	18	17	4

* p < .05; ** p < .01; *** p < .001

Table 7.3: Pearson Correlation Coefficients between Country Features and Intrinsic Work Qualities

Correlations	Pooled	W. Europe	E. Europe	Africa
Individualism	-0.031	0.459*	-0.102	-0.123
GINI	0.110	0.236	-0.005	0.326
Agriculture	0.001	0.463*	0.052	-0.391
Industry	-0.239	0.049	-0.268	0.096
Service	0.176	-0.360	0.223	0.595
Development	0.066	-0.454*	0.330	0.466
Masculinity	-0.235	0.509*	-0.555**	-0.905*
N	39	18	17	4

* p < .05; ** p < .01; *** p < .001

The characteristics of the labour market in terms of employed people in the different economic sectors do not turn out to be important predictors of people's work orientations. It seems that, taking all countries together, in agricultural societies, extrinsic work qualities are more stressed than in less agricultural societies, but contrary to what was expected, societies with large service sectors do not stress intrinsic work orientations more than agricultural or industrial societies. A society's level of development in terms of life quality and wealth seems to affect the extrinsic orientation only. As such, our hypothesis is confirmed that people in more affluent and less vulnerable societies have a lesser tendency towards an intrinsic work orientation than people in less affluent and less secure societies. Also confirmed seems our hypothesis that the more individualistic a society is, the more people are inclined to stress extrinsic qualities in work. The macro features do not seem to affect people's orientation towards work which stresses expressive or intrinsic qualities.

However, the general pattern cannot be substantiated in the three regions. Not only because in Eastern Europe and Africa the correlations appear less strong (and statistically almost never significant), also because the associations in these two regions appear opposite to what is found in Western Europe. For example, in Western Europe, countries that are more masculine stress expressive or intrinsic work qualities, which is opposite to what was expected. In Eastern Europe and in African contexts, that hypothesis can be confirmed. The intrinsic work qualities are emphasised less in more masculine societies. However, our hypothesis that extrinsic work qualities will be stressed in more masculine societies is rejected in Eastern Europe and Africa, but confirmed in Western Europe. It seems as if our arguments 'work' as expected in a Western context, but not in former communist or African contexts.

Individual Determinants

The bi-variate analyses at individual level are simple correlation analyses using Pearson correlation coefficients. These coefficients have been calculated for the pooled data set as well as for the three regions. The results are displayed in Tables 7.4 and 7.5 and Figures 7.2 to 7.5.

The older age groups are not more, but less extrinsic as far as work orientations are concerned. This is opposite to what was expected. In all three regions this is found, whereas in Western Europe (and on the pooled data) the adherence to extrinsic work qualities declines more or less linear with age, in Eastern Europe and Africa this relationship is not linear. In Eastern Europe, people aged 55-64 are (somewhat) more inclined to favour extrinsic work qualities than people aged 45-54. Eastern Europeans between 65 and 75 are far less in favour of such qualities. In Africa, the pattern is even more whimsical. As in Europe, the adherence is less among older age groups, but there is not a steady decline when one moves from the youngest to the oldest group. The adherence declines, increases, declines steadily and then increases again among the oldest age group.

Table 7.4: Pearson Correlation Coefficients between Individual Characteristics and Extrinsic Work Qualities

	Pooled	W. Europe	E. Europe	Africa
Age 18-24	0.038***	0.031***	0.036***	0.068***
Age 25-34	0.025***	0.032***	0.028***	-0.013
Age 35-44	0.012*	0.014*	0.012	0.003
Age 45-54	-0.010*	-0.008	-0.007	-0.035*
Age 55-64	-0.028***	-0.041***	-0.011	-0.045***
Age 65-75	-0.048***	-0.038***	-0.065***	-0.011
Education low	0.021***	0.040***	0.016*	-0.036*
Education medium	0.012*	-0.011	0.029***	0.037*
Education low	-0.042***	-0.035***	-0.058***	0.000
Income low	-0.004	0.012	-0.005	-0.061
Income middle	0.013**	0.014*	0.006	0.043**
Income high	-0.014**	-0.035***	0.000	0.014
Income missing	0.006	0.011	-0.004	0.012
Female work	0.021***	0.019**	0.040***	-0.048**
Housewife	0.013**	0.012	0.021**	-0.007
Male	-0.017**	-0.015*	-0.024**	0.002
N	36.945	16.683	16.409	3.853
Reference country	**MT**	**TR**	**BY**	**ZA**

* $p < .05$; ** $p < .01$; *** $p < .001$

The hypothesis that housewives stress extrinsic qualities more than working females and males can be substantiated in Europe, but not in Africa. In Africa, males appear more in favour of such qualities than housewives. Contrary to what we expected, African women who are working outside their homes are least in favour of extrinsic work qualities.

Table 7.5: Pearson correlation coefficients between individual characteristics and intrinsic work qualities

	Pooled	W. Europe	E. Europe	Africa
Age 18-24	0.055	0.048***	0.064***	0.050**
Age 25-34	0.043***	0.050***	0.045***	0.004
Age 35-44	0.006	0.004	0.015*	-0.024
Age 45-54	-0.008	- 0.019**	0.005	-0.021
Age 55-64	-0.040***	-0.040***	-0.045***	-0.014
Age 65-75	-0.073***	-0.057***	-0.097***	-0.020
Education low	-0.137***	-0.138***	-0.151***	-0.079***
Education medium	0.045***	0.038***	0.049***	0.060***
Education low	0.113***	0.121***	0.119***	0.040**
Income low	-0.086***	-0.072***	-0.085***	-0.139***
Income middle	-0.007	-0.019**	-0.005	0.036*
Income high	0.082***	0.078***	0.095***	0.045**
Income missing	0.015**	0.016*	-0.010	0.084***
Female work	0.019***	0.021**	0.035***	-0.055***
Housewife	-0.042***	-0.053***	-0.040***	-0.002
Male	0.038***	0.031***	0.053***	0.006
N	36.945	16.683	16.409	3.853
Reference country	**MT**	**TR**	**BY**	**ZA**

* $p < .05$; ** $p < .01$; *** $p < .001$

Contrary to our expectation is also that people with higher levels of education in Africa turn out to be more inclined to stress the importance of extrinsic work qualities. In Europe the relationship is reversed, although far from linear. In particular, the upper levels of education in Europe are not so much in favour of extrinsic work qualities.

A similar opposite result is found with regard to income categories. The higher income groups in Western Europe stress such extrinsic qualities least. In Africa, however, such qualities are stressed more by middle and high-income groups.

The multi-variate regression analyses that we performed for each region separately show that the explanations for individual differences in extrinsic work orientation do, indeed, differ in Africa from what is found in European countries. The individual socio-demographic characteristics are of less importance in African context than in European context and some of the effects are reversed in Africa to what is found in Europe. While in Europe working females stress extrinsic work qualities more, in the African context, working women stress such qualities less than men and housewives. In Africa, middle and higher income earners are more in favour of extrinsic work attributes, while in Europe income hardly affects this work orientation. In Europe, the age factor and level of education appear important attributes to understand the differences in this extrinsic work orientation. These factors do not matter in the African context.

Figure 7.3: Comparing Work Orientations in Regions between Age Groups

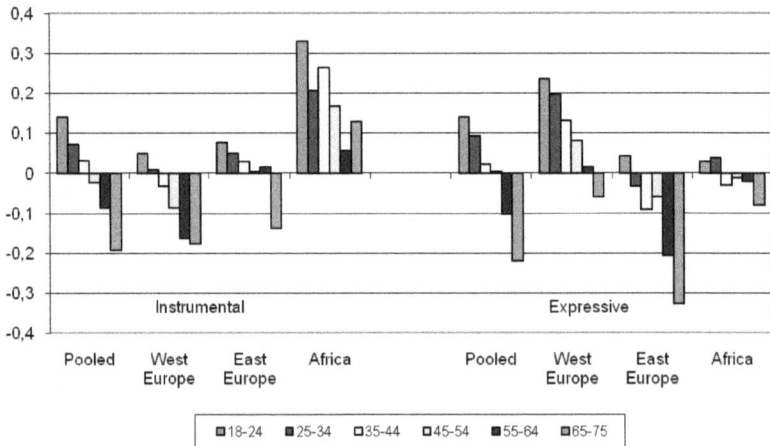

Figure 7.4: Comparing Work Orientations in Regions between Education Levels

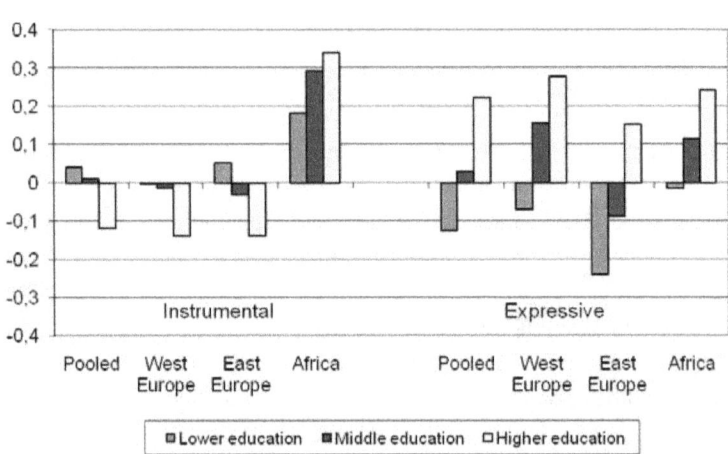

Figure 7.5: Comparing Work Orientations in Regions between Income Levels

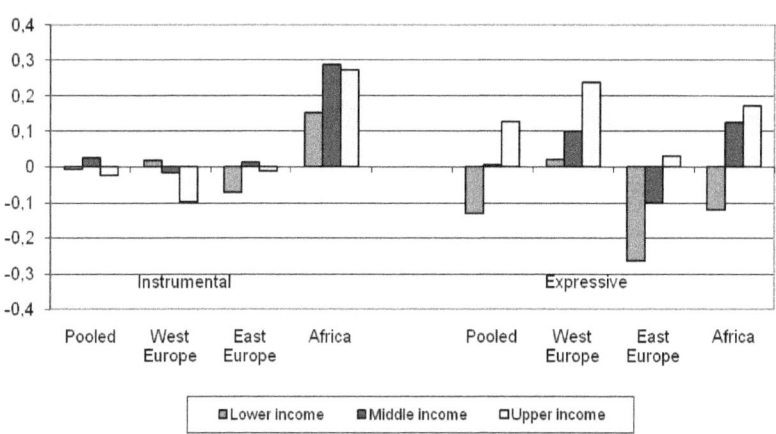

Figure 7.6: Comparing Work Orientations in Regions between Gendered Groups

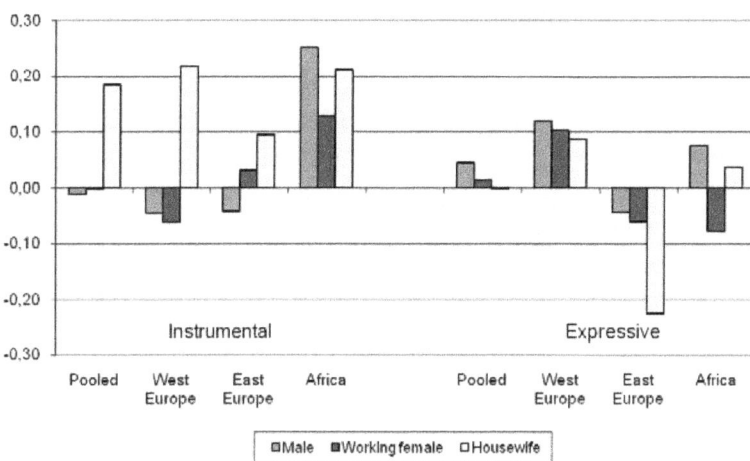

With regard to the intrinsic work orientation, it seems clear that age has the effect as predicted: older people find such qualities less important than younger people. In Africa the various age groups do not differ much. As expected, housewives in Europe are least in favour of such intrinsic work attributes at least when compared with men and working females. The differences are bigger in Eastern Europe than in Western Europe. In Africa, housewives resemble the men in this respect; and working females appear to stress such qualities much lesser than men and housewives. Level of education has an effect as expected in all three regions:

people with higher levels of education are much more in favor of such intrinsic work values than those with lower levels of education; and the same counts for income: the higher the income the more such intrinsic work qualities are considered important.

Multi-variate regression analyses performed for each region separately reveal interesting differences not only between Africa and Europe, but also in Europe between Eastern and Western European countries. The age differences are particularly important in Eastern European context. In Western Europe income differences appear slightly more important. In Africa, age is not important, but education and income appear to generate similar effects as in Europe. In both contexts, intrinsic work qualities are stressed more by people with higher education and those from higher-income groups. As such, our hypotheses are confirmed.

Work Ethos in Southern Africa Analysed

Work ethos is often portrayed as a determining factor in the economic success of a country, individuals and communities. It is seen as a factor in productivity, corruption, saving patterns and consumer behaviour at least. How work ethos compares to other important determining factors in economic success cannot be decided here. However, work ethos develops in a context in which many different processes and aspects may create the conditions for a particular work ethos or make another work ethos difficult to sustain. We would like to look at religion as one specific aspect of the context that is often deemed an important factor in the development and maintenance of a particular work ethos. In the past, it has often been argued that religion would be a determining factor for the development of a particular work ethos. We investigate this matter in a comparison between three Southern African countries and on the basis of the data provided in the survey of the 1999/2000 World Values Survey. Considering the importance of being able to control for the influence of other social dimensions of the context when investigating the role of religion in work ethos, we intended to take into account a number of other macro social dimensions of possible difference between the three African countries. This proved to be an unrealistic aspiration for our study as comparable data for a large enough sample of Southern Africa does not exist and the conclusion of the first part of the survey destroys most of the expectations that structure the usefulness of such multi-level analysis.

Our strategy is to focus simply on the claim that religion has an important influence on work ethos. We discuss the Weberian origins of this claim, some recent research on the matter and some competing theories as to the relationship between work ethos and religion. However, Weber enables us to define particular aspects of religion that should be considered in our analysis and that helps us establish an empirical argument about the matter. However, we have to define

Table 7.6a: Results Regression Analysis Extrinsic Work Orientation

	Pooled			West Europe			East Europe			Africa		
	B	SE	Beta	B	SE	Beta	B	SE	Beta	B	SE	Beta
(Constant)	0.416***	0.036		0.902***	0.041		-0.240***	0.037		0.237*	0.104	0.065
Age 18-24	0.247***	0.020	0.091	0.230***	0.030	0.081	0.257***	0.029	0.092	0.148	0.101	0.015
Age 25-34	0.210***	0.019	0.086	0.211***	0.028	0.087	0.227***	0.029	0.090	0.033	0.100	0.026
Age 35-44	0.179***	0.019	0.073	0.170***	0.028	0.069	0.189***	0.028	0.077	0.063	0.101	-0.010
Age 45-54	0.129***	0.020	0.049	0.113***	0.028	0.043	0.153***	0.028	0.060	-0.031	0.105	-0.025
Age 55-64	0.071***	0.020	0.024	0.011	0.029	0.004	0.141***	0.028	0.050	-0.101	0.112	-0.047
Male	-0.014	0.014	-0.007	0.007	0.023	0.004	-0.005	0.019	-0.002	-0.096*	0.045	0.003
Education medium	-0.067***	0.012	-0.033	-0.113***	0.018	-0.055	-0.061**	0.018	-0.031	0.006	0.038	0.000
Education high	-0.158***	0.016	-0.060	-0.148***	0.022	-0.060	-0.208***	0.024	-0.079	0.001	0.072	-0.073
Female work	0.030	0.016	0.013	0.041	0.026	0.018	0.087***	0.024	0.038	-0.176**	0.053	-0.027
Housewife	0.024	0.021	0.007	0.035	0.029	0.012	0.056	0.035	0.013	-0.101	0.071	0.066
Income middle	0.018	0.013	0.009	-0.005	0.020	-0.002	0.002	0.019	0.001	0.153***	0.043	0.048
Income high	-0.014	0.014	-0.006	-0.070*	0.022	-0.030	-0.002	0.020	-0.001	0.121*	0.050	0.030
Income missing	0.005	0.017	0.002	-0.005	0.023	-0.002	-0.031	0.031	-0.008	0.074	0.050	
R^2	0.019			0.026			0.019			0.014		
Adjusted R^2	0.018			0.025			0.018			0.011		
R^2 with country dummies	0.131			0.146			0.132			0.038		
Adjusted R^2 with country dummies	0.130			0.145			0.130			0.034		

Table 7.6b: Results Regression Analysis Extrinsic Work Orientation

	Pooled			West Europe			East Europe			Africa		
	B	SE	Beta	B	SE	Beta	B	SE	Beta	B	SE	Beta
(Constant)	0.416***	0.036		0.902***	0.041		-0.240***	0.037		0.237*	0.104	0.065
Age 18-24	0.247***	0.020	0.091	0.230***	0.030	0.081	0.257***	0.029	0.092	0.148	0.101	0.015
Age 25-34	0.210***	0.019	0.086	0.211***	0.028	0.087	0.227***	0.029	0.090	0.033	0.100	0.026
Age 35-44	0.179***	0.019	0.073	0.170***	0.028	0.069	0.189***	0.028	0.077	0.063	0.101	-0.010
Age 45-54	0.129***	0.020	0.049	0.113***	0.028	0.043	0.153***	0.028	0.060	-0.031	0.105	-0.025
Age 55-64	0.071***	0.020	0.024	0.011	0.029	0.004	0.141***	0.028	0.050	-0.101	0.112	-0.047
Male	-0.014	0.014	-0.007	0.007	0.023	0.004	-0.005	0.019	-0.002	-0.096*	0.045	0.003
Education medium	-0.067***	0.012	-0.033	-0.113***	0.018	-0.055	-0.061**	0.018	-0.031	0.006	0.038	0.000
Education high	-0.158***	0.016	-0.060	-0.148***	0.022	-0.060	-0.208***	0.024	-0.079	0.001	0.072	-0.073
Female work	0.030	0.016	0.013	0.041	0.026	0.018	0.087***	0.024	0.038	-0.176**	0.053	-0.027
Housewife	0.024	0.021	0.007	0.035	0.029	0.012	0.056	0.035	0.013	-0.101	0.071	0.066
Income middle	0.018	0.013	0.009	-0.005	0.020	-0.002	0.002	0.019	0.001	0.153***	0.043	0.048
Income high	-0.014	0.014	-0.006	-0.070*	0.022	-0.030	-0.002	0.020	-0.001	0.121*	0.050	0.030
Income missing	0.005	0.017	0.002	-0.005	0.023	-0.002	-0.031	0.031	-0.008	0.074	0.050	
R^2	0.019			0.026			0.019			0.014		
Adjusted R^2	0.018			0.025			0.018			0.011		
R^2 with country dummies	0.131			0.146			0.132			0.038		
Adjusted R^2 with country dummies	0.130			0.145			0.130			0.034		

work ethos as well. In a second section we seek a normative but non-religious definition of work ethos that can be operationalised given the data sources that we have.

The third section is a discussion of the individual aspects that may play a role in the development of a particular work ethos – like age, gender and level of education.

However, before we get to this we need to reflect on the place of religion in development in order to place the discussion of work ethos and religion in a broader context.

Religion and Development in African Society

Religion and development have been tied together at least since Karl Marx argued that the liberation of humankind will only take place if religion and philosophy can be understood to be reflections of human desires and suffering and that a new theology should make man 'the highest being for man' (McLellan 1977:73). This is the context of the discussion of religion as the 'opium of the people'. The question is how Germany will be liberated and the answer is that religion needs to be unmasked for what it is, philosophy should become active rather than abstract and the proletariat should be aligned with the aims of the revolution. The suffering which religion is an expression of can be equated with the poverty of a society. But most importantly, the kind of philosophy that is needed is a philosophy that sets the consciousness free. How does one locate the question of work and labour in this starting point?

The very simple point is that religion, as a source of motivations and orientations has to be reflected on in a study of the role of values in development. Furthermore, work and labour are critical elements of socio-economic development and the role of religion in the mobilisation of work has to be considered. It is already clear in Chapter 4 that the missionaries often had very clear ideas about the role of religion in forming good workers and the convergence between their ideas and the development of a labour force accepting of the new notion of wage-labour is discussed in Chapter 4.

It is in this larger context that the Weberian question on the relation between work ethos and religion can be posed. Max Weber was not interested in proposing a solution to the problem of creating good workers for the industrial complex. He was sociologically and historically describing the interesting coincidence that capitalism and ideas about frugality, hard work and commitment to hard work that was associated with the Protestant theology of early Calvinism seem to support each other. We similarly do not argue for a particular worldview, but would like to investigate the purchasing power of a similar argument in our time, and specifically in Africa. The reason for this is the very clear implication in much of what has been said in the rest of the book that values and culture matter in development.

The Work Ethos and Religion Constructs

One does not have to search very hard to find Western business people claiming that there is an important difference between the work ethos and general work culture in Africa and Europe. Steve Murphy, Managing Director of a large insurance company, speaking at an eminent South African business school, argued that this difference is critical to business in Africa. He differentiates between a South African, approach and an African approach, ignoring the fact that South Africans are also African, and thereby demonstrating the sense of comparing South Africa and other African countries.

'He said with reference to South Africans; "We are not patient." South African businessmen need to learn that patience is a virtue. Our impatience is a big turn-off to potential African partners. There is a much slower business ethos in Africa, in comparison to South Africa... These social rules cover the whole gamut of business and social conduct. African culture is different... In Ghana, the work ethos is slow...' (Heald 2001). One might surmise that his version of South Africans would be pretty pale.

A very different take on the matter comes from philosophical and cultural studies intent on giving perspective on unique aspects of African culture. From a point of departure that takes African community orientation as the most distinct moral and religious framework for African culture, it follows that 'the worker and the community are fused into oneness' (Teffo 1999:162). In fact, Teffo finds a clear difference 'between the African and the European attitude of concept of a worker' in that 'it acknowledges that in each and every normal person, there is a skill, knowledge or expertise potential that can contribute to, and be utilised in, the development and the advancement of the human race' (Teffo 1999:162). The European concept of a worker would presumably not acknowledge this. In all fairness, one has to note that Teffo's argument is pitched in a context of serious unemployment problems in South Africa and may be intended to argue for a re-evaluation of the humanity of workers under such conditions. He argues further that the 'communeocentrism', said to be typical of African work ethics, is 'anti-individualism' that 'relies on equal collective participation in whatever is being done' (Teffo 1999:163). African culture and work ethic is said to be imprinted by the notion of *ubuntu*, i.e. the 'basic respect for human nature as a whole' that is a 'common spiritual ideal by which all black people south of the Sahara give meaning to life and reality' (Teffo 1999:153-154).

Contrasting a European business perspective on African work ethos with that of an African philosopher is useful in that it enables one to get a sense of how much might be in the eye of the beholder. What a European may describe as 'slow' could just as well be described as taking care that all participants are persuaded that a particular decision is the right one. The more fundamental issue is obviously the alleged anti-individualism of African people. It is then striking that the formulation of both the European businessman and the African philosopher's depiction of African culture and work ethos are so utterly a-historical and, therefore, constitute a reification of culture.

Teffo does not contextualise his own argument about the anti-individualism of African culture. He makes no explicit mention of the impact of changing labour conditions (outsourcing, retrenchment, unemployment rates, etc.) in the South African situation. Moreover, communalism can been seen as is a survival strategy for the poor that is not exclusive to Africa, but can be found amongst the poor across the world as resources are shared within families and communities. The matter is further complicated in South Africa, given the presence of an extensive social welfare programme which results in the congregation of the unemployed around family members that receive government grants. The central concept of *ubuntu* is presented by Teffo as something all Africans share. *Ubuntu* does not seem to have any historical imprint – even if he later argues that moral degeneration of African values in the workplace takes place through the mixing of ethical norms of Western and African origins. It is implied that 'mixing' means degeneration and, thereby, any question about the historical nature of the concept of *ubunthu* is precluded (for a collection of perspectives on the matter see van den Heuvel et al. 2006).

Murphy's comment about the slow work ethos in Ghana is similarly a-historical. No attempt is made to understand whether there is any link between culturally required consultative processes, regulatory pressures, capacity in organisations, infrastructure, etc. and the so-called slow work ethos. There may be a variety of explanations for variations in work ethos and the cultural explanation is itself a construct that requires some unpacking. One does not expect a business person to delve into the complexities of such explanations but the a-historical depiction of an African work ethos is instructive in itself.

A different picture emerges when looking at an in-depth anthropological perspective on the changing definition of productive processes and work in the history of colonial influence in Africa. The colonial and post-colonial relationship between Europe and Africa were not only relationships of material oppression and exploitation but also processes of cultural and religious exchange. Due to the efficacy of modern technology and the political and economic processes, there is no way in which the cultural exchange could be an exchange between equals. The inequality of the cultural process does not make it less interesting to consider though. The case of the Southern Batswana in Southern Africa is a particularly interesting one if one considers the arguments of the Comaroffs about the exchange between Evangelical Protestantism and a particular African society.

They make the case that Evangelical Protestantism 'sought to reconstruct the inner being of the Tswana chiefly on the more humble ground of everyday life, of the routines of production and reproduction' (Comaroff and Comaroff 1992). The discussion of the Methodist and Wesleyan attempts to change the political and gender economy from pastoral agriculture and limited dry-land crop production to an irrigated gardening system is instructive. 'The mission garden, clearly, was also meant as a lesson in the contrast of "labour" and "idleness" – and, no less, in the relative value of male and female work... The men, whose herds were tended by youths and serfs, appeared to be lazy "lords of creation", their political and ritual exertions not signifying "work" to the missionary eye' (Comaroff and Comaroff 1992:113, quoting Moffat). However, '[i]n stark contrast to the images of work to be nurtured by the mission, then *tiro* and *itirela* invoked a world in which the making of the person, the accumulation of wealth and rank, and the protection of an autonomous identity were indivisible aspects of social practice' (Comaroff and Comaroff 1991:142-143). The work (*tiro*) that is at stake here is work that creates a social and individual self through being active in society at large.

The truly interesting part of this history is that the history of Methodism in Southern Africa may just as well be taken as part of a larger but structurally similar history of Protestantism in Europe. Industrialisation in Europe had the same dynamics of material and cultural change. E.P.Thompson's celebrated analysis of the making of the English working class proves the point (Thompson 1963). The conclusion, therefore, is that we have every reason to be curious about the effect of such religious interventions in African conceptions of work while we should at the same time also be aware that African work ethic may well carry notions that tie work to a broader and fulfilling notion of identity.

Religious Beliefs and Religious Practice
We need to explain where the fascination with religion and its effects on work ethos came from historically. Max Weber is, of course, seen as the originator of the sociological argument that particular beliefs lead to a particular work ethos. He argued that a partial explanation for the different economic development trajectories of different parts of the world should be sought in the relationship between the content of particular beliefs and capitalism. The beliefs and resultant practices of Protestants and Catholics, Hindus, Confucians, etc. were said to have had a particular influence on work ethos. Although Weber argued that no simple answer will satisfy and noted that that the historical context is obviously important, he saw prescribed practices and beliefs as being underrated aspects of the interaction between religion and economy (Weber 1904/1993:2-3). In fact, he argues that the difference between the Catholic and the Protestant success in the development of Capitalism lay above all in the 'inneren Eigenart... der Konfessionen' (1904/1993:5). Most of the rest of what is today known as the

Protestant Ethic and the 'Spirit' of Capitalism is devoted to an analysis of the practices and beliefs found among Protestants in early capitalism in Europe.

It hardly needs mention that the influence of religion in everyday life and public life in Europe has seen a steady decline over the past decades (Dobbelaere 1981; Wilson 1982). In Eastern and Central Europe, religion and religious organisations were put under severe pressure during the Communist era and we are now seeing a resurgence of religion in some countries. The patterns are not the same everywhere, as religion in some formerly Catholic countries now has significant public and everyday life influence while in other countries this is not the case. The same variety of post-Communist religious patterns can be seen in formerly Orthodox, Muslim and mixed-religion countries (Casanova 1994). These changes mean that even in Europe the Protestant ethic cannot be expected to find clear expression – even if Weber was correct about its role in early capitalism. However, the more fundamental question of the influence of religion as a source of moral ideas and notions of duty and meaning in work remains interesting – especially in the African context where African Christianity (Gifford 1998) and African Islam (Rosander and Westerlund 1997) have grown rather than declined.

Rachel McCleary and Robert Barro's article (2003) outlining an empirical and comparative case for the respective effects of religious service attendance and religious beliefs on economic growth is relevant to positioning our research here. They conclude that economic growth responds positively to religious beliefs, but negatively to religious service attendance and that 'these results accord with a model in which religious beliefs influence individual traits that enhance economic performance' (2003:760). They then conjecture that 'stronger religious beliefs stimulate growth because they help sustain specific individual behaviours that enhance productivity' and foresee that it would be useful to examine 'the links between religious beliefs and individual behaviors or values, such as… honesty, thrift, work ethic, and openness to strangers' (2003:779).

There is a difference between values and behaviour and, therefore, the causality that Barro and McCleary suppose in their conjecture as to the factors that determine economic growth may be too complex to decide. We limit ourselves to one aspect of the argument and that is the supposed links between religious beliefs and practices and work ethos. The specific values that McCleary and Barro name are listed as 'honesty, thrift, work ethic and openness to strangers'. This can be translated as having three components, i.e. work ethos, particular values or attitudes (honesty and thrift) and what may be defined as potential bridging social capital (openness to strangers may lead to networks that cut across existing social relations, i.e. bridging social capital (Beugelsdijk and Smulders 2003)). We will only be investigating the work ethos dimension of the equation. An investigation as to the link between religious beliefs and individual behaviour lies outside the scope of our investigation.

The question then remains, are Barro and McCleary guessing correctly that particular religious beliefs support a particular work ethos? They found that economic growth responds positively to religious beliefs but negatively to 'church attendance', and work ethos is seen as a possible intervening variable. We, therefore, need to distinguish beliefs and religious service attendance. In fact, we would like to investigate a slightly wider spectrum of religious activities in our analysis. Religious service attendance is one aspect of a composite of practices including membership of any religious organisation as such, unpaid voluntary work in religious organisations and prayer, among others. We would also like to draw the notion of belief a little wider to distinguish particular objects of belief like God or some supernatural being or force, heaven, hell, life after death, etc. as well as membership of particular denominations and religions (as particular religious traditions are associated with particular beliefs even if not all members hold the orthodox line). We would then also like to distinguish a further aspect, namely religiosity. This dimension would include aspects of religion that would not necessarily be excised in a formal context. They include defining yourself as a religious person, saying that you derive comfort and strength from your religion, saying that God is important in your life, etc. Lastly, we would also like to see what the effects of different kinds of religion-state relationships are. Here, we would like to be looking at the effect of religious freedom and religious pluralism. The practical problem is that the available data in the sets that we have do not allow all of these additional ideas, and we are restricted to religious denomination and two constructs for intensity of religious belief and time spent on religious practices.

But first one has to sketch out the religious situation that is at issue. It is assumed in the analysis that work ethos is of religious origin to some extent. This assumption relates to the Weberian argument. We are interested in the role of religion in African work ethos in the current context. That means a number of other dimensions have to be noted. First of all, African religion is not only Protestant or Catholic. It is also Muslim and traditional. African religion is also a fluid mixture of these traditions, and it may be wholly spurious to analyse denominational influence with the expectation that these denominations relate to distinct groupings and influences. Furthermore, African religion is a complex interaction between traditional religion of a local nature and 'foreign' religion in the forms of Catholic and Protestant mission and Muslim increase over time. Lastly, African communities have also been affected to various degrees by the processes of secularisation, secular socialism of various kinds and industrialisation and modernisation in general.

Data, Measurements and Analytical Strategy

The data which we have available comes from the World Values Survey 1999-2000. Only three countries from Southern Africa – South Africa (3,000), Zimbabwe (1,002) and the Republic of Tanzania (1,171 – excluding Zanzibar) –

were surveyed and only South Africa had been surveyed previously.[10] This takes away the option of analysing any changes over time and limits the claims that can be made about Southern Africa as a region and Africa as a whole. The sampling has already been described in the previous section.

The first step is the evaluation of work ethos items. The items were taken as possible indicators of the relative intensity of commitment to work, and thus work ethos responses on a five-point scale to the statements indicated in Figure 7.6. On the basis of the pattern of analysis established by De Witte upon using the European Values Study survey data (De Witte 1992; Vandoorne and De Witte 2003), we constructed a factor analysis of five items, dealing with dimensions that indicate commitment and perspectives on work that could be read together as signifying work ethos. On first glance, the three African countries in our analysis seem to have high scores on work ethos items. However, these matters are always relative, and a comparison with the rest of the world would be an important step in testing that impression. The object here is a comparison between the three African countries though.

It is clear that all three countries present similar structures of work commitment and work ethos, with the country with the highest poverty levels at the time scoring the highest on the items and the country with the highest average income and most developed formal economy (material advancement clearly dependent on formal employment) scoring the lowest.

Figure 7.7: The positions of South Africa, Zimbabwe and Tanzania with Respect to the Items of Work Ethos (Percentage of the respondents that agree or strongly agree)

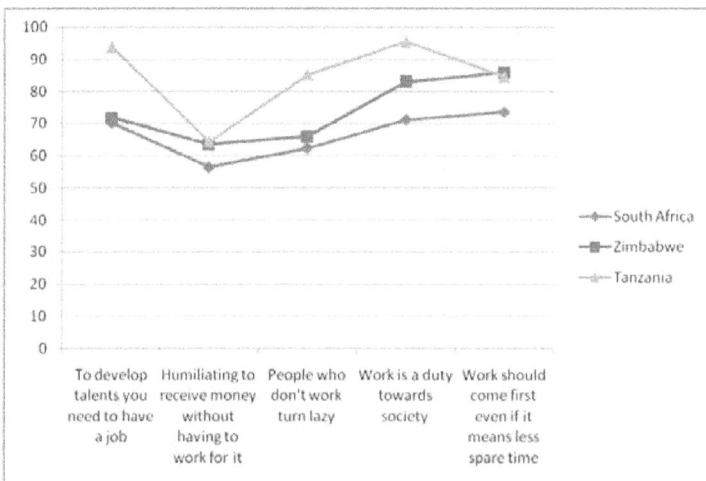

The factor score for Zimbabwe at least is clearly a problem (Table 7.7) and the Zimbabwe analysis is therefore in doubt from the beginning.

Table 7.7: Work Ethos Factor Analysis

	South Africa	Zimbabwe	Tanzania	All Three Countries
		Rotated Factor Loadings		
To develop your talents you need to have a job	0.64540	0.50318	0.65526	0.65520
Humiliating to receive money without having to work	0.47804	0.64724	0.53504	0.52004
People who don't work turn lazy	0.45393	0.51693	0.70820	0.65559
Work is a duty towards society	0.61840	0.48855	0.75138	0.69662
Work should come first even if it means less spare time	0.58602	0.45267	0.60220	0.56080
Cronbach's Alpha	0.5249	0.3337	0.6092	0.5942

The relationship between work ethos and religion is the primary interest of this section. Therefore, we tried to get as close as possible to a sensible analysis of religious aspects as we could. Two kinds of arguments pertain. One is the Weberian argument and the other is the more recent Barro and McCleary argument.

In terms of the Weberian thesis on the Protestant ethic, an association of a specific kind may be expected between Protestant or similar religious worldviews and a high work ethos. We need to remember that the African version of Protestantism cannot be what Weber was analysing when he proposed his study more than a century ago. Thereforee, the expectation is that there may be some positive or negative effect emanating from specific religious denominations, depending on a variation of outlook on savings, thriftiness and deferred gratification. We would specifically expect a high work ethos from religious worldviews that value the accumulation of material wealth as a sign of religious commitment or purity. The Protestantism of Weber's time could not be the only candidate for such a worldview. We would hypothesise that the so-called prosperity gospel (Gifford 1998) may have had an effect in Pentecostal and Evangelical circles where it is found most purchase, as this seems to have been the case both in Africa and in Latin America (Corten and Marshall-Fratani 2001). In terms of the Prosperity Gospel, wealth is a sign of faith and a reward for belief.

The Barro and McCleary argument calls for a seemingly simple analysis of time spent in religious practice and intensity of religious belief. A valid and reliable analysis of these items is difficult in principle as the notion of religious practice is quite wide (it could be very significant or insignificant whether weekly religious services are attended as these could be very long – many African Christian services are; or very brief or very central to religious practice – Catholic church services are; or almost unknown – many forms of traditional African religion do not have a service that takes place on a regular basis); and the intensity of beliefs difficult to measure with a scale of increasing difficulty in view of the increasing variety of cultural expression (Clarke 2001; Van Herk et al. 2004).

The practical problems of constructing valid and reliable indices of intensity of religious belief and time spent in religious practice proved even more difficult than the conceptual problems. We constructed a factor analysis proxy for religious belief by taking belief in God, life after death, people having a soul, hell and heaven as collective indicators of intensity of belief. These items are notoriously bound to the culture and religion of Western Christianity and have been in use in the World Values Survey since its inception. An alternative is not available and despite our reservations on a substantive level, a statistically agreeable factor reduction of intensity of belief could be executed for the three countries (Table 7.8). The fact that the work ethos factor is not deemed to be reliable in the case of Zimbabwe means that the eventual regressions for this country will have to be discounted, though.

Table 7.8: Belief Factor Analysis

	South Africa	Zimbabwe	Tanzania	All Three Countries
	Rotated Factor Loadings			
Belief in God	0.36807	0.36040	0.54001	0.45296
Belief in Life After Death	0.68300	0.68085	0.77817	0.71704
Belief in: People have a Soul	0.68743	0.65527	0.76736	0.70681
Belief in Hell	0.73836	0.77060	0.87157	0.78167
Belief in Heaven	0.71889	0.81790	0.82018	0.77727
Cronbach's Alpha	0.6968	0.6958	0.8155	0.7297

The standard procedure for religious practice analysis would be to take the items that indicate the time spent on religious ceremonies and procedures and form a factor analysis from that. The three items that were available for the three countries were limited to answers to the questions on 'how often do you attend' religious services, take moments of prayer, meditation; and pray to God outside of religious services. Not only is this a small number of items, but items are very much couched in the frame of Western Christianity. It is, therefore, no wonder that the barely acceptable Cronbach alpha score of the religious belief factor score was here followed up with a factor score that proves that the data reduction for religious practice was not successful in the case of Tanzania (Table 7.9).

Table 7.9: Religious Practice Factor Analysis

	South Africa	Zimbabwe	Tanzania	All Three Countries
	Rotated Factor Loadings			
How often do you attend religious services?	0.78196	0.84607	0.82162	0.80717
Moments of prayer, meditation	-0.68298	-0.77417	-0.09668	-0.64272
Pray to God outside of religious services	0.85673	0.89609	0.82371	0.85555
Cronbach's Alpha	0.5970	0.6639	0.3785	0.5874

Because of the disappointing results on the data-reduction attempt at constructing an indicator for religious practice, we decided to at least use the average of the two items that seemed to be most associated and created a proxy item for religious practice per country by taking the average of attendance of services and praying outside of services (Table 7.10). We are not satisfied that this carries the weight of the Barro and McCleary notion of time spent on religious practices, but through the summative factor we were at least able to create a variable that has some reliability.

Table 7.10: Mean Factor Scores and Averages

	Work Ethos	Belief	Religious Practice
South Africa	-0.0348501	0.3086758	2.092208
Zimbabwe	-0.0109466	0.1814599	1.73268
Tanzania	0.0317047	0.0304777	1.781296
All Three Countries	**0.1499098**	**0.1406586**	**1.95922**

The next logical step was to explore the significance of individual characteristics that are directly related to the arguments about the origins of work ethos and then control for individual characteristics that are more or less standard for such regressions (age, gender, educational level and class – and seeing that the data is from the World Values Survey, the Materialism-Postmaterialism dimension). We then added aspects that would be associated with the question of work, namely occupation and level of responsibility.

Results

We cannot expect much from correlation or the regression analyses, as the constructs are not reliable in all cases and will have to be disregarded systematically, but we did find some interesting results for specific religious denominations and for religion as a category of explanatory variables when considering work ethos as a whole on aggregate level. We present the results on two phases with the first focus on religion and work ethos only, and then a regression analysis for the individual countries and for the aggregate of the three countries.

The fact that the aggregate analyses have been presented from the first table and figure does not mean that we consider such an aggregate to be significant on its own. What is significant is that an analysis of three countries in the region differs very much from an analysis for the aggregate. One important factor to explain that variance is, of course, the comparative size of the South African sample, but this would not account for the variation throughout. We consider the variance between the three individual countries and the aggregate analyses to be a warning for continental and regional analyses that work with large data-sets across seemingly coherent regions or continents. It is clear that the data reduction works better when considering aggregate data of different countries. It is also clear that seeming significant patterns are found in the regional data. Figure 2 shows that only the Protestant group seem to be associated positively with the positive work ethos of South Africans. We cannot take Zimbabwe into account in this analysis and we then find a seemingly clear situation in Tanzania where Muslims associate negatively with work ethos. When we consider the aggregate picture, we suddenly seem to find massive confirmation of an extended Weberian thesis in that Protestants and Evangelicals are associated with high work ethos (Independent African Churches as well) and Catholics and Muslims not. Part of the problem emanates from the use of Zimbabwe in the aggregate data while it is clear that the work ethos construct is inadequate there. However, such detail can get lost in large continental comparisons based on items that were formulated in secular Europe and meant to elicit understanding of that situation!

Figure 7.8: Mean Work Ethos Factor Scores by Religion For Each Country

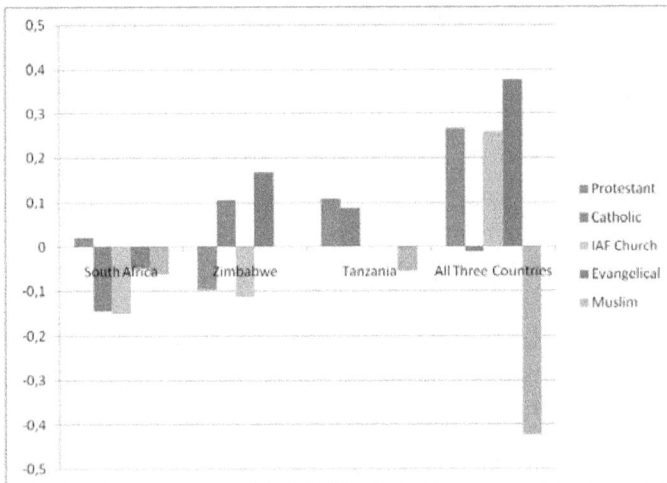

Figure 7.7 attempts to display more detail by combining the denominational and faith categorisation with the religious belief and practice aspects. The data was divided by splitting the belief and practice items on the point of their mean. From this, it seems as if South Africa and Tanzania have significantly different belief structures, but relatively similar practice structures, in that Tanzanian belief patterns are (irrespective of denomination) strongly negative to work ethos, confirming the Barro-McCleary idea, while South Africa is only relatively negative on that relationship. The pattern switches around, seemingly dramatically on the aggregate of the three countries. The real question is the source of that relationship and for that reason the regression analyses are presented as well.

Figure 7.9: Mean Work Ethos Factor Scores by Religion, Religious Practice and Belief for Each Country

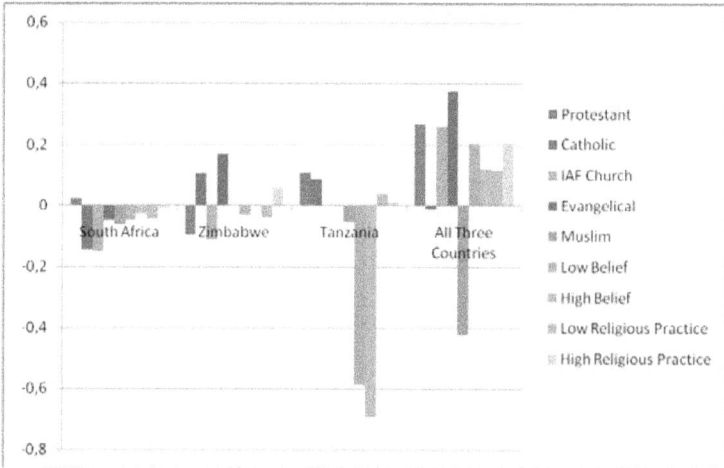

Table 7.11 presents the regression analysis. Due to Zimbabwe's religious ethos factor not being reliable, we discount Zimbabwe's results here as well. It is interesting, that with one exception, no item seems to contribute in significant manner to the Zimbabwe work ethos, if what we are measuring there is indeed in any way related to the Zimbabwean work ethos. Tanzania also delivers no confirmation of the hypotheses regarding the relationship between denomination, intensity of beliefs or time spent on religious practices. The only country that confirms any of the aspects of the theory regarding work ethos and religion is South Africa. The constructs are more or less satisfactory and Protestants seem to be inclined to be the ones who also have a relatively high work ethos.

One cannot explain here, and on the basis of material that we have before us, why Protestants and Catholics are not significant in explaining work ethos and why Evangelicals and Independent African Churches are significantly linked to a high work ethos in the regression analysis. We have speculated on the possible dynamics regarding religion and work ethos among Evangelicals. It may be that a significant part of the Independent churches are independent in the historical sense – i.e. independent of the founding churches like the Methodist, Presbyterian, Anglican and other early missionary churches from which the South African independent churches split off, but not independent of the influence of American Zionist churches that are also often the sources of Prosperity Gospel themes that echo in the Pentecostal and Evangelical churches (Meyer 2004a). On the other hand, it may also be that the self-sufficiency themes that contributed to these churches becoming independent originally are continued in economic and work terms. The Zionist churches in South Africa are similar to the Aladura in Nigeria and the main characteristics are summarised by Ukah as being i) self-financing, ii) self-governance and, iii) self-supporting (Ukah 2007:8). Both these types of explanation could be useful and should be investigated.

The other interesting contradictory finding is that high religious practice, even though we know that the construct is not particularly reliable for what it was meant to elicit, is strongly associated with high work ethos. One can at least argue that it does not confirm the Barro-McCleary arguments, neither on the level of the impact of intensity of belief, nor on the level of time spent on religious practice.

When considering the other aspects that are significant, the role of class seems clear in the case of middle class and up having a high work ethos and unskilled and skilled manual labour having a low work ethos. The mixed category in the materialism-postmaterialism dimension is nothing less than awkward for the theory if the extremes of that dimension are not significant at all. It means that the dimension measures something that is significant but the defining parameters of the dimension is not what is at stake. We will not consider the gender aspect again here. The arguments about the relatively confused state of conclusions in this regard have been presented in the section on work orientations.

With its very specific history of social, cultural, legal and religious divisions in terms of ethnically-constructed identities, the South African data predictably has information on the ethnic differences and these were tested in the analysis. They are significant and the most important pattern that can be found is the difference between English-speaking and vernacular language groups, with the mostly white and mixed decent group making up most of the English group. This group seems to be highly associated with a high work ethos while the rest are associated mostly with a low work ethos. This would probably be taken as a confirmation of the views Murphy on business people in Ghana. We have shown how difficult and dependent on selected items and meaning of the items in particular groups and context such views are, and take the result to confirm only that in terms of the factor constructed, a significant difference is shown.

Conclusions

In this chapter, we have explored work orientations and work ethos in Europe and Africa. Although for most people on the two continents work is (still) highly important, and in the three countries that we investigated on the work ethos aspect it seems as if work ethos is high, the contexts differ in so many respects that differences in work orientations and work ethos were to be expected.

As such, we opted for a most dissimilar systems design in the continental comparison (Przeworski and Teune 1970). Such a design enables researchers to eliminate apparently irrelevant factors to explain differences in a certain dependent variable. We also explored the notion of work ethos and its religious associations in social theory and economic analysis to some extent.

Work orientations and work ethos have been investigated before in numerous studies and publications, but such studies were merely confined to countries and populations of the Western world. A very well-known and often applied distinction is made in extrinsic or extrinsic and expressive or intrinsic work orientations. A very well-know category of relative work ethos exists as well. The two work orientations are linked to ideas of modernisation of society in the sense that modernisation means that extrinsic or extrinsic work gradually declines in importance while expressive or intrinsic work attributes become increasingly important. One of the issues to be addressed, of course, is whether similar developments can be expected to have occurred also in other than Western contexts and, further, if similar work orientations can be found in very different contexts? The work ethos argument is part of another notion associated with modernisation, i.e. secularisation through religious transformation.

Our analyses suggest that, indeed, intrinsic and extrinsic work orientations can be found in African countries and that the meaning and interpretation resembles the meaning and interpretation in Europe to a large extent. The two orientations appear highly similar so that comparisons can be made. The notion of work ethos seems to work on an aggregate level, but we are not confident that the construct is valid across countries.

The comparisons on work orientation and the less successful work ethos comparisons, however, do not yield a clear and obvious pattern. Africans do not appear to have exceptional or unusual orientations compared with Europeans with regard to work orientation; and Africans do not seem to have a clearly religious origin in their work ethos – for as much as we can use that construct. European countries are much more extreme in their work orientations. Latvia and Turkey, for example, are each other's opposites, while African countries display more modest positions on both work dimensions. At the same time, the work ethos aggregate analysis indicates that internal differences may be smoothed out unduly if a regional or continental analysis is done.

When considering the work orientation analysis, it is not a big surprise that the countries' features do not explain much in the differences between African and European countries. We argued that differences in work orientations could be attributed to country differences in the degree to which populations are individualised, 'developed', masculine, working in agriculture, industry or services and living in equal or more unequal societies. It may be due to a poor

Table 7.11: Regression Analysis

Dependent Variable: Work Ethos (SA) Explanatory Variables	South Africa Coefficient	A.V.S+	Zimbabwe Coefficient	A.V.S	Tanzania Coefficient	A.V.S	All Three Countries Coefficient	A.V.S
Education and Experience Variables								
Education Years	0.0002298	0.03	0.0258792	1.73	-0.0100134	0.83	-0.0053383	1.00
Potential Experience	(-0.008553)*	2.22	0.0145975	1.84	-0.0000513	0.01	-0.0031112	1.07
Post-Materialism Index								
Mixed	0.17195**	3.44	0.0427529	0.46	0.0110649	0.12	0.0494725	1.38
Post-Materialism	-0.020361	0.20	-0.1527914	0.85	-0.3192825	1.11	-0.0852984	1.11
Social Class Variables								
Upper Class	(-0.5054442)**	3.15	(-1.301646)*	2.25	0.1575239	0.56	-0.2486411	1.91
Upper Middle Class	0.2031878**	2.61	0.0710238	0.38	0.387206**	2.64	0.216584**	3.79
Lower Middle Class	0.3783031**	5.22	-0.0878125	0.84	0.155433	1.31	0.0704844	1.56
Working Class	-0.0341257	0.50	-0.1299979	0.96	0.3145565*	2.45	-0.0758959	1.57
Employment Variables								
Employer/Manager Cat 1	0.1578803	0.78	-0.8740672	1.64	0.1423267	0.38	0.0652337	0.40
Employer/Manager Cat 2	0.5852225**	4.10	0.702523	0.91	1.375123	1.63	0.886249**	5.90
Professional	0.0554248	0.48	0.4715981*	2.17	-0.2152193	1.28	-0.1036627	1.40
Supervisory	-0.1315179	1.14	0.5472015	1.86	-0.1840856	0.75	0.0616153	0.66
Office worker	-0.0744553	0.78	-0.110457	0.32	(-0.3866747)*	2.32	(-0.1841107)*	2.43
Foreman	-0.4022279	2.02	-0.3677639	0.68	-0.1612334	0.52	-0.2080455	1.35

Table 7.11: Regression Analysis (Continued)

Dependent Variable: Work Ethos (SA) Explanatory Variables	South Africa Coefficient	A.V.S+	Zimbabwe Coefficient	A.V.S	Tanzania Coefficient	A.V.S	All Three Countries Coefficient	A.V.S
Skilled Manual Labourer	(-0.2868954)**	2.92	0.0861362	0.42	-0.1428133	0.76	-0.0086545	0.12
Unskilled Manual Labourer	(-0.2252852)*	2.16	0.2114362	1.05	0.0076423	0.03	0.2054601*	2.58
Semi-Skilled Manual Labourer	-0.1103182	1.44	0.3115313	1.93	0.61331	1.26	0.1565654*	2.53
Farmer	-0.0449101	0.09	-0.540749	0.90	(-0.318427)*	2.12	(-0.5384679)**	5.77
Agricultural Worker	-0.3146217	1.87	0.0270013	0.19	-0.3559171	0.82	0.0277196	0.42
Armed Forces	-0.1900488	0.89	-0.5220403	1.60	-0.2233339	0.78	-0.2227617	1.72
Unemployed	-0.0389896	0.67	0.2952747*	2.26	0.3219039*	2.53	0.1087623*	2.40
Belief Variables								
Protestant	0.1385006	1.21	-0.0954851	0.78	0.0445943	0.42	0.4060122**	6.73
Catholic	0.0327099	0.25	-	-	0.0246497	0.24	0.2604675**	4.08
Independent African Church	0.6027161**	4.67	-0.1320374	1.01	-	-	0.577812**	8.22
Evangelical	0.4839887**	3.88	0.1292545	0.89	-	-	0.6808186**	9.27
Belief (SA)	0.0388344	1.27	0.1405543*	2.53	-0.0156758	0.35	0.0517533**	2.64
Religious Practice	0.1168799**	5.69	-0.0284564	0.60	-0.0173255	0.44	0.0522254**	3.40
Gender and Age Variables								
Female	0.1515623**	3.10	-0.1087376	1.07	0.0941572	1.03	0.1039906	2.84
Youth	-0.2556588	1.74	0.8629995**	2.82	-0.2474147	0.88	0.1151285	1.04
Middle Aged	-0.1193582	1.15	0.5517567*	2.57	0.0381041	0.22	0.0694637	0.92

Table 7.11: Regression Analysis (Continued)

Dependent Variable: Work Ethos (SA)	South Africa		Zimbabwe		Tanzania		All Three Countries	
Explanatory Variables	Coefficient	A.V.S+	Coefficient	A.V.S	Coefficient	A.V.S	Coefficient	A.V.S
Ethnic Group Variables								
English	0.4242712**	5.54						
Ndebele	(-0.796407)**	2.87						
Northern Sotho	0.0665837	0.60						
Southern Sotho	(-0.2314759)**	2.64						
Swazi	0.3193999	0.77						
Tsonga	(-0.7228232)**	3.70						
Tswana	-0.0631996	0.67						
Venda	(-0.4791816)*	2.36						
Xhosa	(-0.2671197)**	2.69						
Zulu	(-0.22765531)**	3.30						
Constant Term	-0.4546	1.77	-1.114492	2.33	0.1510444	0.34	-0.5239172	2.94
Adjusted R-Squared	0.1651		0.0742		0.0124		0.1484	
Number of Observations	1583		502		409		2495	

*Significant at the 5% Level

**Significant at the 1% Level

+ Coefficient Absolute Value of t Statistic

operationalisation of these concepts, but we cannot find much evidence that country differences in intrinsic and extrinsic work orientations can be explained on the basis of differences in such issues. Thus, we should continue our efforts to find explanations for differences and similarities in work orientations. It seems, however, that such characteristics do seem to matter in a European, that is Western, context, but not in Eastern European and African settings. Hence, our argumentation, mainly grounded in modernisation theories, may be too much western and not universal. Modernisation is apparently a Western concept and thus it does not provoke similar outcomes in non-western contexts. It can further be noticed that individualism and development are not two sides of one coin. Contrary to our expectations, the empirical analysis demonstrates that extrinsic work orientations are more stressed by people in more individualistic societies. Our guess was the opposite, the more individualistic a society would be, the less material-oriented, and the more intrinsic and the less extrinsic the dominant work orientation would be. This may be due to the way the concept of individualism was tapped empirically. We measured it by the percentage of people in a country that shared the opinion that people should take their own responsibility and not rely on the state. It is likely that this is more a distinction between socialism and liberalism and does not quite designate individualism. If that is indeed the case, then the result indicates that the more people in a country favour liberal instead of socialist ideas, the more extrinsic work qualities are stressed. We do not have strong theoretical arguments to explain this result. Development, in terms of life expectancy, adult literacy, welfare etc, has the effect as expected. The more developed a society is in such terms, the less extrinsic work qualities are emphasised.

The results of our analyses of work orientation at individual level also seem to suggest that the theoretical arguments have a Western or European bias. The suggested effects of individual characteristics on work orientations can be confirmed more or less in European countries, but less so, or even in the opposite direction, in African countries. This is also true in the case of the work ethos analysis and the aspects that are supposedly contributing factors to a relatively high or low work ethos. The work values themselves may be comparable to a large extent, but the impact of individual characteristics to explain differences in these orientations is not the same. It may be that work ethos is a useful construct and that with a better set of variables one would be able to find a stable and reliable construct. However, since most theories are confined to Western societies, it is an easy guess to conclude that different theories are needed to understand and interpret the situation in African societies, and to a lesser extent also the situation with regard to work orientations in Eastern Europe. The existing theories appear too general and do not take into account all kinds of country and regional peculiarities that may have serious effects on people's work orientations or work ethos. As such, our analyses seem to confirm the idea that societies develop in their own speed following their own path, although perhaps at a very abstract level in the same direction. One of these differences in tracks and speed certainly concern the life circumstances. Many people in Africa, and perhaps also in some Eastern European countries, are still more concerned with pure survival, not only in the context of work, but also more general aspects.

The confusing results may thus be the result of our poor or even simply wrong theoretical reflections and considerations, but they may also be caused by the limitations in the data we were able to analyse. Perhaps we just have been trying to explain work orientation with categories that contained too much variance in them or with the wrong dimensions as such. We are quite sure that the work ethos notion has to be improved for it to have any purchase in African countries. We are even more convinced that the constructs of religious belief and practice require a full overhaul for them to work in our context if they are required at all.

Notes

1. This chapter contains large sections of an article published in the International Journal of Comparative Sociology Copyright © 2006 SAGE Publications. L.Halman, & H.P. Müller, 'Contemporary Work Values in Africa and Europe Comparing Orientations to Work in African and European Societies', IJCS, 47(2): 117–143 (2006). My appreciation again goes to Loek Halman as well for allowing me to use it extensively here.
2. The African data in the World Values Survey is limited to South Africa, Zimbabwe, Tanzania, Uganda and Nigeria. Sampling was stratified for each country by region, sex and community size, and respondents were randomly selected. The questionnaire was translated (in the case of South Africa and Uganda, multiple languages were used while in Tanzania Kiswahili is the lingua franca of 90 per cent of the population and in Zimbabwe English, Shona and SiNdebele cover 95 per cent of the population) and back-translated and piloted. Mother tongue speakers were used as interviewers as a rule and concepts that could not be translated adequately were excluded from these surveys. For more detailed information we can refer to the EVS and WVS/EVS sourcebooks (Halman 2001; Inglehart, Basáñez, Díez Medrano, Halman & Luijkx 2004).
3. The question was: 'Here are some aspects of a job that people say are important. Please look at them and tell me which ones you personally think are important in a job?' The answer categories were mentioned = 1, not mentioned =0 (see Halman 2001: 303; Inglehart et al. 2004: 420, 450).
4. Country samples were weighted in such a way that samples sizes were set to 1,000 in each country.
5. Gini-coefficients for Albania and Macedonia are from Human Development Report 2004, while figures for Malta are from personal communication with the EVS representative in this country. Data for Iceland can be found in Jonsson et al. (2001).
6. The question was to place oneself on a ten-point scale with two opposite positions. 1 = Individuals should take more responsibility for providing for themselves; 10 = the state should take more responsibility to ensure that everyone is provided for (Halman 2001: 316). The codes 1-3 indicate a more individualistic society.

7. The respondents were asked to indicate whether it would be a good thing or a bad thing if in the near future there would be less emphasis on 'Money and material possessions' and 'Decrease in the importance of work in our lives'. The percentages of people who considered it as a bad development were included in our analyses.
8. The respondents were asked to place themselves on a ten-point scale with two extreme positions. 1= Competition is good. It stimulates people to work hard and develop new ideas; 10 = competition is harmful. It brings out the worst in people. The percentages of people in each country with scores 1-3 are included in our analyses.
9. A list of qualities that children can be encouraged to learn at home was presented and the respondent was asked to choose up to five of the qualities that he/she considered important. 'Hard work' and 'determination' were two of these qualities. The percentages of people mentioning these two qualities are used in our analyses.
10. Missing values of various kinds (missing, don't know, etc.), for the indicators used are deleted pair-wise throughout.

8

Conclusion

Hans Müller, Pinkie Mekgwe and Marvellous Mhloyi

Introduction

The quest for comparative perspective on the role of values and culture in development in African societies continues. If there is one matter that has become clear in the process of putting together the results of this book, it is that there are all sorts of gaps in what we can put together without comprehensive new research. The aim of this section is not to try to summarise the results of each section, but to reflect on where the different inputs have brought us in terms of the research questions posed at the beginning and to reflect on the current limitations and future possibilities of our work. However, we need to elucidate the gaps in what has been possible to do on the basis of the material that is available for comparative research first.

The first level of problems emanate from the fact that the research that has been done ever since independence came to Southern African countries has always been dominated by models and theoretical frameworks that are a product of the industrialised and primarily Western countries; and therefore, the dynamics, problems and consciousness that framed the research has been less than appropriate for the African situation.

A second problem is simply that we do not have enough data collected systematically and over a long period of time to be able to assess dynamics as they play out in African societies. This is partially due to the instability of many African countries; but mostly because central institutions like universities and government institutions have not had the funding and the capacity to develop long-term processes and maintain them. A bare minimum of statistics is available in most countries, but the data is mostly standard demographic and economic data and one does not have anything to work with that helps the cause of establishing the impact of values and culture in society. If one compares what would be possible in terms of analysis on the basis of the General Social Survey in the USA and what is possible in Southern Africa, the point becomes clear enough.

The third problem is ideological. The research that has been done in African societies that would be relevant to our quest, has been couched in terms that are often very relevant in Europe and North America but not so clearly relevant here. Research in Africa has also been dogged by ideological limitations emanating from the very clear and continuing need to make the point that African societies have been decimated by the effects of colonial and post-colonial structures. This has very often meant that the research done by Africans stops at the point where the connection between exploitation and African underdevelopment has been made. To go further seems too much like blaming the victim to be politically feasible; it will not attract government funding or funding from large local agencies and to strive for support from multi-lateral and international bodies may mean that the agenda for the research is again determined elsewhere. These are issues that CODESRIA has been dealing with since its inception and the aim of fostering and developing comparative research is a clear attempt to do something about the problem. The development of the Afrobarometer has helped a lot in generating data that can assist; but an opinion survey that is dominated by issues of public concern cannot deliver the full scope of aspects that is required for a values and cultural analysis.

Reflection on Research Questions

We asked whether values can explain poverty and continuous exploitation in Southern Africa. It is not clear that values can do so. The work values and work ethos arguments would seem to be good candidates to support such claims. The assumption that while people are poor and desperate they have a short-term and instrumental approach to work and to the fruits of labour and no real commitment to work as such is not borne out by the analysis. In fact, Southern African countries (or at least the countries that we were able to survey) are moderately European in their approach to these matters.

We asked whether it was possible to explain the fact of survival on the basis of values; and in that played to the gallery that would say that African communalism and social solidarity is a fundamentally African characteristic. We found some historical and anthropological evidence of solidarity constructs that could be enduring, but quite importantly, also evidence of competitiveness among African siblings and family that could be argued to facilitate an opposite argument. None of these directions could be confirmed in data analysis. There is evidence of consensus seeking and the variation point more or less in the direction of survival as the more desperate countries are more consensus-seeking. However, the analysis itself is limited in that it does not attempt a multilevel explanation of the aspects analysed, partly because the nature of the investigation is explorative and partly because the data that would enable a multilevel analysis is not always easy to find. In the work value analysis we found that it was impossible to locate a reliable set of information on unemployment in a particular country, and could not control for that variable in our analysis (we were later on informed that such data does exist, but at the time of the analysis this was not possible to find).

We asked whether values or cultural aspects could be defined that could play a pivotal role in development in the future in Southern Africa. There are many aspects that one could speculate on, but to claim that we have identified such notions would be dishonest. One of the aspects that we would like to consider as candidates is the work values that do seem to exist. When given the opportunity, and in the right structural framework, it seems that African workers can be incredibly productive and deliver quality (the BMW plant in Pretoria South Africa has achieved the top industry award for quality production in the world, 2003b). Another aspect that we would like to investigate more fully is the balance between competitive and social solidarity aspects. We know that productivity as measured in industry is also a function of cost and that the kind of sibling competitiveness that is balanced by matrilineal solidarity in communities that we have put forward material on could also have downsides. Investigation is needed.

We asked whether political-economy dynamics, demographic change and geographic features can be understood better in development terms by the addition of the values question. It seems to be clear that demographic change, on the most fundamental level, is affected by values and these values are in turn affected by demographic change (Chapter 4). It seems clear that particular political choices and frameworks are related to values that we have identified (Chapter 5). The nature of these relationships is a difficult question though. We were not able to establish the causal direction in many analyses that are presented. It is always difficult; but it is just about impossible if the range of questions addressed is as wide as what we discuss and many of the macro-variables are so difficult to obtain.

We asked whether different development paths in different countries could be explained by virtue of insight into the values variations that may exist. We have found some variation in values between countries, but the number of countries that we have data on and the failure of important constructs that we imported from other analyses in Europe and the developed world precludes a definitive answer to the question. The question has to be delimited more carefully, and more specific analyses would have to be done to answer the matter in any sensible way.

Reflection on Key Concepts

The research questions that we posed led us to the concepts discussed in Chapter 3. We indicated the exploratory and tentative nature of our detailing of the conceptual scheme while expressing a stronger commitment to the idea that a values perspective will have to deal with cosmology, power, human relationships and human qualities. Having gone through the list of items that we produced in our initial reflection on the matter with more attention to the content of the basic concepts, and with due attention to the aspects listed under these concepts, we might consider reducing or even reordering the structure of the argument.

The fundamental realisation has been that power, cosmology and relationships cover the ground in a quite balanced way and the fact that the rest of the concepts were put in a basket with a label of human qualities was the result of less than fundamental conceptualisation in the initial phases of the project. It becomes clear what the logic is when a serious and contextualised discussion of any cosmological aspect points to the power relationships and the social nature of the cosmological aspect that the triangle between cosmology, power and relationships would be a more fundamental conceptualisation.

The interesting part of this has been the quite important role of anthropological material on cosmological concepts. These kinds of arguments are often missing in sociological analyses and do not feature in any significant way in political or economic analyses. The logical direction of any attempt at discussion of values and culture has to be that meaning is at stake and that the meaning that is at stake is not only instrumentally and functionally defined. The methodologies of anthropology help elicit these kinds of meaning much better, and although we were not able to present our own qualitative material as we intended to, it is clear that this aspect of the triangulation that the methodological section speaks about is of critical importance in a full analysis of the role of values in development. It is even more important in the African context as the concepts that are to be investigated in the quantitative dimensions of such studies have to be developed from the ground up and cannot be assumed to be clear and available as seems to be the case in Europe and the industrialised and developed countries in the world that the European Values Study and the World Values Survey serve well enough.

African Research Required

We would like to take most of the concepts that we have developed some understanding of and ask ordinary people to respond to the aspects in terms of whether it could be the reason for various dynamics in the development of their well-being. This would make an African comparative study of the role of values in development possible. It is the proper way of developing constructs for quantitative analysis to investigate preliminary ideas in available literature and in the field adapt and learn from those encounters before venturing out with quantitative constructs and the items that support such constructs. This has to be done in the African context in a manner that is not as dependent on the existing pattern of quantitative research in African values as is the case in the World Values Survey. We propose that we have done some of the work that proves the need for alternative constructs and that we have done some of the work needed to facilitate the first phase of qualitative investigation of the relevant constructs. This can now be taken further in a meaningful manner. The dialogue that we are hoping for could consider the concepts and arguments put forward in Section 2 of the book.

Appendix: Country Reports[1]

Botswana

Since attaining independence in 1966, Botswana has emerged as one of Africa's most stable democracies, performing well on issues such as human rights and corruption (BBC News 2007). Its last democratic election was held in 2004 when Festus Mogae was re-elected as president for a second term. Although Botswana is considered to be a relatively stable democracy, with a score of 0.7 on the World Bank political stability ranking, the government has been criticised for its treatment of the Barsawa Bushmen. According to some accounts, the Barsawa have been forcefully removed from their traditional homes in the Central Kalahari Game Reserve, causing tension, not only between the Bushmen and the Botswana government, but also between the Botswana government and the international community. Nevertheless, the various ethnic groups in Botswana (the Tswana, Kalanga, Kgalagadi and Europeans) generally live in relative harmony. Christianity is the dominant religion in Botswana (having 71.6 per cent of the population confirmed), while atheism is also widespread (20.6 per cent) (CIA World Fact Book 2007, Country Watch 2007).

Despite its democratic success, HIV/Aids has proven to be a major threat in the country. In 2003, it was established that 37.3 per cent of Botswana's 1.6 million inhabitants are infected with HIV/Aids. This has had a major impact on life expectancy, which has dropped to 33.74 years. HIV/Aids has also had a negative impact on population growth, creating a negative growth rate of -0.04 per cent, which is a new precedent for Africa. Yet, in reaction to the devastation that HIV/Aids has caused, Botswana has instituted 'one of Africa's most advanced treatment programmes' (BBC News 2007).

Botswana is considered to be politically free according to the Freedom House rankings (Piano & Puddington 2005). However, its human rights record presents some obstacles. Although human rights are generally respected, press freedom has sometimes been limited by the government, prison conditions are poor and overcrowded, child abuse is rising and ethnic violence against the Barsawa has emerged. Nevertheless, Botswana is ranked 131st out of 177 countries on the Human Development Index (Country Watch 2007, World Fact Book 2007).

Despite Botswana's democratic success, gender equality and representation continues to be a problem. In parliament, only 11.1 per cent of MPs are women, a relatively low percentage for Southern African standards considering that more than a third of MPs are women in Mozambique, South Africa and Tanzania (Parliament of South Africa 2007). Although Botswana is slowly moving towards gender equality, the customary nature of its legal system remains problematic in terms of gender equality. Offences such as rape within marriage are yet to be classified as such, and it remains legal for girls to marry at the age of 14, while boys may only marry at the age of 16 (SARPN Wade 2004). Civil society too, remains relatively weak and underdeveloped in Botswana. This is largely attributed to a 'lack of financial resources', 'lack of ideological consciousness', 'lack of capacity' and 'lack of solidarity amongst organisations' (Tlale 2005). The one area where civil society has been relatively successful has been in women's organisations. Although women's representation and equality is not yet at ideal levels, it has improved a great deal since independence, largely as a result of civil society activism (Tlale 2005).

Since independence in 1966, Botswana has boasted of one of the highest economic growth rates in Africa. Currently, GDP stands at $18.72 billion and the GDP growth rate is a stable 4.7 per cent. However, despite its stable GDP, Botswana still struggles with inflation (which is currently at 11.4 per cent), unemployment (23.8 per cent) and poverty (30.3 per cent of the population living below the poverty line) (World Fact Book 2007).

Mozambique

Mozambique attained independence in 1975, after having waged a bloody civil war against the Portuguese. Since then, Mozambique has managed to maintain some degree of political stability, achieving a -0.15 political stability ranking according to the World Bank (2004). Mozambique was, however, only declared 'partly free' according to the Freedom House ranking system in 2005. Contributing to these ratings is large-scale corruption and impunity, as well as disrespect for human rights in the country. The government of Mozambique also has the power to restrict the freedom of the press, political parties and party members, if it is seen as necessary. Discrimination against peoples with disabilities, HIV/Aids and women is also evident (Country Watch 2007). Although Mozambican women hold 34.8 per cent of seats in the national parliament, women are far from equal. The literacy rate in Mozambique averages at only 47.8 per cent, yet the national average for women is even lower at only 31.4 per cent, while for men the figure rises to 62.3 per cent. This may largely be the result of poor school enrolment amongst girls (38 per cent) (Government of Mozambique n.d.).

Even though Mozambique has a better track record in containing HIV/Aids than many of its neighbours, having an adult prevalence rate of only 12.2 per cent, life expectancy remains low at only 39.82 years. Another testament to Mozambique's relatively low HIV/Aids prevalence rate is population growth, which remains steady at 1.38 per cent. Economically, Mozambique has maintained a very high growth rate (7.9 per cent in 2006). Unfortunately, inflation too has remained high (12.8 per cent in 2006). Despite only 21 per cent of citizens being unemployed, 70 per cent of Mozambicans continue to live below the poverty line (CIA World Fact Book 2007). One of the major causes of poverty in Mozambique has been the intermittent droughts and floods that the country has experienced, the most recent of which occurred in February 2007 (BBC News 2007). Demographically, Mozambique is nearly 100 per cent African, of which the largest ethnic tribes are the Makhuwa, Tsonga, Lomwe and Sena. Thirty per cent of Mozambicans are Christian, 20 per cent Muslim and 50 per cent have retained their indigenous beliefs (Country Watch 2007).

Crime has continued to plague Mozambique after the end of the civil war. Some of the major reasons for this have been the widespread availability of weapons after the war, and the high incidence of poverty in the country. Due to ineffective law enforcement and police oversight, Mozambique is a major interim destination for drugs, as well as money laundering. The incidence of organised crime remains quite high, as well as child labour, child prostitution and child abuse. Crime in Mozambique is facilitated by the understaffed and ineffective police and judicial system (Country Watch 2007).

South Africa

Since its peaceful transition to democracy in 1994, South Africa has become Africa's shining example of democracy and economic growth. Although ethnically divided (79 per cent of the population being African, 9.6 per cent European, 8.9 per cent coloured and 2.5 per cent Indian/Asian), South Africa has managed to maintain some degree of political stability, achieving a -0.24 World Bank rating. Freedom House has classified South Africa as completely politically free in 2005. The South African constitution has widely been regarded as one of the most liberal in the world, especially with regard to human rights (Country Watch 2007). As a result, the South African government has instituted an affirmative action policy, aimed at creating racial and gender equality. In terms of gender equality, 32.8 per cent of parliamentary seats are currently held by women (Parliament of South Africa 2007). This achievement is partly due to the involvement of civil society in South Africa, which has been active not only in lobbying for the rights of South Africans, but also in providing services to the poor where government has been lacking (Baden et al. 1999).

Related very closely to gender equality, is income equality. Currently 50, per cent of South Africans live below the international poverty line and the majority of these are women and children. Unfortunately, these inequalities also place women at greater risk of contracting HIV/Aids, which currently has a 21.5 per cent adult prevalence rate. It has become very worrying that these inequalities persist despite the 86.4 per cent literacy rate that South Africa has attained. As seen in the case of Botswana, HIV/Aids in South Africa is having a negative impact on both life expectancy (which is currently at 42.7 years) and population growth (being -0.4 per % in 2006) (Country Watch 2007, CIA World Fact Book 2007).

Economically, South Africa has been doing very well. It has managed to maintain a GDP growth rate of about 4.5 per cent and has also maintained inflation at 5 per cent. Nevertheless, unemployment persists at 25.5 per cent, which contributes to the large-scale inequality in the country (CIA World Fact Book 2007). Crime and the perception thereof remains one of the major obstacles in South Africa. Despite the overall crime rate having decreased since 2003, the widespread media coverage and a number of high profile cases have recently caused outrage amongst South Africans. Even though crime rates have decreased, they remain extremely high, threatening investment and tourism (Louw 2006).

Tanzania

Since independence in 1964, Tanzania has not managed to maintain a great degree of political stability, rated at –0.38 by the World Bank. Tanzania can also not be considered politically free, only being rated as 'part free' in 2005 by Freedom House (Country Watch 2007). One of the reasons for this ranking is that civil society in Tanzania is constrained by law. The Societies Ordinance of 1954 is still in operation, effectively suppressing civil society and political organisations by forcing them to be non-political and declaring their donors (Duhu 2005). Closely related to this problem, is the equality of women in Tanzanian society. Although 30.4 per cent of the Tanzanian parliamentary seats are held by women, women are far from equal. As in many other African states, customary law continues to constrain women in their traditional roles. As a result, women continue to occupy unskilled and low-paid positions. As is the case in South Africa, poverty disproportionately affects women – so much so that up to 60 per cent of Tanzanian women currently live in poverty (Government of Tanzania n.d.).

Although the population of Tanzania is close to 99 per cent African, it is ethnically diverse, consisting of more than 120 different ethnic groups of which not one constitutes more than 15 per cent of the population. In contrast to many other African nations, the HIV/Aids prevalence rate in Tanzania is only 8.8 per cent, and the population growth rate is 0.34 per cent. Life expectancy remains low at only 45.64 years. Religiously, one-third of Tanzanians are Christian, while Muslims and those following indigenous African beliefs also constitute a third of the population (Country Watch 2007).

Economically, Tanzania has proven to be very stable by maintaining a GDP growth rate of 5.8 per cent, as well as keeping inflation below 6 per cent. It has also managed to maintain a literacy rate of 78.2 per cent. Nevertheless, 36 per cent of Tanzanians still live below the poverty line. Despite this poverty problem, Tanzania remains open to African refugees, currently providing asylum for nearly 400,000 refugees from Burundi and 150,000 refugees from the Democratic Republic of the Congo. Although crime rates in Tanzania remain high, the types of crime (such as theft, robbery, fraud and drug trafficking) are much less severe than those found in many other African nations (Country Watch 2007).

Zimbabwe

After attaining independence in 1980, many had very high expectations of Robert Mugabe and the envisaged democratisation process. Today, however, most of these hopes have been shattered by the oppressive Mugabe regime. What began as an attempt to return the land to the people, has become the violent subjugation and intimidation of a nation dissatisfied with its leaders' choices. In 2002, Mugabe censored the press and in 2005, he initiated operation Murambattsvina in which he demolished many informal settlements, leaving Zimbabwe's most destitute without shelter. Unprovoked attacks on opposition party leader Morgan Tsvangirai and his colleagues have also dominated the headlines (BBC 2007). Politically, Zimbabwe is rated as 'not free' by Freedom House, while its political stability is only rated at -1.86 (Country Watch 2007). Life expectancy plummeted to 39.29 years in 2006, which is exacerbated by the HIV/Aids adult prevalence rate of 24.6 per cent, as well as the 1.5 million people who suffer from malnutrition (CIA World Fact Book 2007).

Even though Zimbabwe boasts of an incredible 90.7 per cent literacy rate, unemployment is rampant at 80 per cent, while the same proportion of Zimbabweans live below the poverty line. In ethnic terms, the Shona are by far the largest ethnic group, totalling 82 per cent of the population, followed by the Ndebele and Europeans. Economically, Zimbabwe's GDP growth rate is currently −4.4 per cent, while inflation totals at 1,204.6 per cent (BBC 2007). With regard to human rights, all opposition to the Mugabe government continues to be violently oppressed, while the position of women in Zimbabwe has also deteriorated dramatically (Wines 2003). As a result of the NGO Act, which effectively outlaws the work of aid agencies, they are finding it difficult to continue operating in Zimbabwe. Due to these conditions, riots frequently occur, generally being violently suppressed by the government forces (Country Watch 2007, CIA World Fact Book 2007).

Zambia

Subsequent to achieving independence in 1964, Zambia has not achieved great democratic and economic success. In 2004, Zambia obtained a 'partly free' Freedom House rating and a -0.16 World Bank political stability rating. This could be attributed to the more than 70 different ethnic groups that can be found in the country, as well as the fact that more than half of Zambians are Christian, while the other half are Muslim and Hindu. Zambia, like most Sub-Saharan African countries, is embroiled in a constant struggle with the HIV/Aids epidemic. In 2003, Zambia recorded a HIV/Aids adult prevalence rate of 16.5 per cent, with 89,000 having already died from the disease. Considering that Zambia has a population of only about 11.5 million, this is a significant segment of the population. As is the case in many other African countries, this has an effect on both the life expectancy of Zambians, being about 40 years of age in 2003, as well as population growth rate (2.11 per cent in 2006) (CIA World Fact Book 2007).

Economically, Zambia had a GDP of $11.51 billion in 2006, which translates into an economic growth rate of 6 per cent. However, when taking the inflation rate of 8.8 per cent into account, as well as the 86 per cent of Zambians that live below the poverty line and the 50 per cent of Zambians that are unemployed, a very different picture emerges. In terms of gender equality, Zambia does not match up to other SADC countries. Although the overall literacy rate in Zambia is 80.6 per cent, that of men is 86.8 per cent, while that of women is only 74.8 per cent (2007d). In contrast to most other SADC countries, only 18 out of the 158 members of parliament are women, and only 5 ministers out of 21 are women. Although crime in general remains a problem in Zambia, crimes against women and children have become pervasive (Embassy of Sweden 2005). Despite this disregard for human rights, Zambia does provide refuge for nearly 76,000 Angolan refugees, as well as 61,000 from the DRC and nearly 6,000 from Rwanda (CIA World Fact Book 2007).

Note

1. The appendix provides basic data and does not pretend to be an objective or neutral or complete perspective on the countries surveyed. The references provided are skewed towards the Western press, Western governments and Western dominated multilateral or NGO organisations.

References

Abu-Lughod, L., 1989, 'Zones of Theory in the Anthropology of the Arab World', *Annual Review of Anthropology,* 18, 267-306.

Adams, B., 1993, 'Sustainable Development and the Greening of Development Theory', in F. J. Schuurman, ed., *Beyond the Impasse.* London: Zed Books.

Adelman, I., 2001 'Fallacies in Development Theory', in: G. M. Meier, & J. E. Stigliz, eds., *Frontiers of Development Economics.* Oxford: Oxford University Press.

Adelman, I. & Morris, C., 1965, 'A Factor Analysis of the Interrelationship between Social and Political Variables and Per Capita Gross National Product', *Quarterly Journal of Economics,* 79, 555-578.

Adelman, I. & Morris, C., 1967, *Society, Politics and Economic Development: A Quantitative Approach,* Baltimore: John Hopkins University Press.

Adelman, I. & Morris, C., 1973, *Economic Growth and Social Equity in Developing Countries,* Stanford: Stanford University Press.

Afrobarometer, 2007, *Surveys.* www.afrobarometer.org.

Aka, P. C., 1997, 'Leadership in African development'. *Journal of Third World Studies,* 14, 213-242.

Alcalde, J. G., 1991 *Development, Decay and Social Conflict,* New York: Lanham.

Alkire, S., 2002, 'Dimensions of Human Development', *World Development,* 30, 181-205.

Almond, G. A. V. S., 1963, *The Civic Culture: Political Attitudes and Democracy in Five Nations,* Boston: Little, Brown & Co.

Alverson, H., 1978, *Mind in the Heart of Darkness: Value and Self-Identity Among the Tswana of Southern Africa,* New Haven: Yale University Press.

Amin, S., 1997, *Capitalism in the Age of Gglobalisation,* London: Zed Books.

Anand, S. & Sen, A., 2000 'The Income Component of the Human Development Index', *Journal of Human Development,* 1, 17-23.

Anderson, B., 1983, *Imagined Communities,* London: Verso.

Appadurai, A., 1996, *Modernity at Large: Anthropological Explorations of Globalization,* Mineapolis University of Minnesota Press.

Appiah, K. A., 1992, *In my Father's House: Africa in the Philosophy of Culture,* Oxford: Oxford University Press.

Arendt, H., 1958, *The Human Condition,* Chicago: The University of Chicago Press.

Asad, A. 1983, 'Anthropological Conceptions of Religion: Reflections on Geertz', *Man,* 18, 237-259.

Atkinson, A. B., 1973 'On the Measurement of Inequality', *Journal of Economic Theory,* 2, 244-263.

Bachrach, P. & Baratz, M., 1962, 'Two Faces of Power', *The American Political Science Review,* 56, 947-952.

Baden, S., Hassim, S. & Meintjies, S., 1999, 'Country Gender Profile: South Africa', *Women's Net (Online).*

Barnes, S. B., 1968, 'Paradigms, Scientific and Social', *Man,* 1, 94-102.

Barro, R. J., 1991, 'Economic Growth in a Cross-Section of Countries', *The Quarterly Journal of Economics,* 102, 407-443.

Barro, R. J. & McCleary, R. M., 2003, 'Religion and economic growth across countries', *American Sociological Review,* 68, 760-781.

Bauer, D. F. & Hinnant, J., 1987, 'Normal and Revolutionary Divination', in I. Karp, & C. S. Bird, eds., *Explorations in African Systems of Thought.* Washington, DC: Smithsonian Institution Press.

Bauer, P. T., 1984. 'Remembrance of Studies Past: Retracing First Steps', in G. M. Meier, & D. Seers, eds., *Pioneers in Development.* Oxford: Oxford University Press.

Bauman, Z., 1987, *Legislators and Interpreters,* Cambridge: Polity.

Bayart, J. F., 2000, 'Africa in the World: A History of Extraversion', *African Affairs,* 99, 217-267.

BBC, 2007, *Country Profiles: Zimbabwe.*

BBC, 2007, *Country Profile: Mozambique.*

Beck, U., 1986, *Risikogesellschaft: Auf dem Weg in eine andere Moderne,* Frankfurt: Suhrkamp.

Becker, H., 2003, 'The Least Sexist Society? Perspectives on Gender, Change and Violence among Southern African San', *Journal of Southern African Studies,* 29, 5-23.

Behringer, W., *Witches and Witch-hunts: a Global History,* New Jersey: Wiley Blackwell.

Beidelman, T. O., 1993, 'Review of Risk and Blame: Essays in Cultural Theory', *American Anthropologist,* 95, 1065.

Ben-Amos, P. G., 1994, 'Women and Power in an Edo Spirit Possession Cult', in T. D. Blakely, W. E. A. Van Beek, & D. L. Thompson, eds., *Religion in Africa: Experience and Expression.* London: James Currey.

Ben-Ner, A. & Putterman, L., 1998, 'Values and Institutions in Economic Analysis' in A. Ben-Ner, & L. Putterman, eds., *Economics, Values and Organization,* Cambridge: Cambridge University Press.

Ben Soltake, K. B. & Adam, L., 1999, 'The Role of Information and Communication Technologies in Science and Technology in Africa' in M. W. Makgoba, ed., *African Renaissance,* Sandton: Mafube.

Berg, B. L., 1995, *Qualitative Research Methods for the Social Sciences,* London: Allyn and Bacon.

Bernstein, P. L., 1998, *Against the Gods: The Remarkable Story of Risk,* London: Wiley.

Bernstein, R. J., 1980, *Beyond Objectivism and Relativism,* Oxford: Blackwell.

Berry 2002, *Cross-cultural Psychology: Research and Applications,* Cambridge: Cambridge University Press.

Beugelsdijk, S. & Smulders, S., 2003, 'Bridging and Bonding Social Capital: Which Type is good for Economic growth?' in W. Arts, J. Hagenaars, & L. Halman, eds., *The Cultural Diversity of European Unity,* Leiden: Brill.

Binns, T. & Nel, E., 1999, 'Beyond the Development Impasse: The Role of Local Economic Development and Community Self-Reliance in Rural South Africa', *The Journal of Modern African Studies,* 37, 389-408.

Birbili, M., 2000, 'Translating from one Language to Another' *Social Research update.* Department of Sociology, University of Surrey.

Blunt, P. & Jones, M. L., 1997, 'Exploring the Limits of Western Leadership Theory in East Asia and Africa', *Personnel Review,* 26, 6-23.

Booth, D., 1993a, 'Development Research: From Impasse to New Agenda' in F. J. Schuurman, ed., *Beyond the impasse,* London: Zed Books.

Booth, W. J., 1993b, 'A Note on the Idea of the Moral Economy', *American Political Science Review,* 87, 949-954.

Booth, W. J., 1994, 'On the Idea of the Moral Economy', *American Political Science Review,* 88, 653-667.

Boserup, E., 1970, *Woman's Role in Economic Development,* New York: St Martins Press.

Bourdieu, P., 1992, *Language & Symbolic Power,* Cambridge: Polity Press.

Bratton, M. & Mattes, R., 2001 'Support for Democracy in Africa: Intrinsic or Instrumental?' *British Journal of Political Science,* 31, 447-474.

Bratton, M. & Van der Walle, N., 1994, 'Neopatrimonial Regimes and Political Transitions in Africa', *World Politics,* 46, 453-489.

Breinner, L. ed, 1993, *Muslim Identity and Social Change in Sub-Saharan Africa,* London: Hurst & Company.

Brink, C. H., 2004, *Measuring Political Risk,* Aldershot: Ashgate.

Brislim, R. W., Lonner, W. & Thorndike, R. M., 1973, *Cross-cultural Research Methods,* New York: John Wiley & Sons.

Brown, L. D. & Korten, D. C., 1989, *Understanding Voluntary Organisations: Guidelines for Donors,* Washington: The World Bank.

Browne, B. A., 1997, 'Gender and Preferences for Job Attributes: A Cross Cultural Comparison', *Sex Roles,* 37, 61-71.

Bundy, C., 1988, *The Rise and Fall of the South African Peasantry,* London: James Currey.

Burawoy, M., 1976, 'The Functions and Reproduction of Migrant Labor: Comparative Material from Southern Africa and the United States', *The American Journal of Sociology,* 81, 1050-1087.

Bush, R., 2007, *Poverty and Neoliberalism,* London: Pluto.

Caldwell, J. C. & Caldwell, P., 1987, 'The Cultural Context of High Fertility in Sub-Saharan Africa', *Population and Development Review,* 13.

Carter, M. R. & Maluccio, J. A., 2003, 'Social Capital and Coping with Economic Shocks: An Analysis of Stunting of South African Children', *World Development,* 31, 1147-1163.

Casanova, J., 1994, *Public Religions in the Modern World,* Chicago: University of Chicago Press.

Castells, M., 1996a, *Network Society,* Oxford: Blackwell Publishers.

Castells, M., 1997, *The Power of Identity,* Oxford: Blackwell Publishers.

Castells, M., 1998, *End of Millennium,* Oxford: Blackwell Publishers.

Central Statistical Office, 2003, *2000 Census of Population and Housing: Zambia, Analytical Report,* Vol 10. Lusaka.

Central Statistical Office 2007, *Zambia Demographic and Health Survey 2007,* Lusaka.

Central Statistics Office, 1994, *Census 1992 National Report,* Harare.

Central, Statistics Office, 2004, *Census 2002 National Report.* Harare.

Cernea, M. M., 1988, *Non-governmental Organisations and Local Development,* Washington: The World Bank.

Chambers, R., 1983, *Rural Development: Putting the Last First,* London: Longman.

Chazan, N., 1993, *African Political Culture and Democracy*, Boulder: Lynne Reiner.

Cheater, A. P. & Gaidzanwa, R. B., 1996, 'Citizenship in Neo-Patrilineal States: Gender and Mobility in Southern Africa', *Journal of Southern African Studies*, 22, 189-200.

Cheek, J. & Porter, S., 1997, 'Reviewing Foucault: Possibilities and Problems for Nursing and Health Care', *Nursing Inquiry*, 4, 108-119.

Chilivumbo, A. 1985, *Migration and Uneven Rural Development in Africa: the Case of Zambia*, New York& London: University Press of America.

Chipungu, S., 1992, 'African Leadership Under Indirect Rule in Colonial Zambia', *Guardians in Their Time: Experiences of Zambians Under Colonial Rule*, 50-73.

Chowdhry, G., 1992, Review. *The Journal of Asian Studies*, 51, 132-134.

CIA, 2007, *CIA World Fact Book, Country Reports*.

Clapham, C., 1996, *Africa and the International System*, Cambridge: Cambridge University Press.

Clark, D., 2002a, *Visions of Development: A Study of Human Values*, Cheltenham: Edward Elgar.

Clark, D. A., 2002b, 'Concepts and Perceptions of Human Well-being: Some Evidence from South Africa', Forthcoming in *Oxford Development Studies*.

Clarke, I., 2001, 'Extreme Response Style in Cross-cultural Research', *International Marketing Review*, 18, 301-324.

Coetzee, J. K., ed., 1989, *Development is for People*, Bergvlei: Southern Publishers.

Cohen, B., 2006, 'Urbanization in Developing Countries: Current Trends, Future Projections, and Key Challenges for Sustainability', *Technology in Society*, 28, 63-80.

Cohen, D. & Prusak, L., 2001, *In Good Company: How Social Capital Makes Organisations Work*, Boston: Harvard Business School Press.

Comaroff, J., 1980, 'Healing and the Cultural Order: The Case of the Barolong Boo Ratshidi of Southern Africa', *American Ethnologist*, 7, 637-657.

Comaroff, J., 1985, *Body of Power, Spirit of Resistance*, Chicago: University of Chicago Press.

Comaroff, J. & Comaroff, J., 1992, *Ethnography and the Historical Iimagination*, Boulder: Westview Press.

Comaroff, J. & Comaroff, J. 1993, *Modernity and its Malcontents: Ritual and Power in Postcolonial Africa*, Chicago: University of Chicago Press.

Comaroff, J. & Comaroff, J., 2002, 'Alien-Nation: Zombies, Immigrants, and Millennial Capitalism', *South Atlantic Quarterly*, 101, 779-806.

Comaroff, J. & J. C., 2001, 'On Personhood: an Anthropological Perspective from Africa', *Social Identities*, 7, 267-283.

Comaroff, J. L. & Comaroff, J., 1990 'Goodly Beasts, Beastly Goods: Cattle and Commodities in a South African Context', *American Ethnologist*, 17, 195-216.

Comaroff, J. L. & Comaroff, J., 1991, *Of Revelation and Revolution*, Chicago: University of Chicago Press.

Comaroff, J.L. & Comaroff, J., 1993, *Modernity and its Malcontents*, Chicago: UNiversity of Chicago Press.

Comaroff, J. L. & Comaroff, J., 1997, *Of Revelation and Revolution*, Chicago: University of Chigaco Press.

Comaroff, J. L. & Comaroff, J., 1999, 'Occult Economies and the Violence of Abstraction: Notes from the South African Postcolony', *American Ethnologist*, 26, 279-303.

Commission for Africa, 2005, *Our Common Interest: Report of the Commission for Africa.* London: Penguin.

Cornwall, A. & Brock, K., 2006, 'The New Buzzwords', in P. Utting, ed., *Reclaiming Development Agendas: Knowledge, Power and International Policy Making,* New York: Palgrave MacMillan.

Corten, A. & Marshall-Fratani, R., eds., 2001 *Between Babel and Pentecost: Transnational Pentecostalism in Africa and Latin America,* Bloomington: Indiana University Press.

Coskun Samli, A., Nkonge, J. H. & Foscht, T., 2007, 'The Needed Globalization for African Countries: A Case for Entrepreneurship', *Journal of African Business,* 8, 145-154.

Crush, J. & Fraynes, B., eds., 2010, *Surviving on the Move: Migration, Poverty and Development in Southern Africa,* Cape Town: DBSA and IDASA.

D'Azevedo, W. L., 1994, 'Gola Womanhood & the Limits of Masculine Omnipotence', in T. D. Blakely, , W. E. A. Van Beek, & D. L.Thompson, eds., *Religion in Africa: Experience and Expression,* London: James Currey.

De Jong, F., 2004, 'The Social life of Secrets', in Van W. Binsbergen, & R. Van Dijk, eds., *Situating Globality: African Agency in the Appropriation of Global Culture,* Leiden: Brill.

Department of Trade and Industry, 2003, *Current Developments in the Automotive Industry 2003,* Pretoria.

De Witte, H., 1992, 'On the Impact of Youth Unemployment: Political Radicalization and a Decline of the Work Ethic?' in C. Verhaar, & L. Jansma, eds., *On the Mysteries of Unemployment,* Amsterdam: Kluwer Academic Publishers.

Denzin, N. K., 1978, *The Research Act,* New York: Macgraw Hill.

Diagne, S. B., 2004, 'On Prospective: Development and a Political Culture of Time', *Africa Development,* 29, 55-69.

Dobbelaere, K., 1981, *Secularization,* London: Sage.

Donnelly, T. T., 2002, 'Representing 'others': Avoiding the Reproduction of Unequal Social Relations in Research', *Nurse Researcher,* 9, 57-68.

Douglas, M., 1966, *Purity and Danger: an Analysis of Concepts of Pollution and Taboo,* London: Routledge and Kegan Paul Ltd.

Douglas, M., 1970, *Natural Symbols: Explorations in Cosmology,* London, Barrie & Rockliff: The Cresset Press.

Douglas, M., 1985, *Risk: Acceptability According to the Social Sciences,* London: Routledge and Kegan Paul Ltd.

Douglas, M., 1992, *Risk and Blame: Essays in Cultural Theory,* New York: Routledge.

Drever, J., 1952, *A Dictionary of psychology,* Harmondsworth: Penguin.

Duhu, J., 2005, 'Strengthening Civil Society in the South: Challenges and Constraints - A Case Study of Tanzania', *International Journal of Not-for-Profit Law.*

Durham, D., 2000, 'Youth and the Social Imagination in Africa: Introduction to Parts 1 and 2', *Anthropological Quarterly,* 73, 113-120.

Easterly, W. & Levine, R., 1994, *Africa's Growth Tragedy,* Washington DC: The World Bank.

Eckstein, H., 1997, *Social Science and Cultural Science, Rational Choice as Metaphysics,* Boulder:Westview Press.

Ellis, S., 1999, 'The Frontiers of Crime in South Africa', in J.-F. Bayart, S. Ellis, & B. Hibou, eds., *The Ciminalization of the State in Africa,* Bloomington: Indiana University Press.

Elson, D., 2002, 'Social Policy and Macroeconomic Performance: Integrating «the Economic» and «the Social», *Social Policy in a Development Context.* Geneva, United Nations Research Institute for Social Development.

Embassy of Sweden, 2005, *Annual Country Report Zimbabwe.*

Ember, C. R. & Ember, M., 2001, *Cross-cultural Research Methods,* London: Rowman and Littlefield Publishers.

Ester, P., Halman, L. & De Moor, R., eds., 1994, *The Individualizing Society. Value Change in Europe and North America,* Tilburg: Tilburg University Press.

Etounga-Manguelle, D., 2000, 'Does Africa need a Cultural Adjustment Program?', in L. E. Harrison, & S. P. Huntington, eds., *Culture Matters: How Values Shape Human Progress,* New York: Basic Books.

Evans-Pritchard, E. E., 1937, *Witchcraft, Oracles, and Magic among the Azande,* London: Oxford University Press.

Fabian, J., 1994, 'Jamaa: A Charismatic Movement Revisited', in T. D. Blakely, W. E. A. Van Beek, & D. L. Thompson, eds., *African Religion: Experience and Expression.* London: James Currey.

Fagan, G., Munck, R. & Nadasen, K., 1996, 'Gender, Culture and Development: A South African Experience', *European Journal of Development Research,* 8, 93-110.

Fedderke, J. & Klitgaard, R., 1998, 'Economic Growth and Social Indicators: An Exploratory Analysis', *Economic Development and Cultural Change,* 46, 455-490.

Fine, B., 2001, *Social Capital versus Social Theory,* London: Routledge and Kegan Paul.

Fortes, M., 1978, 'Family, Marriage and Fertility in West Africa', in Oppong et al, eds., *Marriage, Fertility and Parenthood in West Africa.*

Fortes, M. & Dieterlen, G., eds., 1965, *African Systems of Thought: Studies Presented and Discussed at the Third International African Seminar in Salisbury,* December 1960, London: Oxford University Press.

Foucault, M., 1990, *The History of Sexuality: Volume 1: An Introduction,* New York: Vintage Press.

Foucault, M., 1994, 'The Subject and Power', in J. D. Faubion, ed., *Michel Foucault: Power,* New York: The New Press.

Francis, P., 2002, 'Social Capital, Civil Society and Social Exclusion', in U. U. Kothari & M. Minogue, eds., *Development Theory and Practice: Critical Perspectives,* Houndmills: Palgrave.

Friedman, J., 1994a, 'Introduction', in J. Friedman, ed., *Consumption and Iidentity,* Chur, Harwood Academic Publishers.

Friedman, J., 1994b, 'The Political Economy of Elegance', in J. Friedman, ed., *Consumption and Identity.* Chur, Harwood Academic Publishers.

Fukuyama, F., 1995, *Trust: The Social Virtues and the Creation of Prosperity,* London: Penguin Books.

Gabanesch, H., 1972, 'Authoritarianism as World View', *American Journal of Sociology,* 77, 857-875.

Garson, P., 2007, 'SA's Push for Gender Equity', International Marketing Council of South Africa.

Gausset, Q., 2002, 'The Cognitive Rationality of Taboos on Production and Reproduction in Sub-Saharan Africa', *Africa,* 72, 628-654.

Geschiere, P., 1998, 'Globalization and the Power of Indeterminate Meaning: Witchcraft and Spirit Cults in Africa and East Asia'. *Development and Change*, 29, 811-837.

Giddens, A., 1971, *Capitalism and Modern Social Theory: An Analysis of the Writings of Marx, Durkheim and Max Weber,* London: Cambridge University Press.

Giddens, A., 1981, *A Contemporary Critique of Historical Materialism. Vol. 1. Power, Property and the State,* London: Macmillan.

Giddens, A., 1986, *The Constitution of Society,* Berkeley: University of California Press.

Giddens, A., 1991, *The Consequences of Modernity,* Cambridge: Polity Press.

Giddens, A., 1994, 'Living in a Post-traditional Society', in U.Beck, A. Giddens & S. Lash, eds., *Reflexive Modernization: Politics, Tradition and Aesthetics In The Modern Social Order.* Stanford, California: Stanford University Press.

Gifford, P., 1998, *African Christianity: Its Public Role,* London: Hurst.

Goebel, A., 1998, 'Process, Perception and Power: Notes from 'Participatory' Research in a Zimbabwean Resettlement Area', *Development and Change*, 29, 277-305.

Goheen, M., 1992, 'Chiefs, Sub-Chiefs and Local Control: Negotiations over Land, Struggles over Meaning'. *Africa*, 62, 389-412.

Government of Mozambique, n.d., *Gender Information Brief: Mozambique*, EC Gender Helpdesk.

Government of Tanzania, n.d., *Gender.*

Government of Tanzania, n.d., *Global Database of Quotas for Women.* Institute for Democracy and Electoral Assistance, Tanzania.

Graeber, D., 2001 *Toward an Anthropological Theory of Value,* New York: Palgrave.

Granato, J., Inglehart, R. & Lebrang, D., 1996, 'The Effect of Cultural Values on Economic Development: Theory, Hypothesis and some Empirical Tests', *American Journal of Political Science*, 40, 607-631.

Green, R. M., 1983, 'Religion and Morality in the African Traditional Setting', *Journal of Religion in Africa*, 14, 1-23.

Griffith, G., 1967, *Population Problems of the Age of Malthus,* London: Frank Cass.

Grondona, M., 2000, 'A Cultural Typology of Economic Development', in L. E.Harrison, & S. P. Huntington, eds., *Culture Matters,* New York: Basic Books.

Guyer, J. I., 1996, 'Traditions of Invention in Equatorial Africa', *African Studies Review*, 39, 1-28.

Gyekye, K., 1988, *The Unexamined Life: Philosophy and the African Experience,* Accra: Ghana Universities Press.

Gyekye, K., 1997, *Tradition and Modernity,* New York: Oxford University Press.

Habermas, J., 1981, 'Theorie des Kommunikativen Handelns: Zur Kritik der funktionalistischen Vernunft', 2.

Haddad, L., Maluccio, John A., 2003, 'Trust, Membership in Groups, and Household Welfare: Evidence from KwaZulu-Natal, South Africa', *Economic Development and Cultural Change*, 51, 573-602.

Hagen, E., 1962, *On the Theory of Social Change: How Economic Growth Begins,* Homewood: Dorsey Press.

Hagenars, J., Halman, L. & Moors, G., 2003, 'Exploring Europe's basic value map', in Arts, W., Hagenaars, J. & Halman, L., eds., *The Cultural Diversity of European Unity.* Leiden/Boston: Brill.

Hakim, C., 1991, 'Grateful Slaves and Self-Made Women: Facts and Fantasy in Women's Work Orientations', *European Sociological Review*, 7, 101-121.

Halman, L., 1991, *Waarden in de Westerse Wereld*, Tilburg: Tilburg University Press.

Halman, L., 2001, *The European Values Study: A Third Wave. Source Book of the 1999/2000 European Values Study Surveys*, Tilburg, EVS, WORC: Tilburg University.

Halman, L. & Muller, H., 2006, 'Contemporary Work Values in Africa and Europe: Comparing Orientations to Work in African and European Societies', *International Journal of Comparative Sociology*, 47, 117-143.

Halman, L. & Vloet, A., 1994, *Measuring and Comparing Values in 16 Countries of the Western World*, Tilburg: Worc.

Hammond-Tooke, W. D., 1974, *The Bantu-speaking Peoples of Southern Africa*, London: Routledge & Kegan Paul.

Hanmer, L. C., Pyatt, G. & White, H., 1999, 'What do the World Bank's Poverty Assessments Teach us About Poverty in Sub-Saharan Africa?' *Development and Change*, 30, 785-823.

Hannerz, U., 1996, 'The Local and the Global: Continuity and Change', in Hannerz, U., ed., *Transnational Connections: Culture, People, Places*, New York: Routledge.

Harding, S. & Hikspoors, F., 1995, 'New Work Values: In Theory and in Practice', *International Social Science Journal*, 145, 441-456.

Harrison, L. E., 2000, 'Introduction: Why Culture Matters', in L. E. Harrison, & S. P. Huntington, eds., *Culture Matters: How Values Sshape Human Progress*, New York: Basic Books.

Hatch, E., 1983, *Culture and Morality: The Relativity of Values in Anthropology*, New York: Columbia University Press.

Haug, M. R., 1967, 'Social and Cultural Pluralisms as a Concept in Social System Analysis', *American Journal of Sociology*, 73, 294-304.

Heald, G., 2001, 'Reflections on Interview with Steve Murphy Managing Director of Hannover Re about the Business in Africa Elective to be Run by Wits Business School', *Embark Magazine*, Wits Business School.

Herzberg, F., Mausner, B. & Bloch Snyderman, B., 1959, *The Motivation to Work*, New York: John Wiley & Sons.

Hettne, B., 1990, *Development Theory and the Three Worlds*, Harlow: Longman Scientific and Technical.

Hobsbawm, E. & Ranger, T., eds., 1983, *The Invention of Tradition*, Cambridge: Cambridge University Press.

Hofstede, G., 2001, *Culture's Consequences: Comparing Values, Behaviours, Institutions, and Organisations Across Nations*, London: Sage.

Horton, R., 1993, *Patterns of Thought in Africa and the West: Essays on Magic, Religion and Science*, Cambridge: Cambridge University Press.

Hoselitz, B., 1952, 'Non-Economic Barriers to Economic Development', *Economic Development and Cultural Change*, 1, 8-21.

Hountondji, P. J., 1996, *African Philosophy: Myth and Reality*, Bloomington, Indiana University Press.

Hui, C. H. & Triandis, H. C., 1989, 'Effects of Culture and Response Format on Extreme Response Style', *Journal of Cross-Cultural Psychology*, 20, 296-309.

Huntington, S. P., 1993, 'The Clash of Civilizations?', *Foreign Affairs*, 72, 22-49.

Huntington, S. P., 1996, *The Clash of Civilizations and the Remaking of World Order*, New York; Simon & Schuster.

Huntington, S. P., 2000, 'Foreword: Cultures Count', in L. E. Harrison, & S. P. Huntington, eds., *Culture Matters: How Values Shape Human Progress*. New York: Basic Books.

Hyden, G., 2001, 'The Social Capital Crash in the Periphery: An Analysis of the Current Predicament in Africa', *Journal of Socioeconomics*, 30, 161-163.

Inglehart, R., 1977, *The Silent Revolution*, Princeton: Princeton University Press.

Inglehart, R., 1988, 'The Renaissance of Political Culture', *American Political Science Review*, 82, 1203-1230.

Inglehart, R., 1990, *Culture Shift in Advanced Industrial Society*, Princeton, NJ: Princeton University Press.

Inglehart, R., 1995, 'Changing Values, Economic Development and Political Change', *International Social Science Journal*, 47, 379-404.

Inglehart, R., 1997, *Modernization and Postmodernization*, Princeton:Princeton University Press.

Inglehart, R. & Baker, W. E., 2000, 'Modernization, Cultural Change, and the Persistence of Traditional Values', *American Sociological Review*, 65, 19-51.

Inglehart, R., Basanez, M., Diez-Medrano, J., Halman, L. & Luijkx, R., 2004, *Human Beliefs and Values. A Cross-cultural Sourcebook Based on the 1999-2002 Values Surveys*, Mexico: L Siglo XXI Editores.

Inglehart, R., Basanez, M. & Moreno, A., 1998, *Human Values and Beliefs. A Cross-Cultural Sourcebook*, Michigan: The University of Michigan Press.

Inglehart, R. & Welzel, C., eds., 2005, *Modernization, Cultural Change and Democracy; The Human Development Sequence*, New York: Cambridge University Press.

Ingram, D., 1987, *Habermas and the Dialectic of Reason*, New Haven: Yale University Press.

Inkeles, A., 1974, *Becoming Modern*, Harvard: Harvard University Press.

Isaac, J. C., 1987, 'Beyond the Three Faces of Power: A Realist Critique', *Polity*, 20, 4-31.

Jacobson, R., 1999, 'Complicating «Complexity»: Integrating Gender into the Analysis of the Mozambican Conflict', *Third World Quarterly*, 20, 175-187.

Joubert, D., 1992, *Reflections on Social Values*, Pretoria: Human Sciences Research Council.

Kalleberg, A. L. & Stark, D., 1993, 'Career Strategies in Capitalism and Socialism: Work Values and Job Rewards in the United States and Hungary', *Social Forces*, 72, 181-198.

Kamler, B. & Threadgold, T., 2003, 'Translating Difference: Questions of Representation in Cross-Cultural Research Encounters', *Journal of Intercultural Studies*, 24, 137-151.

Kamuzora, C. 1987, 'Survival Strategy: The Historical and Economic Roots of an African High Fertility Culture', in E. van de Walle, ed,., *The Cultural Roots of African Fertility Regimes*.

Kaspin, D., 1996, 'A Chewa Cosmology of the Body', *American Ethnologist*, 23, 561-578.

Katerere, Y., Hill, R. & Moyo, S., 2001, 'A Critique of Transboundary Natural Resource Management in Southern Africa'. Paper No.1, IUCN-ROSA Series on Transboundary Natural Resource Management. Nairobi, The World Conservation Union.

Kebede, M., 2004, 'African Development and the Primacy of Mental Decolonization', *Africa Development*, 29, 107-129.

Keesing, R. M. A. S., 1998, *Cultural Anthropology: A Contemporary Perspective*, Belmont, Wadsworth.

Kluckhohn, C. K., Parsons, T. & Shills, E. A., 1951, 'Some Fundamental Categories in the Theory of Action', in T. Parsons, & E. A. Shills, eds., *Towards a General Theory of Action.* Cambridge: Harvard University Press.

Knack, S. K.,1997, 'Does Social Capital have an Economic Payoff? A Cross-country Investigation', *The Quarterly Journal of Economics,* 112, 1251-1288.

Kopytoff, I., 1987, 'Realization and the Genesis of Cults in Pragmatic Religion', in I.Karp, & C. S. Bird, eds., *Explorations in African Systems of Thought,* Washington, DC.: Smithsonian Institution Press.

Korten, D. C., 1990, *Getting to the 21st Century: Voluntary Action and the Global Agenda,* West Hartford: Kumarian.

Kothari, U. & Minogue, M., 2002, 'Critical Perspectives on Development: an Introduction', in U.Kothari, & M. Minogue, eds., *Development Theory and Practice: Critical Perspectives,* Houndmills: Palgrave.

Kothari, U., Minogue, M. & De Jong, J., 2002, 'The political economy of globalization', in U. Kothari, & M. Minogue, eds., *Development Theory and Practice: Critical Perspectives,* Houndmills: Palgrave.

Kotze, H. & Lombard, K., 2002, 'Revising the Value Shift Hypothesis: A Descriptive Analysis of South Africa's value priorities between 1990 and 2001', *Comparative Sociology,* 1, 1-25.

Kuper, A., 1983, *Anthropology and Anthropologists,* London: Routledge and Kegan Paul.

Kuran, T., 1997, 'Islam and Underdevelopment: An Old Puzzle Revisited', *Journal of Institutional and Theoretical Economics,* 153, 41-71.

Kuran, T., 1998, 'The Genesis of Islamic Economics: A Chapter in the Politics of Muslim Identity', *Social Research Update,* 64, 301-338.

Kuran, T., 2001, 'The Provision of Public Goods under Islamic Law: Origins, Impact, and Limitations of the Waqf System. *Law & Society Review,* 35, 841-897.

Kuran, T., 2003, 'The Islamic Commercial Crisis: Institutional Roots of Economic Underdevelopment in the Middle East', *Journal of Economic History,* 63, 414-446.

Kuran, T., 2004a 'Cultural Obstacles to Economic Development: Often Overstated, Usually Transitory', in V. Rao, & M.Walton, eds., *Culture and Public Action.* Stanford, Calfornia: Stanford University Press.

Kuran, T., 2004b, 'The Economic Ascent of the Middle East's Religious Minorities: the Role of Islamic Legal Pluralism', *Journal of Legal Studies,* 33, 475-515.

Kuran, T., 2004c, 'Why the Middle East is Economically Underdeveloped: Historical Mechanisms of Institutional Stagnation', *Journal of Economic Perspectives,* 18, 71-90.

Kuran, T., 2005, 'The Logic of Financial Westernization in the Middle East', *Journal of Economic Behavior and Organization,* 56, 593-615.

Landes, D., 2000, 'Culture Makes Almost all the Difference', in L. E. Harrison, & S. P. Huntington, eds., *Culture Matters: How Values Shape Human Progress,* New York: Basic Books.

Landes, D. S., 1998, *The Wealth and Poverty of Nations: Why Some are so Rich and Some are so Poor,* New York: W.W. Norton.

Landman, T., 2000, *Issues and Methods in Comparative Politics: An Introduction,* London: Routledge.

Lassiter, J. E., 1999a 'African Culture and Personality: Bad Social Science, Effective Social Activism, or a Call to Reinvent Ethnology?', *African Studies Quarterly*, 3.

Lategan, B., 2000, 'Extending the Materialist/Post-Materialist Distinction. Some Remarks on the Classification of Values from a South African Perspective', *Scriptura*, 75, 409-420.

Lawuyi, O. B., 1998, 'Water, Healing, Gender and Space in African Cosmology', *South African Journal of Ethnology*, 21.

Leatt, J., 1982, 'Astride Two Worlds: Religion and Values among Black Migrant Workers on South African Gold Mines', *Journal of Theology in Southern Africa*, 38, 59-82.

Lee, E., 1968, 'Theories on Migration', *Readings on Population*, 181-201.

Lehmann, D., 1990, 'Modernity and Popular Culture', *European Journal of Development Research*, 2, 1-13.

Levinson, H. S., 1981, 'Traditional Religion, Modernity, and Unthinkable Thoughts', *The Journal of Religion*, 61, 37-58.

Lewis, B., 2003, *Crisis of Islam*, New York, Modern Library.

Lian, B., Oneal, John R., 1997, 'Cultural diversity and Economic Development: A Cross-national Study of 98 Countries, 1960-1985', *Economic Development and Cultural Change*, 46, 61-78.

Likoti, F. J. 2007, 'The 1998 Military Intervention in Lesotho: SADC Peace Mission or Resource War?', *International Peacekeeping*, 14, 251 - 263.

Lindenberg, M., 2002, 'Measuring Household Livelihood Security at the Family and Community Level in the Developing World', *World Development*, 30, 301-318.

Lipset, S., 1996, *American Exceptionalism*, New York/London: W.W. Norton & Company.

Lo Liyong, T., 1988, 'John S. Mbiti is a Thief of Gods', in K. H.Petersen,, ed., *Criticism and Ideology*. Uppsala: Scandinavian Institute of African Studies.

Londregan, J., Bienen, H. & Van de Walle, N., 1995, 'Ethnicity and Leadership Succession in Africa', *International Studies Quarterly*, 39, 1-25.

Long, N. & Villareal, M., 1993, 'Exploring Development Interfaces: From the Transfer of Knowledge to the Transformation of Meaning', in F. J. Schuurman, ed., *Beyond the impasse*, London: Zed Books.

Louw, A., 2006, 'The Start of a «Crime Wave»'?, *Crime Quarterly*.

Louw, D., 1998 'Ubuntu: An African Assessment of the Religious Other', *20th World Congress of Philosophy*, Massachusetts: University of Boston .

Luhmann, N., 1982, *Funktion der Religion*, Frankfurt: Suhrkamp.

Luhmann, N., 1985, 'Society, Meaning, Religion - Based on Self-Reference', *Sociological Analysis*, 46, 5-20.

Luhmann, N., 1993, *Risk: a Sociological Theory*, New York: Walter de Gruyter.

Lukes, S., 1974, *Power: A Radical View*, New York, Macmillan.

Lwanga-Ntale, C. & McClean, K., 2004, 'The Face of Chronic Poverty in Uganda from the Poor's Perspective: Constraints and Opportunities', *Journal of Human Development*, 5, 177-194.

Mafeje, A. 1978, *Science, Ideology and Development*, Uppsala: Scandinavian Institute of African Studies.

Maluccio, J., 1999, 'Social Capital and Income Generation in South Africa 1993-1998', Food Policy Research Institute.

Maluccio, J., Haddad, L. & May, J., 2000, 'Social Capital and Household Welfare in South Africa, 1993-98', *The Journal of Development Studies,* 36, 54-82.

Mamdani, M., 1996, *Citizen and Subject: Contemporary Africa and the Legacy of Late Colonialism,* Princeton: Princeton University Press.

Manji, A., 2003, 'Capital, Labour and Land Relations in Africa: A Gender Analysis of the World Bank's Policy Research Report on Land Institutions and Land Policy', *Third World Quarterly,* 24, 97-114.

Marindo-Ranganai, 1995, 'The Population Dynamics of the Tembomvura People of Zambezi Valley, Northern Zimbabwe: Some Methods of Collecting and Analysing Birth Historical Data, *Zambezia,* XXII, 177-195.

Marini, M., 2004, 'Cultural Evolution and Economic Growth: a Theoretical Hypothesis with some Empirical Evidence', *Journal of Socio-Economics,* 33, 765-785.

Marini, M. M., Fan, P.-L., Finley, E. & Beutel, A. M., 1996, 'Gender and Job Values'. *Sociology of Education,* 69, 49-65.

Martin, R., 1977, *The Sociology of Power,* London: Routledge & Kegan Paul.

Masolo, D. A., 1991, 'An Archaeology of African Knowledge: A Discussion of V. Y. Mudimbe', *Callaloo,* 14, 998-1011.

Matlosa, K., 2004, 'Managing Democracy: A Review of SADC Principles and Guidelines Governing Democratic Elections. *EISA Democracy Seminars Series,* Johannesburg: EISA.

Mattes, R. & Shin, C., 2005, 'The Democratic Impact of Traditional Cultural Values in Africa and Asia: The cases of South Korea and South Africa', Afrobarometer Working Paper No. 50.

Matthews, S. 2004, 'Post-Development Theory and the Questions of Alternatives: A View from Africa', *Third World Quarterly,* 25, 373-384.

May, J. 2008, 'Conceptualising and Measuring Poverty in the SADC region', in M. Pressend, & M. Ruiters, eds., *Dilemmas of Poverty and Development,* Braamfontein: Institute for Global Dialogue.

Mayer, L. C., 1989 *Redefining Comparative Politics: Promise Versus Performance,* Newbury Park, CA: Sage.

Mazrui, A., 1990, *Cultural Forces in World Politics,* London: James Currey.

McClelland, D., 1967, *The Achieving Society,* Princeton, Van Nostrand.

McKeown, T., 1976, *The Modern Rise of Population,* London: Edward Arnold Ltd.

McLaughlin, B., 1965, 'Values in behavioral science', *Journal of Religion and Health,* 4, 258-279.

McLellan, D., ed., 1977, *Karl Marx: Selected Writings,* Oxford: Oxford University Press.

Meier, G. M., 1964, *Leading Issues in Economic Development,* New York: Oxford University Press.

Meyer, B., 2004a, 'Christianity in Africa: From African Independent to Pentecostal-Charismatic Churches', *Annual Review of Anthropology,* 33, 447-474.

Mhloyi, M. M., 1987, 'The Proximate Determinants and their Socio-cultural Determinants: The Case of Two Rural Settings in Zimbabwe', in E.Van de Walle, & K. Omideyi, eds., *The Cultural Roots of African Fertility Regimes,* Philadelphia: Population Studies Centre University Pennsylvania, Proceedings of Ife Conference.

Mhloyi, M. M., 1988, 'The Determinants of Fertility in Africa Under Modernization', in E.Van de Walle, ed., IUSSP.

Mhone, G. & Bond, P., 2002, 'Botswana and Zimbabwe: Relative Success and Comparative Failure', in S. M.Murshed, ed., *Globalization, Marginalization and Development,* London: Routledge.

Mkandawire, T., 2001a 'Social Policy in a Development Context', *Social Policy and Development Programme,* Geneva, United Nations Research Institute for Social Development.

Mkandawire, T., 2001b 'Thinking about Developmental States in Africa', *Cambridge Journal of Economics,* 25, 289-313.

Mkandawire, T., 2010, 'Running while Others Walk: Knowledge and the Challenge of Africa's Development'.

Mopper, B., 2006, 'Religion and Conflict in Africa with Special Focus on East Africa'. Danish Institute for International Studies.

Montaner, C. A., 2000, 'Culture and the Behaviour of Elites in Latin America', in L. E. Harrison, & S. P. Huntington, eds., *Culture Matters,* New York: Basic Books.

Moore, B., 1966, *Social Origins of Dictatorships and Democracy,* Harmondsworth: Penguin.

Morrell, R. 1998, 'Of Boys and Men: Masculinity and Gender in Southern African Studies', *Journal of Southern African Studies,* 24, 605-630.

Mouzelis, N., 1994, 'The State in Late Development: Historical and Comparative Perspectives' in D. Booth, ed., *Rethinking Social Development,* Harlow: Longman.

Mow, I. R. T., 1987, *The Meaning of Working,* London, Academic Press.

Muller, H., 2000, 'The Invention of Religion: Aspects of the South African Case, *Social Dynamics,* 26, 56-75.

Muller, H., 2004, 'The application of Inglehart's Materialism-Postmaterialism Index in Non-industrialised Countries - A critique', *Acta Academica,* 36, 127-156.

Myrdal, G., 1968, *Asian Drama: An Inquiry into the Poverty of Nations,* New York: Pantheon.

Narayan, D., 2000, *Voices of the Poor. Can Anyone Hear Us?* Oxford: Oxford University Press.

Narayan, D. & Pritchett, L., 1997, 'Cents and Sociability - Household Income and Social Capital in Rural Tanzania', Washington DC: The World Bank.

Nederveen Pieterse, J., 1995, 'The Cultural Turn in Development Research: Questions of Power', *European Journal of Development Research,* 7, 176-192.

Neuman, W. L., 2000, *Social Research Methods: Qualitative and Quantitative Approaches,* London: Allen and Bacon.

News, B., 2007 Country Profile: Botswana.

Niehaus, I., 2005, 'Obituary: David Hammond-Tooke', *Anthropology Today,* 21.

Niehaus, I., Mohlala, E. & Shokane, K., 2001, *Witchcraft, Power and Politics: Exploring the Occult in the South African Lowveld,* Ann Arbor: University of Michigan University Press.

Nkrumah, K., 1964, *Concientism: Philosophy and Ideology for Decolonization and Development with Particular Relevance to the African Revolution,* London: Heineman.

Noland, M., 2005, 'Religion and Economic Performance'. *World Development,* 33, 1215-1232.

North, D. C., 2005, 'The Contribution of the New Institutional Economics to an Understanding of the Transition Problem' in G. A. Cornia, M.Pohjola, & A. Shorrocks, eds., *Wider Perspectives on Global Development,* New York: Palgrave Macmillan.

Nussbaum, M. C. & Glover, J., eds., 1995, *Women, Culture, and Development,* Oxford: Clarendon Press.

Nussbaum, M. C. & Sen, A. K., eds., 1993, *The Quality of Life,* Oxford: Clarendon Press.

Nwanko, N. R. L. & Nzelibe, C. G., 1990, 'Communication and Conflict Management in African Development'. *Journal of Black Studies,* 20, 253-266.

Nyamnjoh, F. B., 2004, 'Globalisation, Boundaries and Livelihoods: Perspectives on Africa', *Identity, Culture and Politics,* 5, 37-59.

Odhiambo, E. S. A., 2002, 'The Cultural Dimensions of Development in Africa', *African Studies Review,* 45, 1-16.

Ogura, M., 1991, 'Rural Urban Migration in Zambia and Migrant Ties to Home Villages', *Developing Economies,* 29, 145-165.

Ohadike, P., 1981, *Demographic Perspectives in Zambia,* Manchester: Manchester University Press.

Onimode, B., 1992, *A Future for Africa. Beyong the Politics and Adjustment,* London: Earthscan.

Osaghae, E., 1999, 'The Post-colonial African State and its Problems',in P. Nel & P. McGowan, eds., *Power, Wealth and Global Order,* Cape Town: University of Cape Town Press.

Osmani, S. R., 2005, 'Poverty and Human Rights: Building on the Capability Approach', *Journal of Human Development,* 6, 205-219.

Owusu, M. 1992, 'Democracy and Africa: A View from the Village', *Journal of Modern African Studies,* 30, 369-396.

Oyeshile, O. A., 200,) 'Traditional Yoruba Social-ethical Values and Governance in Modern Africa', *Philosophia Africana,* 6, 81-88.

Oyeshile, O. A.,2004, 'Communal Values, Cultural Identity and the Challenge of Development in Contemporary Africa', 29, 291-304.

p'Bitek, O., 1970, *African Religions in Western Scholarship,* Kampala: East African Literature Bureau.

p'Bitek, O., 1973, *Africa's Cultural Revolution,* Nairobi: Macmillan.

Pallotti, A.,2004, 'SADC: A Development Community without a Development Policy?', *Review of African Political Economy,* 31, 513.

Parliament of South Africa, 2007, *The Parliament of South Africa.* Pretoria: Government Printer.

Patel, V., 2001, 'Cultural Factors and International Epidemiology', *British Medical Bulletin,* 57, 33-45.

Pels, P., 1998, 'The Magic of Africa: Reflections on a Western Commonplace', *African Studies Review,* 41, 193-209.

Peristiany, J. G., ed., 1974, *Honour and Shame: the Values of Mediterranean Society,* Chicago: University of Chicago Press.

Perman, R., Yue, M. & McCgilvary, J., 1996, *Natural Resources and Environmental Economics,* Harlowe: Pearson Addison-Wesley.

Petringa, M., 2006, *Brazza, A Life for Africa,* London; Authorhouse.

Pew Forum on Religion & Public Life, 2006, *Spirit and Power: a 10-country Survey of Pentecostals.* Washington, DC.

Phillips, H. P., 1960, *In Human Organisation Research: Field Relations and Techniques,* Homewood: Dorsey Press Inc.

Piano, A. & Puddington, A. 2005, *Freedom in the World.* Lanham: Rowman & Littlefield.

Pieterse, J. N., 1998, 'My Paradigm or Yours? Alternative Development, Post-Development, Reflexive Development', *Development and Change,* 29, 343-373.

Pithouse, R., 2007, 'Producing the Poor: The World Bank's new Discourse of Domination', in D. Moore, ed., *The World Bank: Development, Poverty, Hegemony,* Scottsville: University of Kwa-Zulu-Natal Press.

Pityana, N. B., 2006, 'Perspectives on Leadership and the Silences of Reason', The Second JD Baqwa Memorial Lecture, UCT.

Popper, K. R., 1963, *Conjectures and Refutations: The Growth of Scientific Knowledge,* London: Routledge.

Population Reference Bureau Inc., 1981, *World Population Data Sheet,* Washington DC.

Population Reference Bureau Inc., 1985, *World Population Data Sheet,* Washington DC.

Population Reference Bureau Inc., 1990, *World Population Data Sheet,* Washington DC.

Population Reference Bureau Inc., 1995, *World Population Data Sheet,* Washington DC.

Population Reference Bureau Inc., 2000, *World Population Data Sheet,* Washington DC.

Pretorius, E., 1989, 'Skakeling tussen tradisionele en modern geneeskunde in Afrika', *Acta Academica,* 21, 101-129.

Pretorius, E., 1994, 'Afrosentriese etiologiese opvattings: empiriese bevindings in Magaung', *Suid-Afrikaanse Tydskrif vir Sosiologie,* 25, 104-113.

Prosterman, R. L., Temple, M. N. & Hanstad, T. M., eds., 1990, *Agrarian reform and grassroots development,* Boulder: Lynne Reiner.

Przeworski, A. & Teune, H., 1970, *The Logic of Comparative Social Inquiry,* New York: Wiley Interscience.

Putnam, R., 1993, *Making Democracy Work. Civic Traditions in Modern Italy,* Princeton: Princeton University Press.

Putnam, R., 1995, 'Bowling alone: America's declining Social Capital', *Journal of Democracy,* 6, 65-78.

Putnam, R., 2000, *Bowling Alone: The Collapse and Revival of American Community,* New York: Simon and Schuster.

Rahnema, M. & Bawtree, V., eds., 1997, *The Post-development Reader,* Cape Town: David Phillip.

Ranger, T., 1995, *Are We Not Also Men? The Samkange Family and African Politics in Zimbabwe 1920-64,* London: James Currey.

Ranger, T., 2003, 'Christianity and Indigenous Peoples: A Personal Overview', *Journal of Religious History,* 27, 255-271.

Rasing, T., 2004, 'The Persistence of Female Initiation Rites: Reflexivity and Resilience of Women in Zambia', in W. Van Binsbergen, & R.Van Dijk, eds., *Situating Globality: African Agency in the Appropriation of Global Culture* Leiden: Brill.

Ratner, B., 2004, '«Sustainability» as a Dialogue of Values: Challenges to the Sociology of Development', *Sociological Inquiry,* 74, 50-69.

Razzell, P., 1974, 'An Interpretation of the Modern Rise of Population in Europe- A Critique', *Population Studies,* 28, 1.

Reynolds, L. G., 1985, *Economic Growth in the Third World, 1850-1980,* New Haven: Yale University Press.

Robertson, C., 1984, *Sharing the Same Bowl: A Socio-economic History of Women and Class in Accra, Ghana,* Bloomington: Indiana University Press.

Robeyns, I., 2005, 'The Capability Approach: a Theoretical Survey', *Journal of Human Development,* 6, 93-114.

Robin, D.M., Larsen, A.R. & Levin, C., 2007, *Encyclopedia of Women in the Renaissance: Italy, France, and England*, Santa Barbara: ABC-CLIO.

Robins, S., 2003, 'Whose Modernity? Indigenous Modernities and Land Claims after Apartheid', *Development and Change,* 34, 265-285.

Robinson, W. S., 1950, 'Ecological Correlations and the Behaviour of Individuals', *American Sociological Review,* 15, 351-357.

Rokeach, M., 1970, *Beliefs, Attitudes, Values,* New York: Jossey-Bass.

Rokeach, M., 1973, *The Nature of Human Values,* Glencoe: Free Press.

Rosander, E. E. & Westerlund, D., eds., 1997, *African Islam and Islam in Africa: Encounters between Sufis and Islamists,* Athens/ Ohio: Ohio University Press.

Rostow, W., 1960, *The Stages of Economic Growth: A Non-Communist Manifesto,* Cambridge: Cambridge University Press.

Rowe, R. & Snizek, W. E., 1995, 'Gender Differences in Work Values', *Work and Occupations,* 22, 215-230.

Ruttan, V. W. (1988) Cultural Endowments and Economic Development: What can we Learn from Anthropology. *Economic Development and Cultural Change,* 36, 247-272.

Rutten, M. & Leliveld, A., 2008, 'Introduction: Inside Poverty and Development in Africa', in M. Rutten, A. Leliveld, & D. Foeken, eds., *Inside Poverty and Development in Africa,* Leiden: Brill.

Sachs, J., 2000, 'Notes on a New Sociology of Economic Development', in L. E. Harrison, & S. P. Huntington, eds., *Culture Matters,* New York, Basic Books.

SADC, 1992, 'Declaration Treaty and Protocol of Southern African Development Community', Gaborone.

Said, E., 1979, *Orientalism,* New York: Vintage Books.

Said, E., 2004, 'Orientalism Once More', *Development and Change,* 35, 869-879.

Sala-I-Martin, X., 2002, 'The Disturbing «Rise» of Global Income Inequality', *NBER Working Paper Series,* Working Paper 8904.

Sala-I-Martin, X., Doppelhofer, G. & Miller, R. I., 2004, 'Determinants of Long-Run Growth: A Bayesian Averaging of Classical Estimates (BACE) Approach', *American Economic Review,* 94, 813-835.

Schattschneider, E. E., 1960, *The Semi-Sovereign People,* New York: Holt, Rinehart & Winston.

Schuster, C. I. & Van Pelt, W. V., 1993, *Speculations: Readings in Culture, Identity and Values,* Englewood Cliffs, NJ: Prentice Hall.

Schuster, I., 1979, 'New Women of Lusaka', *Palo Alto.*

Schuurman, F. J., 1993, 'Modernity, Post-modernity and the New Social Movements', in F. J. Schuurman, ed., *Beyond the impasse,* London, Zed Books.

Schwartz, S. H., 1994, 'Beyond Individualism/Collectivism: New Dimensions of Values', in I. U.Kim, H. C.Triandis, C. Kagitcibasi, S. C. Choi, & G. Yoon, eds., *Individualism and Collectivism: Theory Application and Methods.* Newbury Park: CA, Sage.

Sechrest, L., Fay, T. L. & Zaidi, S. M. H., 1972 'Problems of Translation in Cross-cultural Research', *Journal of Cross-Cultural Psychology,* 3, 41-56.

Seleti, Y. N., 1992, 'Entrepreneurship in Colonial Zambia', in S. Chipungu, ed., *Guardians in Their Time: Experiences of Zambians under Colonial Rule,* London: Macmillan.

Seligson, M. A., 2003, 'Dual gaps: an Overview of Theory and Research', in M. A. Seligson, & J. T. Passe-Smith, eds., *Develoment and Underdevelopment: the Political-economy of Global Inequality* London: Lynne Rienner Publishers.

Sen, A., 1999, *Development as Freedom,* Oxford: Oxford University Press.

Sen, A. 2004a 'How Does Culture Matter?' in V. Rao, & M. Walton, eds., *Culture and Public Action,* Stanford: Stanford University Press.

Sen, A. K., 2004b, 'Capabilities, Lists and Public Reason: Continuing the Conversation', *Feminist Economics,* 10, 77-80.

Serageldin, I. & Taboroff, J., eds., 1994, *Culture and Development in Africa,* Washington DC: IBRD.

Sharp, J. & West, M., 1982 'Dualism, Culture and Migrant Mineworkers: A Rejoinder from Anthropology', *Journal of Theology in Southern Africa,* 39, 64-69.

Sijuwade, P. O., 2006 'Globalization and Cultural Conflict in Developing Countries: The South African Example', *Anthropologist,* 8, 125-137.

Silberschimidt, M., 2001, 'Disempowerment of Men in Rural and Urban East Africa: Implications for Male Identity and Sexual Behavior', *World Development,* 29, 657-671.

Sindima, H. J., 1995, *Africa's Agenda: the Legacy of Liberalism and Colonialism in the Crisis of African Values,* London: Greenwood Press.

Skelton, T., 1996, 'Cultures of Land' in the Caribbean: A Contribution to the Debate on Development and Culture', *European Journal of Development Research,* 8, 71-92.

Sklair, L., 2000, 'Social Movements and Global Capitalism', in J. T. Roberts, & A. Hite, eds., *From Modernization to Globalization,* Malden: Blackwell.

Sklair, R. L., 1998, 'The nature of class domination in Africa', in Lewis, P., ed., *Africa: dilemmas of development and change.* Boulder: Westview Press.

Skorupski, J., 1976, *Symbol and Theory,* London: Cambridge University Press.

Stewart, D. W. & Shamdasi, P. M., 1990, *Focus Groups: Theory and Practice,* Newbury Park: Sage.

Stewart, F., 2005, 'Groups and Capabilities', *Journal of Human Development,* 6, 185-204.

Stiglitz, J., 2002, *Globalization and Its Discontents,* New York: W.W. Norton & Company.

Sutcliffe, B., 2000, 'Development after ecology', in J. T. Roberts, & A. Hite, eds., *From modernization to globalization,* Malden: Blackwell.

Tarnai, C., Grimm, H. & Watermann, R., 1995, 'Work Values in European Comparison: School Education and Work Orientation in Nine Countries', *Tertium Comparationis. Journal für Internationale Bildungsforschung,* 1, 139-163.

Taylor, M., 2002, 'The Shaping of San Livelihood Strategies: Government Policy and Popular Values', *Development and Change,* 33, 467-488.

Teffo, L., 1999, 'Moral renewal and African experience(s)', in M. Makgoba, Ed., *African Renaissance: The new struggle,* Sandton/ Cape Town: Mafube/ Tafelberg.

Thomas-Slayter, B. P., 1992, 'Politics, Class, and Gender in African Resource Management: The Case of Rural Kenya', *Economic Development and Cultural Change,* 40, 809-829.

Thompson, E. P., 1963, *The Making of the English Working Class,* London: Victor Gollanz.

Tlale, B., 2005, 'The state of Civil Society in Botswana', *Mmegi Online.*

Torgerson, W. S., 1958, *Theory and Methods of Scaling,* New York: Wiley and Sons.

Touraine, A., 1974, *The Academic System in American Society,* New York: MacGraw & Hill.

Turaine, A., 1977, *The Self-production of Society,* Chicago: The University of Chicago Press.

Townsend, J., 1993, 'Gender Studies: Whose Agenda?', in Schuurman, F. J., ed., *Beyond the Impasse,* London: Zed Books.

Triandis, H., 1988, 'Collectivism and Development', in Sinha, D. & Kao, H., eds., *Social Values and Development: Asian Perspectives,* New Delhi: Sage.

Tripp, A. M., 1998, 'Gender, Political Participation and the Transformation of Associational Life in Uganda and Tanzania', in P. Lewis, ed., *Africa: Dilemmas of Development and Change,* Boulder CL: Westview Press.

Tucker, V., 1996, 'Introduction: A Cultural Perspective on Development', *European Journal of Development Research,* 8, 1-21.

Turner, J. H., 1997, *The Institutional Order,* New York: Longman.

Tyndale, W. 2000, 'Faith and economics in «development»: A Bridge Across the Chasm?', *Development in Practice,* 1.

Ukah, A., 2007, 'African Christianities: Features, Promises and Problems', Mainz: Institut für Ethnologie und Afrikastudien, Johannes Gutenberg-Universität.

UN, 2005, 'United Nations Millennium Project Investing in Development: A Practical Plan to Achieve the Millennium Development Goals', New York: Earthscan.

UN, 2010, 'The Millennium Development Goals Report 2010', New York: United Nations.

UNDP, 2000, *Human Development Report 2000,* New York: UNDP.

UNDP, 2002, *Human Development Report 2002.* Oxford: UNDP.

UNDP, 2003, *Human Development Report,* New York: UNDP.

UN General Assembly, 2000, *United Nations Millennium Declaration,* New York.

Upton, R. L., 2001, '«Infertility Makes You Invisible»: Gender, Health and the Negotiation of Fertility in Northern Botswana', *Journal of Southern African Studies,* 27, 349-362.

Utting, P., 2006, 'Introduction: Reclaiming development agendas', in P. Utting, , ed., *Reclaiming development agendas: Knowledge, Power and Policy Making.* New York: Palgrave.

Vail, L., 1983, 'The Political Economy of East-Central Africa', in D. Birmingham, & P. Martin, eds., *History of Central Africa,* London: Longman.

Van Binsbergen, W., Van Dijk, R. & Gewald, J.-B., 2004, 'Situating Globality: African Agency in the Appropriation of Global Culture', in W.Van Binsbergen, & R.Van Dijk, eds., *Situating Globality: African Agency in the Appropriation of Global Culture,* Leiden: Brill.

Van de Vijver, F. & Leung, K., 1997, *Methods and Data analysis for Cross-cultural Research,* London: Sage.

Van de Vijver, F. J. R. & Leung, K., 2000, 'Methodological Issues in Psychological Research on Culture', *Journal of Cross-cultural Psychology,* 33, 33-51.

Van de Walle, E., 1987, 'The Diversity of Fertility Behaviour: Bobo-Dioulasso, Bamako, Yaounde and Ngayokheme', in E. Van de Walle, ed., *The Cultural Roots of African Fertility Regimes.*

Van den Heuvel, H., Mangaliso, M. & Van de Bunt, L., eds., 2006, *Prophecies and Protests: Ubuntu in Glocal Management,* Amsterdam: Rosenberg Publishers.

Van der Geest, S., 1997, 'Money and Respect: The Changing Value of Old Age in Rural Ghana', *Africa,* 67, 534-559.

Van Deth, J. W. & Scarbrough, E., 1995a, *The Impact of Values,* Oxford: Oxford University Press.

Van Deth, J. W. & Scarbrough, E., 1995b, 'Introduction', in Van Deth, J. W. & Scarbrough, E., eds., *The Impact of Values,* Oxford: Oxford University Press.

Van Herk, H., Poortinga, Y. H. & Verhallen, T. M. M., 2004, 'Response Styles in Rating Scales: Evidence of Method Bias in Data From Six EU Countries', *Journal of Cross-Cultural Psychology,* 35, 346-360.

Vandoorne, J. & De Witte, H., 2003, 'Arbeidsethos in Vlaanderen. Exploratie van de morele inbedding van arbeid op basis van het APS-survey van 1998', *Tijdschrift voor Sociologie*, 24, 37-62.

Von Bertalanffy, L., 1968, *General System Theory: Foundations, Development, Applications*, New York: George Braziller.

Wade, R., 2004, 'Is Globalization Reducing Poverty and Inequality?', *World Development*, 32, 567-589.

Warner, M. W., Al-Hassan, R. M. & Kydd, J. G., 1997, 'Beyond Gender Roles? Conceptualizing the Social and Economic Lives of Rural People in Sub-Saharan Africa', *Development and Change*, 28, 143-168.

Warwick, D. P. & Osherson, S., 1973, 'Comparative Analysis in the Social Sciences', in D. P.Warwick, & S. Osherson, eds., *Comparative Research Methods: An Overview*. Englewood Cliffs NJ: Prentice-Hall.

Weber, M., 1904/1993, *Die protestantische Ethik un der 'Geist' des Kapitalismus*, Weinheim: Beltz Athenäum Verlag.

Webster, E. C., 2002, 'South Africa', in D. B. Cornfield, & R. Hodson, eds., *Worlds of Work*, New York: Kluwer Academic.

Westerlund, D. & Rosander, E. E., eds., 1997, *African Islam and Islam in Africa*, London: Hurst & Co.

Whiteley, P. F., 2000, 'Economic Growth and Social Capital', *Political Studies*, 48, 443-466.

Widner, J. & Mundt, A., 1998, 'Researching Social Capital in Africa', *Africa*, 68, 1-24.

Wilson, B. R., 1982, *Religion in Sociological Perspective*, Oxford: Oxford University Press.

Wines, M., 2003, 'Reports of Rape and Torture inside Zimbabwean Militia' New York Times, December 28, 2003.

Wiredu, J. E., 1997, 'How Not to Compare African Traditional Thought with Western Thought', *Transition*, 75/76, 320-327.

Wiredu, K., 2001, *Explorations in African Political Thought: Identity, Community, Ethics*, New York: Routledge.

World Watch, 2007, *Country Watch, Country Reports*.

Worsley, P. M., 1957, *The Trumpet Shall Sound: A Study of 'Cargo' Cults in Melanesia*, London: MacGibbon & Keel.

Yamba, C. B., 1997, 'Cosmologies in Turmoil: Witchcraft and AIDS in Chiawa, Zambia', *Africa*, 67, 224-250.

Yankelovich, D., Zetterberg, H., Strumpel, B. & Shanks, M., eds., 1985, *The World at Work. An International Report on Jobs, Productivity and Human Values*, New York: Octogon Books.

Zanders, H., 1994, 'Changing Work Values', in P. Ester, , L. Halman & R. De Moor eds., *The Individualizing Society: Value Change in Europe and North America*, Tilburg: Tilburg University Press.

Zanders, H. & Harding, S., 1995, 'Changing Work Values in Europe and North America. Continents and occupations compared', in R. De Moor, ed., *Values in Western Society*, Tilburg: Tilburg University Press.

Zeleza, P. T., 2002, 'The Politics of Historical and Social Science Research in Africa', *Journal of Southern African Studies*, 28, 9-23.

www.ingramcontent.com/pod-product-compliance
Lightning Source LLC
Chambersburg PA
CBHW032124020426
42334CB00016B/1063